THE TOLERANT POPULISTS

THE TOLERANT POPULISTS

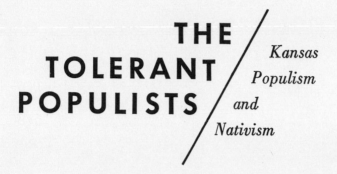

Kansas Populism and Nativism

WALTER T. K. NUGENT

 THE UNIVERSITY OF CHICAGO PRESS

Chicago & London

Library of Congress Catalog Card Number: 63-13069

THE UNIVERSITY OF CHICAGO PRESS, CHICAGO & LONDON
THE UNIVERSITY OF TORONTO PRESS, TORONTO 5, CANADA

25604

To My Parents

PREFACE

This book is an investigation of the attitudes of the Populists of Kansas to foreign-born people and to foreign groups and institutions and of the participation of the foreign-born in the People's, or Populist, party in Kansas from about 1888 to about 1900. During the past decade a body of writing has appeared that accuses the Populists of a number of faults, especially nativism, and the following pages constitute a look into Populism in a key state of its western phase in order to discover how seriously these accusations—nativism, anti-Semitism, protofascism, and others—ought to be taken. I find that they need considerable revision and restatement.

It is not my desire to denigrate the stimulating and valuable work of other historians. I hope it is permissible, however, to revise without rancor some of their apparent overgeneralizations. It seems to me that Populism, or for that matter many movements in American history, ought to be looked at from the standpoint of its operation in a state and local context as well as in comparison to its manifestations elsewhere or to other incidents that may seem to bear to it a superficial similarity. This is especially true in the case of a movement like Populism, which chose the route of party politics to accomplish its objectives. In making that partisan commitment it found itself committed also, willy-nilly, to the ways of compromise, the tactics of group support, and the process, sometimes a painful one, of transmuting logical ideology into manipulable, attainable policies. The commitment further demanded more than passing attention to the particular economic, political, ethnic, and traditional configurations of a given state, which like all others, had a politics that was unique. In short, it is of the essence of Populism that it was the People's *party*.

In order to deal with the criticisms to which Populism has recently been subjected as well as to examine more fruitfully the thing itself, some remarks seemed to be necessary concerning the relation of behavioral science concepts to historical writing. This book, then, deals with this problem too, although far less thoroughly than it treats of nativism in Populism.

Perhaps this book will have another use, and that is to provide some reflections on American democracy. The Populists represent an instance of minority conflict, and their experience may reflect upon the question of the place of elites in a democratic society. But this, too, is much less central than the discussion of Populism and nativism.

Dozens of persons helped me in many different ways in the preparation of this manuscript, and I am deeply grateful to them. Several deserve mention by name for suggestions, criticisms, or other assistance while work was in progress or for careful, helpful readings of the completed version. Some of their suggestions I have incorporated, but others met with too stubborn resistance on my part, and so I am entirely responsible for utilizing or interpreting whatever assistance they gave me. Specifically, I must thank James P. Murphy, whose clear perception into Populism and nativism helped me to formulate their relation as a problem for historical investigation; the staff of the Kansas State Historical Society, especially Nyle Miller, Edgar Langsdorf, and Robert W. Richmond; Walter Johnson, Bernard A. Weisberger, C. Vann Woodward, and Martin Ridge for their much-appreciated comments, criticisms, and thoughtful suggestions; Mrs. Elinor Barber for a critical reading; Rt. Rev. George W. King for his constant support; and my colleagues William T. Doherty, Jr., George Hilton Jones, Philip M. Rice, and Homer E. Socolofsky for criticisms of the manuscript or for allowing me to pester them on various annoying matters. Finally, I thank my wife for many things.

WALTER T. K. NUGENT

KANSAS STATE UNIVERSITY
April, 1962

CONTENTS

LIST OF ABBREVIATIONS

Advocate *The Advocate* (Meriden, August 10, 1889 through December 20, 1889; Topeka, January 9, 1890 through November 17, 1897); *The Advocate and News* (Topeka, November 24, 1897 through April 12, 1889); *The Farmer's Advocate* (Topeka, from April 19, 1899).

CKSHS *Collections of the Kansas State Historical Society* (Topeka).

KSHS Kansas State Historical Society, Topeka.

Nonconformist *The American Nonconformist and Kansas Industrial Liberator* (Winfield).

TKSHS *Transactions of the Kansas State Historical Society* (Topeka).

POPULISM BASTINADOED
AND SOME CAVEATS

OSWALD: What dost thou know me for?
KENT: A knave, a rascal, an eater of broken meats;
a base, proud, shallow, beggarly, three-suited, hun-
dred-pound, filthy, worsted-stocking knave; a lily-
liver'd, action-taking knave; a whoreson, glass-gazing,
super-serviceable, finical rogue; one-trunk-inheriting
slave; one that wouldst be a bawd, in way of good
service, and art nothing but the composition of a
knave, beggar, coward, pandar, and the son and heir
of a mongrel bitch; one whom I will beat into clamor-
ous whining if thou deniest the least syllable of thy
addition.
                    —*King Lear*, Act II, scene 2

CHAPTER ONE

THE POPULIST AS MONSTER

In the National Gallery of Art in Washington hangs Raphael's famous painting of "St. George and the Dragon." One of its happiest qualities is its utter lack of ambiguity: good and evil are unmistakable; moral judgment is simple. For almost half a century, the Populist was one of the St. Georges of American historical writing. Yet suddenly of late it has appeared that he was not that at all but in fact a dragon and a fierce one. The awful truth emerged that in fixing good and evil upon their canvases, historians had got the combatants reversed. The erstwhile hero stood stripped of his shining armor in the harsh glare of behavioral science and "realism." But better to have the truth, however belated, it was said, if truth it was.

The reasons for Populism's long-time favor were several. It was a colorful episode with more than its share of picturesque characters and quotable quotes, such as Mrs. Mary E. Lease's undocumentable but "typical" advice to farmers to raise less corn and more hell. Historians whose outlook had been shaped by liberal reformism in the twenties and thirties regarded it benignly as a vigorous, friendly ancestor. Furthermore, in the days when Frederick Jackson Turner's "frontier thesis" was riding high as an interpretive device for all American history, Populism seemed felicitously to bear it out.

In the 1950's, however, some historians and other writers concerned with the threats to American traditions they saw posed by the Cold War and by McCarthyism took another look at Populism. To them it appeared to be a late nineteenth-century eruption of the same pathological condition that produced the Wisconsin Senator and his growling cohorts. It had been thoroughly egalitarian and had despised aristocratic views and elitism, which some of these writers believed the United States needed more of, not less. A virulent strain of anti-intellectualism seemed to impregnate it. It had been notably unsubdued, unreconstructed, and unorthodox, and thus it was

3

rudely disturbing and ultimately dangerous to any reading of American history that stressed tranquillity and harmonious order as opposed to bumptious reform and raucous protest. Treatments of Populism by earlier writers had been innocent, moreover, of the behavioral science approaches then beginning to become fashionable among historians. It was a richly endowed whipping boy indeed.

"Populism" simply identifies a movement of political and economic protest that rose out of the Farmers' Alliances in about 1890, made its vehicle the Populist, or People's, party in several southern and western states in the nineties, reached a high point nationally in the Bryan-McKinley campaign of 1896, and then went rapidly downhill. The interpretation of Populism that scholars as well as college students have come to accept over the past thirty years is nearly as unadorned as that. Until very recently, standard college texts followed John D. Hicks's study, *The Populist Revolt* (1931), which has been cited widely in American history bibliographies as the most comprehensive book on the subject.[1] It presented Populism as a frontier phenomenon, a political answer to agrarian economic difficulties in a newly settled area. In his widely used text on post-Civil War American history, *The American Nation,* Hicks again viewed Populism as a political revolt against hard times, a program of positive action that tried to relieve specific economic distresses. Much the same presentation appeared in H. U. Faulkner's extremely popular textbook for survey courses, *American Economic History,* with an added emphasis on class tensions in that Populism was seen as an attempt to tie farmer and labor interests together under a radical program. A slightly more elegant but basically similar view was taken by Morison and Commager in *The Growth of the American Republic,* wherein Populism was described as having been rooted in, and in fact created by, a government and society increasingly hostile to agrarian interests, insufficiently democratic, and unresponsive to a very severe agrarian economic distress. As for Kansas Populism specifically, the most thorough study of it, by Raymond Miller, also interpreted it as a political outgrowth of economic trouble in a frontier situation and "the simple demand of an independent and aggressive people, de-

[1] Minneapolis: University of Minnesota Press.

manding that the government perform its legitimate functions."[2]

It must have been with some dismay that a student in the 1950's who had been nurtured on this view of the Populists as an injured, honest, alert citizenry striving only for economic fair play and democratic treatment arrived in graduate school only to find that such an approach had suddenly become hopelessly out of date. As irresponsible disturbers of the peace, the Populists were in disgrace. The employment of certain behavioral science concepts was revealing that they had been neurotic, anxious, ethnocentric, anti-Semitic, and fear-ridden and that their kind of democracy was noxious since it later produced McCarthy. They had not been torchbearers of democracy but incipient fascists.

Some adjustments were in order, too, if the well-read graduate student approached the problem from the opposite side, from the place of Populism among the roots of American nativism and anti-Semitism, especially in the late nineteenth century. Up until the last ten years or so, nativism and anti-Semitism were not often written about—certainly far less than Populism—but a few books discussed these attitudes, which were, moreover, embedded in some of the classic works of American historiography. Yet the student might recall that Rabbi Lee J. Levinger placed none of the onus for anti-Semitism on the Populists in his book of 1925; he might also remember that Carey McWilliams in 1947 saw anti-Semitism not as a farmer-labor fantasy but as a device employed by late nineteenth-century tycoons to gull a free and democratic-minded public into swallowing the subjugation of industrialism; and he might search in vain through Humphrey Desmond's book on the American Protective Association for a mention of the Populists as supporters of the most widespread nativist movement of the time. Furthermore, if he had read his Henry Adams, Parkman, Theodore Roosevelt, Woodrow Wilson, his

[2] John D. Hicks, *The American Nation: A History of the United States from 1865 to the Present* (3d ed.; Boston: Houghton Mifflin Co., 1958), especially Chap. xi; Harold Underwood Faulkner, *American Economic History* (8th ed.; New York: Harper & Bros., 1960), pp. 367–68, 462, 521–22; Samuel Eliot Morison and Henry Steele Commager, *The Growth of the American Republic* (New York: Oxford University Press, 1953), II, 236–41; Raymond C. Miller, "The Populist Party in Kansas" (Ph.D. dissertation, Department of History, University of Chicago, 1928), pp. 173 and *passim*.

Schouler, von Holst, Rhodes, McMaster, and Oberholtzer, he
would have found that these very un-Populistic historians
shared in greater or lesser degree a distaste for immigrants
and Jews. And if he had studied the writings of some of the
outstanding reformers, academicians, and educators of the
turn-of-the-century years, he might have gained the impression
that anti-Semitism and nativism in that period were chiefly
well-bred eastern affairs and, therefore, probably appeared less
strongly if at all among the unlettered Populists of the western
prairie.[3]

Somewhere between college and graduate school, the vexed
student of the fifties discovered that the Populist had been
changed in his role. New casting directors had switched him
from the sympathetic hero to the villain of a melodrama, howl-
ing calamity through a spade beard. The student was to replace
a good stereotype with an unfavorable one—one less pleasant
to behold but certainly, it seemed, one more in accord with
social science concepts, one more profound, less idealistic, and
therefore more truly historical.

In this case the re-writers of history were a disparate group.
By no means all of them were professional historians or even
amateurs. Many of them used the word "Populist" to refer only
very tenuously to the specific party and movement that historians have called by that name and much more directly to a
state of mind whose roots they were seeking. Very often the
Populism of history was left unanalyzed, undescribed, and un-
researched while its name became a handy catch-all word of
reprobation. The depth and vigor of the criticism varied
greatly, with the historians tending as a rule to be much more
discreet than the others, but a general impression was left, a
"climate of opinion" created, in which Populism became the

[3] Lee J. Levinger, *Anti-Semitism in the United States: Its History and
Causes* (New York: Bloch Publishing Co., Inc., 1925); Carey McWilliams,
A Mask for Privilege: Anti-Semitism in America (Boston: Little, Brown &
Co., 1948), pp. 69 and *passim*; Humphrey J. Desmond, *The A.P.A. Move-
ment: A Sketch* (Washington, D.C.: New Century Press, 1912); Edward N.
Saveth, American Historians and European Immigrants, 1875–1925 (New
York: Columbia University Press, 1948), *passim*; Saveth, "Henry Adams'
Norman Ancestors," *Contemporary Jewish Record* (June, 1945), pp. 250–61
and *passim*; Barbara Miller Solomon, *Ancestors and Immigrants* (Cam-
bridge: Harvard University Press, 1956), pp. 104, 127, 168, 170 and *passim*.

bearer of many of the more shameful trends in American cultural history. The process of changing the Populist stereotype from glamor to repulsiveness was in no instance supported by direct, thorough investigations in the form of scholarly monographs, as had been the views of Hicks and several others who had dealt with Populism in several of the states in the twenties and thirties. The new view was arrived at, even in its most creditable presentations, by studies dealing mainly with other, broader subjects and actually only impressionistically and obliquely with Populism itself.

Perhaps the most concentratedly venomous of the new views was the one that appeared as something of an obiter dictum in an article concerned mainly with the place of Ezra Pound, the poet, in the mainstream of "American fascism." the author was Victor Ferkiss, a political scientist and at one time a psychological warfare officer for the United States Army. His indictment of Populism, given unfortunately without any proof, was succinct as well as acrid:

American fascism had its roots in American populism; it pursued the same ends and even used many of the same slogans. Both despaired of achieving a just society under the joined banners of liberalism and capitalism. The attacks on finance capitalism, the hatred of social democracy and socialism, the belief that representative democracy is a mask for rule by a predatory economic plutocracy, and that a strong executive is essential for the creation and preservation of a middle-class society composed of small independent landowners, suspicion of freedom of the press and civil liberties generally as the shields and instrumentalities of the plutocracy, ultra-nationalism, anti-Semitism (both latent and active), and, finally, a peculiar interpretation of history which sees in events a working-out of a dialectic which opposes the financier and the producer—these populist beliefs and attitudes form the core of Pound's philosophy, just as they provide the basis of American fascism generally.[4]

Another critic of the Populists who went at his task with no less verve, but with more pungency and ingenuity than Ferkiss (and certainly at greater length) was the well-known poet,

[4] Victor C. Ferkiss, "Ezra Pound and American Fascism," *The Journal of Politics*, XVII (May, 1955), 174. For an able critique of Ferkiss' view of Populism, see Paul S. Holbo, "Wheat or What? Populism and American Fascism," *Western Political Quarterly*, XIV (September, 1961), 727–36.

pundit, social critic, and sometime historian, Peter Viereck. In 1955 Viereck contributed an essay to a book that attempted to explain the roots of the McCarthy phenomenon, and in 1956 he brought out a book of his own that was meant to be an apologia for limited democracy, representative government, and a conservative tradition based on ideas of John Adams, Burke, Calhoun, Disraeli, and others. In both works Populism was a source of the bad and an obstacle to the good. In neither was there any analysis of the economic conditions that triggered the Populism of the nineties, no history of the party, no comparison of the Populists with other Americans of that time.· Instead, Populism was the possessor of several horrid traits and was chiefly important for that reason. In the first place, it was irrational, the product of "lower-class resentment" against upper-class status and privilege, the vehicle of an "emotional desire . . . concealed beneath the top-of-the-brain economic slogans of 'free silver' . . . to smash the egalitarian west down upon old New England and Wall Street."[5]

Second, Populism was important not as an historical product of a specific time, place, and set of circumstances but as a manifestation of a trend or tradition that has inhered in American culture long before and long after the specific outburst of the nineties. It is as though historical events sprang to life only when the inherent idea or culture-factor breathed its spirit into them rather than that the idea was a function of the events. As in other cases of putting the cart before the horse, this approach to history gives the illusion of speed, freshness, and originality in covering historical ground. Said Viereck: a "Populist tradition" spoke through Paine, Jefferson, and Jackson, through Weaver, Bryan, and La Follette, and on through Father Charles Coughlin in the thirties to McCarthy in the fifties. Father Coughlin, the anti-Roosevelt, anti-banker, isolationist, anti-Semitic, hyperdemocratic "radio priest" of the New Deal years, hated many of the same enemies that the Populists hated, and so did McCarthy. It is true that the first two flourished during depressions, and McCarthy during pros-

[5] Peter Viereck, "The Revolt against the Elite," *The New American Right*, ed. Daniel Bell (New York: Criterion Books, 1955), pp. 91–116, esp. p. 93; see also Viereck, *The Unadjusted Man: A New Hero for Americans; Reflections on the Distinction between Conforming and Conserving* (Boston: Beacon Press, 1956), esp. pp. 194, 195, 198, 200, 203.

perity, but they all used a "radical-seeming scapegoat." Not only were the Populists of the nineties irrationally possessed in many forms, not only did they render a disservice by "habituating the midwest" to these irrationalities, but they were lineal forebears of Coughlin, pre-World War II American fascism, and McCarthy.[6] "Populism" in Viereck's lexicon lost its quality as a proper noun and became a blanket term for a bundle of irrationalities, and wherever these seemed to have appeared they were "Populist" *ex hypothesi.*

Third, the Populists and their scabrous successors were extreme nationalists, as their isolationism and a somewhat selective nativism showed. This conclusion follows easily once it has been established that Populism, Coughlinism, American fascism, and McCarthyism were only different excrescences of the same thing, because the anti-English sentiment of the Populists on financial matters can be read forward into the isolationism of the Coughlinites and the McCarthyites, and the pro-German or -Irish nationalist stands of the later groups can be read backward into Populism. Populism, therefore, although not strictly speaking nativistic, since it had some support from Scandinavian, Irish, and German farmers for reasons of group nationalism, was extremely Anglophobic, chauvinist, and isolationist.[7]

Fourth, since all these groups were Anglophobic, conscious of Jewish finance capitalism, pro-German, and protofascist, they were characterized also by anti-Semitism. "Beneath the sane economic demands of the Populists of 1880–1900 [*sic*] seethed a mania of xenophobic, Jew-baiting, intellectual-baiting, and thought-controlling lynch-spirit."[8] And, moreover, ". . . Coughlin's right-wing fascist anti-Semitism sounds word for word the same as the vile tirades against 'Jewish international bankers' by the left-wing egalitarian Populist, Ignatius Donnelly."[9] The same chauvinism that made Anglophobia a Populist trait made anti-Semitism another.

Fifth, on this basis the "Populists" of the 1950's continued the fascistic trend of their predecessors; they led an anti-

[6] Viereck, "Revolt against the Elite," p. 94; *The Unadjusted Man,* pp. 180, 195, 197, 205, 208–9.

[7] Viereck, *The Unadjusted Man,* pp. 196, 201, 203, 204.

[8] *Ibid.,* p. 201; cf. pp. 202–4.

[9] Viereck, "Revolt against the Elite," p. 94.

Communist crusade because it was a device for concealing their anticapitalistic spirit; their next step would have been, while they kept up their lip-service to democracy, "to set up an undemocratic terrorist dictatorship in order to purge these 'unnatural' aristocrats or plutocrats." Overtly democratic, these people were actually thorough-going authoritarians.[10]

Sixth, in order to convince themselves and their potential supporters of the rightness and the feasibility of their cause, these groups insisted that bands of international bankers, Wall Streeters, Jewish capitalists, Eastern intellectuals—"some small aristocratic or plutocratic 'conspiracy' "—continued to defraud the people of their rights.[11]

Finally, for all these reasons, the Populists (old and new) preached an unalloyed egalitarianism and a demand for direct democracy. They were anti-intellectual and had no respect for elites, for, it was assumed, fancy ideas and fancy people—who were usually English, Jewish, Eastern, and conspiratorial— cheat the people of what is rightfully and naturally theirs. This was a ruse, however—"The spread of democratic equal rights facilitates, as Nietzsche prophesied, the equal violation of rights"—and instead of the conspirators, it was the egalitarians who were the great danger:

The new would-be rulers include unmellowed plebeian western wealth (Chicago, Texas, much of Detroit) and their enormous, gullible mass-base: the nationalist alliance between the sticks and the slums, between the hick-Protestant mentalities in the west (Populist-Progressive on the Left, Know-Nothing on the Right) and the South Boston mentalities in the East.[12]

In rare instances, the "humane reform" of the "often noble, idealistic Populist-Progressives" got a compliment from Viereck, but he made it clear that his "legitimate target" was "Populist proto-fascism and proto-McCarthyism," and the net impression of his writings was to caricature the Populist as a bigoted, vicious, authoritarian, xenophobic anarchist. It is

[10] Viereck, *The Unadjusted Man*, p. 209; see also pp. 196, 201–2.
[11] Viereck, "Revolt against the Elite," p. 98; *The Unadjusted Man*, pp. 195, 204, 208–9.
[12] Viereck, "Revolt against the Elite," pp. 96, 111–12; *The Unadjusted Man*, pp. 131, 204.

regrettable that Viereck's intriguing, if choleric, view was documented scantily, inappropriately, or not at all.

A third tradition-seeker who found in Populism (or rather, populism) a whipping boy for America's cultural lapses was an eminent anthropologist, Edward A. Shils. Shils brought out a book in 1956 investigating secrecy, conspiracy, and security policy in the United States, in which, especially in a section that dealt with "The Deeper Sources" of security-mindedness, the word "populism" was used very frequently.[13] Perhaps it is unfair to include him among the critics of Populism because his "populism" almost never referred to the specific movement of the nineties but rather to a kind of "political response," an expression of direct democracy and hyperegalitarianism, an example of conspiracy-mindedness that intimidates politicians and intellectuals whose thoughts might be unpopular. Yet Populism, upper case, typified populism, lower case; and more important, this book heightened and again disseminated the general impression that Populism in the concrete was the forerunner of all the unfortunate tendencies of populism in the abstract. Populism was a spirit that had moved horizontally across space:

. . . for many years, there flourished in the Middle West of the United States, the belief that the bankers on the Eastern seaboard were in a secret alliance with the City of London and the British Foreign Office. This fear of the conspiracy of bankers against the rest of society is a common feature of the conspiratorial conception when it becomes populistic. It was found in the National Socialist movement in Germany, in British fascism, in American populism and more broadly in Bolshevist and Fascist movements in all countries.

And vertically through time:

There is a straight line from Ben Tillman to Huey Long and Eugene Tallmadge; from Bryan and LaFollette to Gerald L. K. Smith, Father Coughlin and Senator McCarthy, Gerald Nye, William Langer and many others.

As one of the "deeper sources" of a mentality that felt threatened by conspiracies and secrecy and then became excessively

[13] Edward A. Shils, *The Torment of Secrecy: The Background and Consequences of American Security Policies* (Glencoe, Ill.: Free Press, 1956).

security-minded and persecutory itself, Populism spread, together with hyperpatriotism, xenophobia, isolationism, fundamentalism, and the fear of revolution. Granted that American Populism had its progressive side and its "great humanitarians," such as Senators Norris and La Follette, Shils added, "but Populism has many faces"—and it was the grotesque and menacing faces that peered through his pages.[14]

The noted sociologist, Seymour Martin Lipset, joined Populism's critics with his essay, "The Sources of the 'Radical Right,' " which appeared in 1955 in the same volume that included Viereck's first outburst.[15] Here again a picture emerged of irrational Populists fostering McCarthy, hating the East, despising the Jews. Lipset carefully explained something that other critics seldom did—that protest movements may occur during depressions for reasons rooted in real abuses but that they often emerge in times of prosperity (as was true of the Know-Nothings, the American Protective Association, the second Ku Klux Klan, and other movements), and when they are prosperity-based their impulse is status-seeking or status-keeping; in other words, they are an attempt to halt a downward slide in social prestige. Movements with irrational roots such as this may easily begin to look for scapegoats, i.e., minority groups, on which to heap their resentment. But Lipset in effect bypassed this distinction between prosperity-based and depression-based protest movements and made an exception for the Populists, who had been clearly depression-based but also anti-Semitic, just as Father Coughlin was. He generously pointed out that "both of these movements focused primarily on proposed solutions to economic problems rather than racism"; but again the damage had been done: the Populists became scapegoat-seekers, proto-McCarthyites, anti-Semites, motivated in good part irrationally and by resentment.

In the same collection of essays, the sociologists David Riesman, Nathan Glazer, and Talcott Parsons expressed somewhat similar views.[16] None of them dealt with Populism systematically, but Riesman and Glazer referred to "Wilsonian and

14 *Ibid.*, pp. 31, 77–98, 103.

15 Daniel Bell (ed.), *The New American Right*, pp. 166–233, esp. pp. 172–74, 191–92, 210, 219–20.

16 Riesman and Glazer, "The Intellectuals and the Discontented Classes," *ibid.*, pp. 56–90; Parsons, "Social Strains in America," *ibid.*, pp. 117–40.

Populist rhetoric" as the basis for more radical accretions and
to McCarthy's "gruff charm and his Populist roots." Parsons
found not only that Populism prefigured McCarthyism but also
that it was anti-intellectual and anti-Eastern. The status-
mobility concept reappeared—and along with it a view like
Viereck's about Populist egalitarianism and anti-elitism—in
the form of an assertion that "new ideas have their headquarters in New York" and "often originate with, or are medi-
ated by, Jews, who have more reasons for hesitation and are
perhaps psychologically as well as sociologically more vulnerable to pressure than the New Englanders." This is an assertion
that is deserving of some close analysis in itself, but it is enough
to say here that once again "Populism" and "Populistic" became opprobrious terms and once again without benefit of
documentation.[17]

All of the critics of Populism discussed thus far have shown
at least that a strong assertion is easier to make than a strong
case. All of them have used Populism as evidence to support
some other discussion, usually the question of the origins of
American culture or some part of it as it existed in the 1950's
and usually in connection with the McCarthy phenomenon.
Some, though not all, took the trouble to cite a few examples of
unsavory statements made by a few Populists in the nineties,
but none pretended that he had made a thorough investigation of the subject or referred to anyone else who had done so.
Since any unification of history and the social sciences seems
to be yet a thing of the future, these social scientists, at least,
cannot be censured for being behind the times.

Only a few historians joined Populism's critics in the fifties,
but they were among the luminaries of the historical profes-
sion, and their work went far to reverse the image of Populism.
As a rule, they hedged their statements much more cautiously
than the social scientists did, and such of their opinions as are
open to question usually appeared in works that seem otherwise solidly founded and permanently valuable, at least to the
extent that historiography ever permits. Here such imputations
as anti-Semitism, irrationality, a deluded view of society, ex-

[17] Riesman and Glazer, *op. cit.*, pp. 64, 65, 80–81; Parsons, *op. cit.*, pp. 133,
136.

treme nationalism, and the like, were definitely subordinated, at least in the authors' intent, to the over-all view that the Populists were well meaning if radical and naïve reformers who worked under difficult economic and political conditions. But if the authors cannot be blamed for being quoted out of context or without the qualifications that they indicated should be made, the effect of their writing on many of their readers has been simply to reverse the stereotype of the Populist and to do it in an apparently more credible way than anyone else.

Max Lerner was one of these historians, and in his widely circulated *America as a Civilization,* a survey of the historical roots of present-day American culture published in 1957, he left the reader with a generally unfavorable impression of the Populists. Lerner did not downgrade Populism's tangible, rational roots in economic depression, but he believed that there had been irrational factors in the origin of the movement too. The 1890–1910 period, Lerner stated, was one of four great seedbeds of change in American history, when Populism, led by Bryan and La Follette (neither one a Populist), raised its clamor to end monopoly and renew American equality. The emphasis on property-holding and renewal of past traditions indicated that the Populists were more interested in reinvigorating the ideal of agrarianism than in doing anything really novel. But if this were true, Lerner said, it was also true that Populism contained strong draughts of anti-Semitism and isolationism, although these traits did not seem to him to have come to the surface in the Populist period itself but decades later, especially in the thirties. Populism proper fused antimonopoly sentiment with a kind of evangelical moralism, as in Bryan's "Cross of Gold" speech, although later expressions of the same spirit substituted hatred of labor, Jews, and Negroes for the quondam antimonopoly impulse.[18]

Some of these points appeared again in certain of Oscar Handlin's works. Handlin has written frequently and ably on American immigration and American Jewish history, and to include his generally sober, well-balanced writing in the same pages with the writings of some of the other critics of Populism may be unjust and invidious. Yet some of his discussions have

[18] Lerner, *America as a Civilization* (New York: Simon and Schuster, 1957), pp. 49, 146, 707–8.

described the Populists as one of several sources of twentieth-century American nativism or anti-Semitism. This conclusion seems to me to be an overstatement resting on a very few, and rather atypical, statements by people in one way or another connected with the Populist movement. Here again a few ugly aspects of Populism received an undue stress because they seemed to shed light on the particular problem at hand. The full story of Populism, including its favorable side, was not germane and remained unmentioned. The result—the author's intentions aside—was that the reader tended again to recast the Populist in the role of villain from that of hero.

The main burden of Handlin's criticism was something like Lerner's. It was a little stronger in that he said the Populists were personally guilty of some degree of overt anti-Semitism, but their chief culpability for him lay in an ugly legacy: "Millions of well-intentioned Americans would find the later anti-Semitic libel credible because they had already accepted its ingredients in a form that was not anti-Semitic." Trade unions and certain genteel Eastern people were also to blame for the later libel, but, he felt, the stigma should lie heavily on Populism.[19]

Several indictments were dismissed by Handlin although an overzealous critic might have found the Populists guilty. For example, he said they meant no harm when they damned the "Shylocks," because until sometime in the nineties the Shylock image "involved no hostility, no negative judgment." If they shuddered at the name of Rothschild and seemed convinced that Jews were natural money-makers, it was also true that Oscar Straus soon after subscribed to much the same idea, and certainly Alfred de Rothschild, Montefiore Levi, and Perry Belmont were prominent in international finance. Dialect poems and stories might be in bad taste today, but when Populism was flourishing they were "intended to be funny, but no more hostile, than the Mr. Dooley of the same period." Tom Watson of Georgia, the Populist vice-presidential candidate in 1896,

[19] Handlin, "American Views of the Jew at the Opening of the Twentieth Century," *Publication of the American Jewish Historical Society*, XL (June, 1951), 340; Handlin, *Race and Nationality in American Life* (Boston: Little, Brown & Co., 1957), pp. 54, 93; Handlin, *Adventure in Freedom: Three Hundred Years of Jewish Life in America* (New York: McGraw-Hill Book Co., Inc., 1954), pp. 183 ff.

stood in the dock in Handlin's 1954 book as a Populist anti-Semite because he helped to incite the 1915 lynching of Leo Frank, a young Jewish factory manager in Atlanta; but earlier Handlin had given Watson credit for "still vigorously condemning medieval prejudices against the Jews" in 1899, just before Populism gave up the ghost.[20]

On the other hand, the Populists did not get off scot-free. Handlin thought that their repeated use of Christian imagery, as in the closing lines of Bryan's "Cross of Gold" speech, together with their "religious intensity," had anti-Semitic overtones. Rothschild was to them a stereotype, a bogeyman, not a real person. Ignatius Donnelly's futuristic novel, *Caesar's Column*, was, in Handlin's opinion, studded with anti-Semitic references, and it became his prime proof for Populist anti-Semitism. Finally, the Populists had swum with the spreading racist current of the period and helped to pump an ominous stereotype of the Jew into popular American opinion. Handlin pointed out that while it might have been true that William Allen White mixed freely with the few Jewish boys in his boyhood home of El Dorado, Kansas,

there were others, many others, who believed "all trade is treachery," who believed that commerce "by the manipulation of Satan" has become "a curse to humanity" dominating all the peoples of the earth. To those people every Jewish shopkeeper . . . bore the standard of all the dread forces that threatened their security.

If the Populist was not a dangerous, active anti-Semite, he was at least willing to believe the worst, and when he publicized anti-Semitic stereotypes along with the more essential parts of his program, he helped provoke the more virulent hatreds of later decades.[21]

Only one writer of the fifties dealt with Populism directly rather than as contributory to some other study, and he has been its most influential critic—the historian, Richard Hofstadter. In a Pulitzer Prize book, *The Age of Reform: From Bryan to F.D.R.* (1955), Hofstadter did many things. He fitted Populism into a general interpretation of American liberal re-

---

[20] Handlin, "American Views . . . ," pp. 324, 328, 329, 331, 333; Handlin, *Adventure in Freedom*, pp. 183, 201.

[21] Handlin, *Adventure in Freedom*, pp. 185–90, 191 ff.; Handlin, "American Views . . . ," pp. 333, 340.

form since the late nineteenth century. He arrived at many of the same conclusions as the social scientist critics but in a much more coherent and striking manner. He added fresh insights and new indictments to the case. He placed such social psychological concepts as scapegoat-seeking and status-resentment at the core of his argument. And all this he achieved so convincingly that the reader could set the book down with the impression that the scapegoat-seekers had become themselves scapegoats for many of the most censurable elements in American life today.[22]

Very possibly this impression was not intended, because Hofstadter often pointed out that Populism had a rational, productive, valuable side and that he was simply interested in showing that it had "an ambiguous character." He praised the "reform tradition" for discovering "real and serious deficiencies in our economic system," and Populism, as "the first such movement to attack seriously the problems created by industrialism," for trying to remedy these deficiencies. The Populists' faults were not theirs alone, and he readily granted that

to discuss the broad ideology of the Populist does them [sic] some injustice, for it was in their concrete program that they added most constructively to our political life, and in their more general picture of the world that they were most credulous and vulnerable. Moreover, any account of the fallibility of Populist thinking that does not acknowledge the stress and suffering out of which that thinking emerged will be seriously remiss.

Hofstadter's book went some distance toward a balanced view of Populism not only by presenting warnings such as these to less cautious critics but also by some insights that call for solid endorsement. As his book pointed out, the Populists were heirs and perpetuators of the American "agrarian myth," a view of life to which a once-rural country could naturally assent, a view that glamorized farming, country life, the self-sufficient yeoman, an economy of freeholders, as things pecul-

---

[22] Hofstadter, *The Age of Reform* (New York: Alfred A. Knopf, 1955). The same basic approach to Populism also appeared in Hofstadter's essays, "The Pseudo-Conservative Revolt," in *The New American Right*, ed. Daniel Bell, pp. 33–55; and "Manifest Destiny and the Philippines," in *America in Crisis* (New York: Alfred A. Knopf, 1952) ed. Daniel Aaron, pp. 173–200.

iarly and supremely conducive to virtue, both moral and civic.[23] Hofstadter did not remind his readers, however, that since in the Populists' day most Americans still lived in rural areas, their devotion to rural values was not so surprising; but he did render a service by recalling the deep roots of this outlook, from Jefferson, Crèvecoeur, Paine, and Freneau through the nineteenth century.

Another useful insight of Hofstadter's was that this "agrarian myth" existed alongside a very practical devotion to money-making through the cultivation and marketing of crops. If the farmer was a yeoman in theory, said Hofstadter, he was an entrepreneur in practice, and such a "double personality" led him to use the rhetoric of the "agrarian myth" to protect his commercial existence.[24]

Hofstadter made two other points in his book that were all to the good in revising the previous writing on Populism. In the first place, *The Age of Reform* freed Populism from the toils of the Turner "frontier thesis," through both direct criticism and the suggestion of a plausible alternative. Secondly, it declared that "liberal intellectuals . . . readily succumb to a tendency to sentimentalize the folk . . . [and] remake the image of popular rebellion closer to their heart's desire."[25] Previous writers on Populism may well have taken too romantic a view, and a stronger dose of realism would not be out of place.

These helpful insights and careful qualifications did much to make *The Age of Reform* the valuable book that it is. But along with them went some severe criticisms. The Populists were conspiracy-minded, nativists, chauvinists and jingoes, anti-Semites, part of a long-time "undercurrent of provincial resentments," founders of a legacy of virulence, part of a credulous age but more credulous and vicious than their contemporaries, rebellious, suspicious, irrational. To arrive at these criticisms Hofstadter seems to have relied heavily and consistently on three things: several behavioral science concepts, especially status mobility; a somewhat elitist frame of reference

[23] Hofstadter, *The Age of Reform*, pp. 17, 20, 23–36, 61, 71, 78, 90–93.
[24] *Ibid.*, pp. 47 ff.
[25] *Ibid.*, pp. 18–19, 49 ff.

in dealing with social structures; and what has been called the "consensus" approach to American history.

Populist conspiracy-mindedness, the suspicion that a gang of knife-in-teeth plutocrats threatened their every act, was an irrational outgrowth of the "agrarian myth":

The agrarian myth encouraged farmers to believe that they were not themselves an organic part of the whole order of business enterprise and speculation that flourished in the city, partaking of its character and sharing in its risks, but rather the innocent pastoral victims of a conspiracy hatched in the distance.

The Populists, Hofstadter maintained, particularly "loved the secret plot and the conspiratorial meeting," believed that "all American history since the Civil War could be understood as a sustained conspiracy of the international money power," felt the need of a melodramatic villain or scapegoat, and blamed this villainy not simply on the domestic enemy, Wall Street, but on a foreign conspirator, Lombard Street, as well. No one could deny that there have been conspiracies *in* history, but the Populists went overboard by "saying that history *is,* in effect, a conspiracy"; therefore they were not just "singling out those conspiratorial acts that do on occasion occur" but were "weaving a vast fabric of social explanation out of nothing but skeins of evil plots."[26] For these conclusions, *The Age of Reform* gave as primary sources eight references from four books by Populist or radical writers, especially Mrs. S. E. V. Emery.

Populist nativism also sprang from the "agrarian myth," said Hofstadter, who was the only critic of Populism discussed here to make a firm allegation of nativism, although others had hinted at it, and in his view it was perhaps their chief fault. If the Populists were dedicated to "agrarian life" and "personal entrepreneurship and individual opportunity," they also wanted "to maintain a homogeneous Yankee civilization." Populism, coming as it did in an age of mass immigration, was "in considerable part colored by the reaction to this immigrant stream among the native elements of the population" and rose out of "the indigenous Yankee-Protestant political traditions." It in turn left a legacy of "hatred of Europe and Europeans,

[26] *Ibid.,* pp. 5, 35, 71–74.

racial, religious, and nativist phobias" that has seemingly re-appeared in "the cranky pseudo-conservatism of our own time." Its connections with "nativism and nationalism" have been overlooked up until now, Hofstadter declared:

The conspiratorial theory and the associated Anglophobic and Judophobic feelings were part of a larger complex of fear and suspicion of the stranger that haunted, and still tragically haunts, the nativist American mind. This feeling, though hardly confined to Populists and Bryanites, was none the less exhibited by them in a particularly virulent form.[27]

To document these changes, *The Age of Reform* listed several pages in a book by Mary E. Lease (which were written at a time when she was only very tenuously connected with the People's party and which were cited elsewhere in support of conspiracy-mindedness) and one page each from a book by Tom Watson and a book by "Coin" Harvey.

Chauvinism and jingoism derived directly from nativism. "Nativism and nationalism" were coupled, and if the Populists were "nationalistic and bellicose" it was because they exemplified so well "the nativist mind." They became bumptious jingoes, supported President Cleveland's aggressive policy in the Venezuela boundary dispute in 1895, and more important, helped lead the advocates of war with Spain in 1898 ostensibly to free Cuba from Spanish torture. Fundamentally, these attitudes rested largely on irrational resentments and impulses, Hofstadter contended in *The Age of Reform*.

It is no coincidence, then, that Populism and jingoism grew concurrently in the United States during the 1890's. The rising mood of intolerant nationalism was a nationwide thing, certainly not confined to the regions of Populist strength; but among no stratum of the population was it stronger than among the Populists. . . . Their pressure went far to bring about a needless war. When the war was over, the economic and emotional climate in which their movement had grown no longer existed, and their forces were scattered and confused.[28]

Anti-Semitism followed *a fortiori* from nativism and conspiracy-mindedness. Populism had a "frequent link with a kind

[27] *Ibid.*, pp. 5, 8–9, 11, 19, 61, 81–82.
[28] *Ibid.*, pp. 61, 85–91, esp. pp. 87–88, 90. See also Hofstadter, "Manifest Destiny and the Philippines," and chaps. viii and ix in this book.

of rhetorical anti-Semitism," and for this "tincture" it should be brought to task. Hofstadter agreed with Handlin that Populist scorn for "Shylock" was unimportant, but felt that "the frequent references to the House of Rothschild make it clear that for many silverites the Jew was an organic part of the conspiracy theory of history." The Populists were at once more credulous and vicious than their contemporaries:

While . . . this prejudice existed outside Populist literature, it was chiefly Populist writers who expressed that identification of the Jew with the usurer and the "international gold ring" which was the central theme of the American anti-Semitism of the age.

And perhaps more virulent than the twentieth-century anti-Semites they spawned. Although it was "entirely verbal," a "mode of expression, a rhetorical style, not a tactic or a program," Populist anti-Semitism was important

as a symptom of a certain ominous credulity in the Populist mind. It is not too much to say that the Greenback-Populist tradition activated most of what we have of modern popular anti-Semitism in the United States.[29]

Aside from four books by three authors (Mary E. Lease, "Coin" Harvey, and Gordon Clark) brought in elsewhere in *The Age of Reform* to establish the case for conspiracy-mindedness and nativism, Hofstadter cited two sources for the charge of anti-Semitism: a statement by a New Jersey granger at the Second National Silver Convention in Washington in 1892 and the same novel that Handlin had flayed, Ignatius Donnelly's *Caesar's Column*.

Finally, the fact that Populism so effortlessly jettisoned the great bulk of its reform program to embrace fusion with the Democrats in 1896 on the previously secondary issue of "free silver" indicated their fundamental lack of principle—that their vaunted program was just a cover for a drive to regain agrarian power and prestige.[30]

In *The Age of Reform*, three interlocking points form a base from which the qualifications, the valuable insights, and the severe criticisms rise in a cohesive structure. These three points

[29] Hofstadter, *The Age of Reform*, pp. 61, 77, 78, 80–81.

[30] *Ibid.*, pp. 104–8. For a discussion of *Caesar's Column*, see chap. v in this book.

are an adherence to the "consensus" approach, a querulous view of popular movements, which seem to threaten the leadership of an urbanized, often academic, intelligentsia or elite, and the use of concepts that originated in the behavioral sciences. Given proper analysis and careful application, each of the three may become a very useful tool for understanding the past; in particular, the use of behavioral concepts is quickly becoming a *sine qua non* in many areas of historical writing. Yet some exceptions seem to be in order regarding the use of these points in *The Age of Reform.*

The book exhibits the "consensus" approach mainly in three ways. In the first place, American farmers (including the Populists) are for the first time described as strongly entrepreneurial and devoted to commercial enterprise. Although their "agrarian myth" came to deviate from it, their practical economic orientation was much the same as everybody else's: the Populists, in practice if not in theory, were part of the American "consensus" on economic beliefs. Secondly, although liberal historiography seemed to fix the Populists irrevocably in a stance of protest against an established order, as a group obviously out of the mainstream, the whole period they lived in was "an age of reform." Therefore, the Populists were not protestants against the evils of their time but exemplars of its chief trend. True enough, the Populists battled certain other groups very vigorously, but both of the contending elements agreed on important fundamentals (profit-taking, especially) and really should be interpreted as parts of a consensus rather than as opposites in a dialectic. When "consensus" history replaced "New Dealish" dualistic history in this way, the ideologies of the Populists and their opponents became not the uniforms of warring armies, but different patches on the same quilt of history, beneath which the two elements jostled each other for the bigger half of the same good old American bed.

The third use of "consensus" placed the Populists at some disadvantage. To the extent that they actually believed the "agrarian myth" and became oversold by their own propaganda, they engendered in themselves the neurotic aberrations of nativism, anti-Semitism, chauvinism, and conspiracy-mindedness; they deluded themselves with dualisms, golden

ages, and conspiracies, and thus placed themselves outside the
serene, cautious, capitalistic "consensus." Such a deviation,
and much of the resulting protest, became in Hofstadter's view
irrational—to such an extent, in fact, that the rational roots of
the whole Populist movement were obscured. Since his book
omitted any discussion of the Populist reform program and
its basis in actual historical conditions, since his discussion was
pitched entirely at the subliminal level of the group and its
place in an assumed "age of reform," it thereby located the
Populists outside the "consensus" as an lunatic fringe mainly
deserving reproof.

Perhaps it is worth adding a comment. It is one thing to say
that a consensus on some vague, broad fundamentals existed
among the political parties and movements of the eighties and
nineties (although there certainly were plenty of differences in
the programs and origins of many of them); it is another to
assert some consensus between one or all of these movements,
on the one hand, and present-day American thinking, on the
other. This is an error that leads easily to the mistaken belief
that minority protests were a matter of rabble-rousing, not reform. Furthermore, he who commits it lays himself open to the
charges of being anti-intellectual (since fresh ideas in economic
or political affairs would become worse than useless) and un-
historical (since it effectually denies both specific causation and
intrinsic differentiation between phenomena).[31]

Although other writings of Hofstadter's more clearly reveal a distrust of popular democracy and a confidence in an
educated elite than *The Age of Reform* does, these views show
through this book in statements such as: the Populists typified
"a kind of popular impulse that is endemic in American culture," "an undercurrent of provincial resentments, [plus]
popular and 'democratic' rebelliousness and suspiciousness," a
demand for "popular government," and the wish to "topple

---

[31] *Ibid.*, pp. 3, 8, 12, 62; chaps. i–iii *passim*. See John Higham, "The Cult
of the 'American Consensus,'" *Commentary*, XVII (April, 1959), 93–100, a
general discussion of the "consensus" approach; and Norman Pollack, "Hofstadter on Populism: A Critique of 'The Age of Reform,'" *The Journal of
Southern History*, XXVI (November, 1960), 479–81, for Hofstadter's use of
"consensus," although Pollack's discussion is somewhat different from mine.
I am indebted to both articles for formulating the "consensus" idea in such
a way as to afford its use in examining Populism.

the established political structure and open new opportunities for the leaders of disinherited farmers."[32] Populism was thus largely motivated by the dwindling of the farmers' social status at a time when the status of a conservative elite, led by the "money power," was rising. In a separate essay Hofstadter pictures popular democracy as clearly threatening a socially valuable but insecure elite. In discussing McCarthyism, the most dangerous manifestation of a "new American Right," he states that it would probably not degenerate further into out-and-out fascism, but it was ominous nevertheless:

However, in a populistic culture like ours, which seems to lack a responsible elite with political and moral autonomy, and in which it is possible to exploit the wildest currents of public senti-ment for private purposes, it is at least conceivable that a highly organized, vocal, active and well-financed minority could create a political climate in which the rational pursuit of our well-being and safety would become impossible.[33]

Perhaps it is ironic that while "consensus" may have been good enough for interpreting the past, in the contemporary crisis of the early fifties it was a dualism that mattered—a dualism with hyperdemocracy, provinciality, and social and political irresponsibility, on one side, conspiring against ration-ality, well-being, public safety, and an educated intellectual elite, on the other. The valid place of education, responsible elites, and the rule of law in a democratic society is beyond doubt, but to seek to describe that place, as a philosophic prob-lem alone and without reference to history, requires much more discussion than any single author, or obviously a line or two here, can possibly give. In fact, to strike a balance among the legitimate claims of classes and masses, of individual citi-zens, minority groups of whatever type, and the total com-munity, has been a constant issue in the United States begin-ning at least as early as the First Continental Congress. And it ought to be an issue in any society that is not to be static. One may hope rather than fear that it will never be settled con-clusively in favor of either side of the argument. The point is that the values of elites and majorities to each other and to an

[32] Hofstadter, *The Age of Reform*, pp. 4, 5, 93.
[33] Hofstadter, "The Pseudo-Conservative Revolt," pp. 53–54.

organic society are not absolute but a function of shifting historical contexts; and surely the context shifted greatly from the time of Populism to that of McCarthyism.

Yet Populism is peculiar in that it may serve either side of the argument. From one viewpoint, it is a mob attempting to bludgeon a respectable elite and a well-ordered society into abject submission. From the other, it is a case study in the democratic process in which a minority, viciously trodden down by certain economic and political evils, struggles manfully to free itself by well-considered institutional correctives. Since the party failed and the program succeeded, it becomes accordingly either a narrow escape from totalitarianism—which threat perdures with the "populistic spirit"—or a notable enrichment of American politics and culture. Either of these views would be a caricature, however, and the truth lies much deeper. The older writers on Populism, most of them inheritors of Wilsonian idealism, practitioners of Turnerian historiography, and participants in the reform urge of the thirties, erred by investing the Populists with an aureole of democratic dedication and by painting out their grimy overalls and shiny frock coats. But Hofstadter and the other new critics also erred. They sketched too starkly what they took to be Populism's tendencies toward a dull gray *petit bourgeois* authoritarianism running roughshod over the rights of individuals and minorities. With the demagogue McCarthy enjoying the support of one out of every two Americans in the year preceding the publication of *The Age of Reform,* it is easy to understand how the strength of popular movements might suddenly become frightening and how the democratic impulse itself, together with such an outstanding example of it as Populism, might become suspect.

The third basic point that underlies *The Age of Reform* is a series of concepts that originated in the behavioral sciences. Four of these are particularly important. First is status resentment: social groups have at any time a certain place, or status, in a social hierarchy, are very conscious of this status, and if their status becomes lower (i.e., if they are "downwardly mobile"), they tend to resent it. As Hofstadter saw it, farmers were downwardly mobile, and Populism was an expression of their status resentment. The second concept is scapegoat-seeking: the status-losing group attempts to fix the blame for its downward mobility on some definite minority group, or scapegoat, which may or may not have anything to do with the real causes of their status loss. The Populists, according to Hofstadter, found a scapegoat in the "money power," foreign elements, and so on. Third, scapegoat-seeking and status resentment are pervasive: they are not restricted to isolated attitudes or actions but underlie a general state of mind tending toward neurosis of a paranoid type. Populist "conspiracy-mindedness," Anglophobia, and anti-Semitism were "part of a larger complex of fear and suspicion of the stranger that haunted . . . the nativist American mind."[34] The fourth concept is irrationality of motivation: the conscious actions of an individual or a group may or may not be well founded in reality, but in any case they spring from the irrational, subconscious, libidinous, or psychopathological drives inherent in everybody, which increase in significance as the person or group shuns reality and moves toward neurosis. The Age of Reform gave very little notice to the concrete economic and political reality involved in Populism and therefore left it to be viewed fundamentally in terms of the psychopathological and irrational.

A survey of what certain prominent behavioral scientists have had to say about prejudice, nativism, and anti-Semitism follows in a few pages, but perhaps it is worth reiterating here that The Age of Reform was not in any sense a diatribe or a one-man mudslinging contest. It is a significant reassessment of a critical problem in American historiography. It warned the reader against extreme or overly simple views. It was a reinterpretation that contained many new and valuable insights and in some ways was a fresh contribution to historical methodology. Like any historical interpretation, however, it must end with a question mark. Hofstadter cannot be blamed if, after the book left his hands, the question mark was answered with so resounding a "yes" that the qualifications were drowned out, that a new, demoniacal stereotype rushed to replace the overly angelic one of earlier liberal historians. So while The Age of Reform improved our knowledge of Populism in several ways, it still has left us in need of a corrective. This corrective should

[34] Hofstadter, The Age of Reform, pp. 81–82.

be more than simply the striking of a mean between Hicks and Hofstadter. It should try to answer both of their sets of questions and some new ones. In particular, it must emanate from a more direct and thorough contact with the primary sources. This book is not that corrective, but I hope it is at least a step in the right direction.

CHAPTER TWO

REVISING THE REVISIONISTS

Until now the criticisms of Populism made in the fifties have not been met by thoroughgoing revisions, but a few articles in scholarly journals have appeared that should help because of the methodological suggestions they have made.

Norman Pollack's "Hofstadter on Populism" in the *Journal of Southern History* is the most biting criticism so far. Pollack argues that Hofstadter constructed his scheme of Populism's main themes arbitrarily and at random, that he depended much too strongly on the "consensus" idea, and that he assumed the irrationality of Populism from the outset. "In presenting this critique," Pollack said, "it was necessary to confine the remarks to Hofstadter's own evidence and in that way raise questions concerning the validity of his scholarship," and he accordingly restricted himself to a purely methodological criticism of Hofstadter's main points, which he hoped would lead to a full-scale revision:

It is suggested, however, that a re-searching of Populist manuscripts and newspapers shows even more effectively the weaknesses of his interpretation, for the evidence on each of his themes points to an entirely different conclusion. For example, the Populists were far from adopting a retrogressively utopian view towards society; many of them accepted the fact of industrialism and sought to democratize its impact through highly specific measures. They did not hold to outdated producers' values but reasoned that farmers and workers were being placed in precisely the same economic position vis-à-vis the total society; hence, actual attempts at coalition between the two groups were made. Tens of thousands of Populist statements show that anti-Semitism was so infrequently mentioned that it might be contended that there was less, not more, anti-Semitism in the movement than in the rest of society. Finally, the issue of fusion was so complex and rooted so firmly in the difficulties of making protest heard during this period that the charge of a Populist betrayal of principles is not warranted.

And he promised "an intellectual history of Populism" which one would expect would present a different view from Hofstadter's.[1]

Another critic of the critics was the historian, John Higham, who has published two articles on anti-Semitism that deal with the Populist role both methodologically and substantively. For one thing, Higham said, anyone investigating American anti-Semitism (1) should avoid pigeonholing people as pro-Semites or anti-Semites ("many Americans were both . . . at the same time"); (2) should recognize the role of the "enemy" in provoking tension ("one should not blink the fact that Jews themselves contributed to the exaggerated impression of their financial power"); and (3) should use a "consistently comparative approach" by comparing Jewish experiences in the nineties with the experiences of other groups, with other periods in American Jewish history, and with the experiences of Jews in other places. Higham thought that distinctions were always worth making between ideological "gigantic unrealities," "more ordinary antipathies embedded in the mores of a community," social discrimination, and simple stereotypy. These forms of prejudice are related, perhaps, but not the same. As for anti-Semitism in the 1890's, it came from three groups: *"some of the agrarian radicals caught up* in the Populist movement; certain patrician intellectuals in the East, such as Henry and Brooks Adams and Henry Cabot Lodge; and many of the poorest classes in urban centers"* (emphasis added). Populism came off best of the three in this scheme of things because the other groups "lacked the democratic restraints that qualified the thinking" of Populists and because

the Populists and other currency reformers who saw the "Shylocks of Europe" pitted against the "toilers" of America were also the very groups most deeply swayed by the ideals that had made the United States a beloved homeland for thousands of Jews. The whole agrarian crusade of the late nineteenth century drew vitality from the best traditions of American democracy and Christianity.[2]

[1] *Journal of Southern History*, XXVI (November, 1960), 478–500, esp. 499–500. See also Pollack's "The Myth of Populist Anti-Semitism," *American Historical Review*, LXVIII (October, 1962), 76–80.

[2] John Higham, "Anti-Semitism in the Gilded Age: A Reinterpretation," *Mississippi Valley Historical Review*, XLIII (March, 1957), 564, 567, 569,

So far the most eminent defender of the Populists has been the historian C. Vann Woodward, who argues in his essay, "The Populist Heritage and the Intellectual," in the *American Scholar*, that Populism (upper or lower case) is not the threat to stable democratic institutions that the critics seem to have feared. Although the material in his essay was drawn mainly from southern Populism, he objected to the identification of Populism in general with McCarthyism and fascism, to the tendency to ignore Populism's real contributions to American democracy and reform, and to the emphasis on status motivation rather than Populism's rational program. Woodward pointed out that the Southern Populists, at least, were not very status- or class-minded but heavily economics-minded; otherwise they would not have looked for Negro support. Many of the critics' valuable insights were vitiated by taking the Populists out of the context of their time. If they were provincial and ill-informed, so were people in every other region; if they were obsessed with money, so were the gold standard advocates; if they were prone to conspiracies, so too were their opponents who thought them a conspiracy; if they polarized producers and manipulators of wealth, this was standard practice in American political rhetoric.[3]

These perceptive remarks of Woodward, Higham, and Pollack largely concerned the historical methodology of the critics, and they have exposed many major weaknesses from that standpoint alone. The further question should be raised whether the critics used the concepts they appropriated from behavioral science either properly or precisely.

Unfortunately, the critics, in using concepts or terms such as prejudice, nativism, anti-Semitism, scapegoat-seeking, status mobility, and the like, did not always observe sufficiently the qualifications and definitions that behavioral scientists have made. Sometimes the critics endowed these concepts or terms with a certitude that behavioral science does not, and may not ever, give them.

572; Higham, "Social Discrimination against Jews in America, 1830–1930," *Publication of the American Jewish Historical Society*, XLVII (September, 1957), 2.

[3] C. Vann Woodward, "The Populist Heritage and the Intellectual," *American Scholar*, XXIX (Winter, 1959–60), 57–62, 67–69.

Prejudice and nativism, for example, are still largely unexplained either socially or psychologically. A person or a group may be hostile to some other group, but this attitude does not automatically qualify as prejudice unless rational grounds for the hostility are absent. By no means all group hostilities result from the simple, subconscious mechanism of scapegoat-seeking; the scapegoat himself may actually be one of the causes of hostility.[4] Aside from this, not all prejudices or xenophobias are alike; there are differences of kind and of degree. A person who holds a passive stereotype of Jews is hardly in the same category with a Himmler or an Eichmann.[5] As for anti-Semitism, which behavioral scientists seem to think of as a special case of prejudice rather than a unique phenomenon, it has never, apparently, been precisely defined. Whether the term even means anything aside from a catch-all for any anti-Jewish act anytime, anywhere, is still moot.

Not least, to rest a historical interpretation on status resentment or status mobility is a tricky business, since these concepts, as used by behavioral scientists, are more assumed than proven and are built upon kinds of evidence—questionnaires and psychoanalysis—hardly available to the historian, whose subjects are for the most part deceased. Superficial resemblances between mid-twentieth-century psychological mechanisms and late nineteenth-century group behavior do not prove anything about the latter. Social protest, such as the Populists', may be quite rational and independent of irrational drives.[6] These concepts are not sufficiently well-defined to permit their use in historical explanation in anything but hazardous and tentative ways, despite considerable theoretical work by be-

[4] Gordon W. Allport, *The Nature of Prejudice* (Reading, Mass.: Addison-Wesley Publishing Co., Inc., 1954), pp. 87–88, 349–51; Bohdan Zawadski, "Limitations of the Scapegoat Theory of Prejudice," *Journal of Abnormal and Social Psychology*, XLIII (April, 1948), 127–33.

[5] Allport, *op. cit.*, pp. 49, 51, 56, 57; Bruno Bettelheim and Morris Janowitz, *Dynamics of Prejudice: A Psychological and Sociological Study of Veterans* (New York: Harper & Bros., 1950), pp. 8, 9, 13; T. W. Adorno et al., *The Authoritarian Personality* (New York: Harper & Bros., 1950), pp. 74–75, 606–7.

[6] Murray B. Levin et al., *The Alienated Voter: Politics in Boston* (New York: Holt, Rinehart and Winston, Inc. [1960], p. 59; Leo Lowenthal and Norbert Guterman, *Prophets of Deceit: A Study of the Techniques of the American Agitator* (New York: Harper and Bros., 1949), pp. 6, 7, 9; Allport, *op. cit.*, pp. 60, 359–60; Adorno et al., *op. cit.*, pp. 8–9.

havioral scientists. They help to clarify terms but cannot themselves lead to historical conclusions.

Behavioral science may, if anything, lend itself to a favorable view of Populism rather than the reverse. For example, if the Populists were unfriendly to one or two minority groups, they should have been hostile to a great many in order to qualify as "ethnocentric." Probably, too, if they were really ethnocentric they would have left plenty of evidence of other kinds of nasty behavior,[7] but this is not the case. On the other hand, since protest movements can come from realistic sources as well as irrational ones, the question should be raised very sharply whether there were realistic grounds for what the Populists actually did and said.

When all is said and done, however, neither historical methodology nor behavioral science can do more than cast doubt on the new critics' views of Populism. The job of assessing the Kansas Populists falls ultimately upon their own historical remains. Therefore, the chapters that follow attempt to answer two questions: Did the Kansas Populists express any antagonism to non-American groups or persons, and if so, how? If not, what *was* the relation of the foreign-born, then and there, to the People's party—did they flock to it, use it, ignore it, or shun it?

The story presented in the following chapters is a different one from that of the critics. It will not provide a new interpretation of American culture with which to fight the Cold War, and it will not even do Senator McCarthy any appreciable good or harm, but it does provide some answers to the questions just raised. Its results apply only to Kansas; but Kansas was the heartland of Great Plains Populism.[8]

[7] Allport, *op. cit.*, pp. 68, 396–400, 404–6, 408; Adorno *et al.*, *op. cit.*, pp. 9, 100, 146–47, 152, 209, 662, 731, 753–55, 759–62; Bettelheim and Janowitz, *op. cit.*, pp. 1, 148; Lowenthal and Guterman, *op. cit.*, pp. 38–48.

[8] Since this story assumes fundamentally that state and local variations and contexts are important for the history of Populism, as well as for practically any American political or social problem, it would be worse than absurd to extend its conclusions even to other western farming states touched by Populism, not to mention the silver states or the South. There are too many variables involved.

PART TWO

THE SALAD DAYS

EDGAR: . . . The gods are just, and of our pleasant vices make instruments to plague us.
—*King Lear*, Act V, scene 3

KANSAS IN THE EIGHTIES

1. The Ethnic Pattern

The fairly common assumption that Kansas is a state of native American stock is true only in a relative sense. Since one out of ten residents in 1890 and one out of twelve in 1900 were foreign-born, it was far from being among the most heavily native American states. Furthermore, many immigrants to Kansas had come shortly after the Civil War, and with the second generation much in evidence by the nineties, Kansas ranked rather high among the other states in its proportion of foreign stock.

Immigrants were encouraged to concentrate in the north central counties by the accessibility by railroad and the availability of railroad grant lands and other staple croplands at the time they arrived, which gave some of these counties a foreign-born population at least twice the state average and very high for the Middle West. These counties together with others directly south of them formed a vast north-south band of wheat fields running through the center of the state, and twenty to thirty years after they were settled these counties came to form a roughly equivalent band of Populism. Other immigrants settled in northeastern Kansas cities such as Leavenworth, Topeka, Atchison, and the towns that later formed Kansas City, and some of them moved into a handful of industrial and mining counties in the extreme southeast corner of the state.[1]

Until after 1900, when Italians and Mexicans began to swell the industrial labor force, new arrivals nearly always found ethnic kinsmen among the oldest pioneers. Aside from

[1] U.S. Census Office, *Report on Population of the United States at the Eleventh Census: 1890*, Part I [Population], Vol. I (Washington, D.C.: Government Printing Office, 1895), pp. 20, 606; U.S. Census Office, *Twelfth Census of the United States, Taken in the Year 1900*, Part I [Population], Vol. I (Washington, D.C.: U.S. Census Office, 1901), pp. xliii, 732; Rebecca Jean King, "The Identification of Foreign Immigrant Groups in Kansas" (Master's thesis, Kansas State University, 1948), pp. 6–7.

the fact that a good many had lived elsewhere in the United States prior to coming to Kansas, they arrived in some places as early or earlier than native stock settlers. For these people, assimilation was as easy and rapid as they might wish. This was true not only in farming areas but in cities like Leavenworth, where the economic interests of the native stock, the Germans, and the Irish were more common than competitive. As was apparently the case elsewhere in the country, early and contemporaneous settlement by native and foreign-born elements together seemed to stave off status rivalries, and the social outlook of the immigrants was very often so much like that of the native stock that assimilation was no problem.

Perhaps this lack of community antagonism toward foreign-born groups lay behind the fact that the sons and daughters of the immigrants behaved politically much as their parents did; they often kept close ties with their ethnic group, and they seldom felt any particular pressure to reject their origins. Some commentators on American immigration have suggested that as a general rule the immigrants' American-born children revolted against most of the things their parents stood for, but in Kansas the second generation seldom seemed to object to being referred to as "Germans" or "Swedes" or "Russians." The label carried no stigma. Even today McPherson county is heavily Swedish, Ellis county is heavily German-Russian Catholic, Marion county is heavily German-Russian Mennonite, and so forth, and social or economic pressures of a kind that would push them into leaving the group, to "move uptown," simply did not operate. The immigrants' children often remained on their parents' farms, or took up land nearby, and identified with their group politically as well as in other ways.

Some post-1900 arrivals such as the Mexicans, Italians, and certain Slavic groups were not so lucky. Land was no longer cheap, and for the most part they found themselves informally separated into their own ghettos in cities and industrial areas.[2]

In 1890, however, the foreign elements then in Kansas had been there for some time. The Germans, the largest foreign

[2] King, op. cit., p. 9; John Higham, "Another Look at Nativism," American Catholic Historical Review, XLIV (July, 1958), 154–57; Carroll D. Clark and Roy L. Roberts, People of Kansas: A Demographic and Sociological Study (Topeka: Kansas State Planning Board, 1936), pp. 53, 57, 60.

ethnic group for most of Kansas history, numbered about two and a half times as many as the English, the second largest, and comprised about a third of the total foreign population. There were only slightly fewer Swedes than Englishmen, and the Irish were close behind in fourth place. The other groups that were at all sizable were linguistic cousins of the first four, with the exception of the Czechs (always called Bohemians in Kansas) and the French.[3]

The Germans arrived steadily from the 1850's onward—singly and in groups, to cities and to farms—and aside from their unity of language really comprised several separate units that behaved differently according to their religious affiliations. A few, such as the forty-eighters, were freethinkers, but the mass of them were either Baptists, Lutherans (in several synods), Methodists, or Roman Catholics.[4]

The Germans were as divided in their political behavior as they were in religion. The Roman Catholics seem to have been mostly Democrats; the Lutherans varied, somewhat according to synod and perhaps according to each synod's position on the liquor question; the Baptists seem to have been generally Republican; and the Methodists apparently went both ways. When the Republican party in Kansas became officially "dry" with the onset of state prohibition in 1881, repeal—called "resubmission" because it could only be done by resubmitting a constitutional amendment to the electorate—became the one great political issue for many Germans, particularly

[3] Clark and Roberts, op. cit., p. 51. In 1890, of about 148,000 foreign-born, the leading ten groups were Germans (46,000), English (18,000), Swedes (17,000), Irish (15,800), Canadians (10,000), Russians of German language and ethnic origin (10,000), Scottish (5,500), Swiss (3,800), Danes (3,100), and Bohemians (3,000). In 1900 this order was the same except that the Swedes slightly outnumbered the English and Austrians had replaced Danes near the bottom of the list.

[4] For general treatments of German and other foreign settlement in Kansas, see King, op. cit.; J. Neale Carman, "Continental Europeans in Rural Kansas, 1854–1861," in Territorial Kansas. Studies Commemorating the Centennial (Lawrence: University of Kansas Press, 1954), pp. 164–96, esp. 184–92); Carman, "Critique of Carruth's Articles on Foreign Settlements in Kansas," Kansas Historical Quarterly, XXV (Winter, 1960), 386–90; W. H. Carruth, "Foreign Settlements in Kansas," Kansas University Quarterly, I (1892–93), 71–84; ibid., III (October, 1894), 159–63; "Ruppenthal Scrapbooks," IX: 21, in KSHS; Evangelical Association [German Methodists] Kansas Conference, Proceedings, II (1890), 20–21; "Lutheran Churches: Clippings," I, in KSHS; Topeka Journal, January 30, 1915, August 4, 1917.

for the German language press, and defections to the Democrats were large and permanent. The Germans simply did not behave as a political unit, however, and after three decades of prohibition many German Protestants were more heavily Republican than they had been in 1880, while the German Catholics had shifted decidedly toward the Democratic party. If one looks at trends rather than at the absolute numbers of Republican or Populist or Democratic votes, it appears that many Germans moved away from Republicanism in the eighties when prohibition went into effect; that in 1890 others turned from the Republicans, some moderately and some strongly, when the Populists conducted their first campaign; and that in the nineties many drifted slowly back toward Republicanism, and some German areas, going counter to the trend for the whole state and for other groups, seem to have voted against Bryan rather heavily. Either they were not greatly affected as a group by the national Republican party's expansionist policy after 1898 or else other factors canceled out what anti-imperialist feelings they may have had. After 1900 they drifted slowly into the Republican column in each successive election.[5]

From territorial times onward, the Germans of Kansas were active voters and officeholders and figured prominently in agrarian reform at least a decade before the birth of Populism. As for the German language press in the eighties and

[5] These political generalizations and following ones concerning other ethnic groups are based on a comparison of two sources: the Kansas State Census of 1895 and official voting returns (for counties, 1880–92; for precincts and counties, 1894–1908) deposited by the secretary of state of Kansas in the KSHS. Voting units of the greatest possible concentration and purity of each ethnic group were isolated from the Census; the voting returns from these units were plotted on graphs; and some obvious conclusions were drawn from them. The generalizations are highly tentative, both because the samples were unavoidably small and because many variables were not or could not be eliminated. The Republican vote for secretary of state was used to measure trends because it appeared in every election, was never fused with another party's vote, and reflected less ticket-splitting than any other office. While the generalizations do not derive from any very sophisticated statistical method, they do seem useful to indicate certain facts and trends. I owe great thanks to J. Neale Carman, chairman of the Department of Romance Languages and Literatures at the University of Kansas, who eased this work and helped to make it much more accurate by supplying me with a statistical breakdown of the 1895 Kansas Census by language groups and townships as well as with an abundance of other material preliminary to his *Foreign-Language Units of Kansas: I. Historical Atlas and Statistics* (Lawrence, 1962).

much of the nineties, its feeling was largely, "Praise God! We vote Democratic!"[6]

Closely related in many respects to the Germans were three groups called collectively the German-Russians. All three were people of German ethnic stock who had emigrated from various parts of Germany and the Netherlands to Russia in the eighteenth century and had lived there in colonies for about a century. They had enjoyed certain privileges, such as exemption from Russian military conscription, and when these privileges ceased in the 1870's, many of them emigrated to Kansas. In every respect except their collective title, the Lutheran, Mennonite, and Roman Catholic German-Russians were separate groups.[7]

The German-Russian Lutherans settled primarily in Russell county in the west central part of the state, although they later overflowed into neighboring townships of other counties. The German-Russian Lutheran was a Republican more often than not and remained so throughout the 1880–1908 period.[8]

The more widely known German-Russian Mennonites massively invaded large parts of the central counties of Marion, McPherson, Harvey, and Reno in the midseventies on grant lands of the Atchison, Topeka, and Santa Fe Railroad. A religious sect in the strict sense of the word, the Mennonites believed that the church congregation provided all the social organization that they needed and found such political institutions as voting an unnecessary intrusion. This attitude waned in their children, and when they came of voting age in the nineties, solid Mennonite townships turned in solid Republican majorities. By that time, two almost purely Mennonite townships in Marion county had three to four hundred voters between them,

[6] Harley J. Stucky, "The German Element in Kansas," in *Kansas: The First Century*, ed. John D. Bright (New York: Lewis Historical Publishing Co., Inc., 1956), I, 350; "List of Subordinate Farmers' Alliances in the State of Kansas on April 1, 1881, and the Addresses of Their Secretaries" (printed slip), "Populist Party Pamphlets," I, in KSHS; *Kansas Telegraph* (Topeka), November 1, 1888.

[7] For the exodus of the Germans, see Stucky, *op. cit.*; Mabel Ranney Wheeler, "The Germanic Element in the Settlement and Development of Kansas" (Master's thesis, Department of Sociology, University of Kansas, 1920), esp. pp. 15, 17, 21, 54.

[8] Interview with J. C. Ruppenthal in Russell, Kan., September 16, 1960; J. C. Ruppenthal, "The German Element in Central Kansas," *CKSHS*, XIII (1913–14), 513–34.

and practically every voter was a Republican. A separate Mennonite township around Inman, in McPherson county, was very much less Republican, however. Although the Mennonites, like everyone else, were beset with rock-bottom crop prices in the late eighties and the nineties, they spread the burden evenly throughout their tight-knit communities and escaped the black disaster that blanketed their neighbors. Their honesty and practicality were universally praised, even by wistful Populist or Democratic politicians who stared lugubriously at their bedrock Republicanism.[9]

The third group, the German-Russian Roman Catholics, began to arrive in force in 1876 on grant lands of the Kansas Pacific Railroad in Ellis county, where they still predominate. Lacking the political austerity of the Mennonites, they soon made Ellis the banner Democratic county in the state, especially after prohibition made the trip to the polls such a thirsty one. Apparently only a minority of them became out-and-out Populists, but they cheerfully helped nominate and elect Populists on the frequent fusion tickets.[10]

In 1926 there were an estimated 24,473 Jews in Kansas, but there were only about 3,000 in 1904 and apparently far fewer in 1890, although several hundred had been in the state since before the Civil War. Eudora, in Douglas county, had had a certain number of German Jews since territorial times, probably but few of them farmers. By 1890 they doubtless made less than a fourth of the population, had mixed thoroughly with the other Germans in the neighborhood, and were subject to the usual Republicanism of small eastern Kansas towns.

[9] C. B. Schmidt, "Reminisces of Foreign Immigration Work for Kansas," *TKSHS*, IX (1905–6), 485–97 [Schmidt was the commissioner of immigration for the Santa Fe and was instrumental in the Mennonite settlement]; Cornelius Cicero Janzen, "Americanization of the Russian Mennonites in Central Kansas" (Master's thesis, Department of Sociology, University of Kansas, 1914), pp. 100–103, 112–13; letter from James C. Malin to writer, in Lawrence, Kan., December 24, 1959; Wheeler, *op. cit.*, p. 70; *Advocate*, July 31, 1895; *Council Grove Guard*, November 9, 1894.

[10] For early Republicanism in Ellis county, see *Ellis County Star* (Hays), September 11, November 13, 1879; B. M. Dreiling (comp.), *Golden Jubilee of the German-Russian Settlements in Ellis and Rush Counties, Kansas* (Hays: Ellis County News [1926]), pp. 14–17, 107; letter from C. B. Schmidt to Bishop Louis M. Fink, Topeka, Kan., March 15, 1876, in St. Benedict's College Archives, Atchison; Francis S. Laing, "German-Russian Settlements in Ellis County, Kansas," *CKSHS*, XI (1909–10), 489–528; Wheeler, *op. cit.*, pp. 56–57.

Several Jewish agricultural colonies were started or were rumored to have been started during the boom of the eighties in a few economically doomed western counties, but they quickly blew away, like the hopes and the topsoil of many others in the region. The only one that outlasted a single season was at Ravanna, near Garden City; however, although individual Jews were mentioned warmly enough in the local press, the colony itself very seldom appeared in print. Neither these nor the Jewish families scattered across the state, one, two, or a handful in a town, were concentrated sufficiently in any one place to permit even the most hazardous political generalizations.[11]

A native-born group with many characteristics of an immigrant ethnic group was the Germanic "Pennsylvania Dutch," most of whom arrived in Kansas from 1870 onward after more than a century in Pennsylvania. Some settled in Dickinson county, some in Russell, some in Franklin, and they went by such various names as German Baptists, River Brethren, Dunkards, or simply "Pennsylvania Dutch." For religious reasons many of them did not vote, and such political activity as they undertook was probably Republican, except perhaps for the Franklin county Dunkards, who may have contributed to the Populist majorities in their townships.[12]

Several smaller European groups were widely diffused geographically and politically. Hungarian Germans at Herndon, in Rawlins county, leaned toward Republicanism. Austrians in Barton county were Democrats eight or ten to one. Townships in Phillips and Smith counties with Dutch settlements consistently approximated the Republican state average. A township in Nemaha county that included German Swiss immigrants was quite Democratic during the nineties but moved toward the Republican party thereafter, and another Nemaha township

[11] *Topeka Journal*, July 24, 1928; Sigmund Frey, "Kansas," in *Jewish Encyclopedia*, VII, 433; George M. Price, "The Russian Jews in America," *Publication of the American Jewish Historical Society*, XLVIII (December, 1958), 87; Leonard G. Robinson, *The Agricultural Activities of the Jews in America* (New York: American Jewish Committee, 1912), pp. 44, 59, 75; *New Kansas Magazine* (Atchison), I (May, 1892), 1; *Kansas Sod House* (Ravanna), April 29, 1887; *Ravanna Record*, September 7, 1888.

[12] Stucky, *op. cit.*, I: 330–32, 350; *Topeka Capital*, October 28, 1900, April 10, 1938; *Topeka State Journal*, September 12, 1957; Waldron, *op. cit.*, pp. 102–3; *Ottawa Republican*, August 9, 1877; interview with J. Neale Carman in Lawrence, Kan., August 31, 1960.

with many French Swiss in it usually voted above the Republican state average.[13]

Of the major English-speaking groups, the English, Canadians, and Scottish did not form large enough permanent colonies to permit generalizations about their political behavior, except to say that very likely none of them voted overwhelmingly for any single party.

The Welsh, too, were usually scattered, but some of them concentrated around Emporia, at Bala in Riley county, and at Arvonia in Osage county, where they mined and farmed. Arvonia was the most heavily Welsh and the most heavily Populist of these settlements, but after the mid-nineties it reverted to its once customary Republicanism.[14]

The Irish usually preferred to settle as individuals, which makes their political appraisal difficult. In one township that was certainly Irish and several that were more or less so, however, the vote was Democratic except when three-ticket elections gave the residents the opportunity to vote Populist, which they did in good numbers. Blaine precinct in Pottawatomie county, which began as a colony of the Irish Catholic Benevolent Union, was heavily Populist in the three-ticket campaign of 1894 and fusionist or Democratic in other years, depending upon the label. It would seem that the Irish usually avoided the Republican party. Populist orators and writers often drew parallels between Irish absentee landlordism and land tenure problems in Kansas, and this may explain some of their friendliness to Populism. Whether the Irish liked that feature of Populism or whether the Populists used the land argument to attract the Irish is problematical, but in any case Irish-American nationalism very probably contributed to the strength of Populism in Kansas.[15]

Scandinavian immigration was heaviest in the seventies and eighties and resulted in large measure from planned colonizing

[13] King, op. cit., p. 78; official voting returns, 1880–1908.

[14] King, op. cit., pp. 29–30; Nell B. Waldron, "Colonization in Kansas from 1861–1890" (Ph.D. dissertation, Northwestern University, 1932), p. 51.

[15] Louis M. Fink, Kansas, Its Resources, Capabilities, Etc. (Leavenworth, 1883), pp. 5–8; James P. Shannon, Catholic Colonization on the Western Frontier (New Haven, Conn.: Yale University Press, 1957), pp. 30, 81, 135, 244; Smoky Valley News (Lindsborg), October 8, 1886; letter from T. J. Downey to Louis M. Fink, Holy Cross, Kan., December 23, 1884, in St. Benedict's College Archives.

ventures. The Swedes settled rather densely along the Smoky Hill, Republican, Neosho, and Blue rivers, and although they split denominationally into Lutherans (Augustana Synod), Baptists, Methodists, and Mission Covenanters, all groups had generally Republican leanings. The largest Swedish settlement, Lindsborg, in McPherson county, was a Republican fortress, in part because of the granite Republicanism of its preceptor, Rev. Dr. Carl Swensson, president of Bethany College. Peculiarly, however, some nearby Swedish farming townships were as strongly Populist as Lindsborg was not, and heavily Swedish McPherson county was one of the leading third party counties in the eighties. In the politically and economically fractious decade of the nineties, the voting pattern of Swedish precincts was much more disturbed and heterogeneous than in more peaceful times, which may indicate that they and other groups showing similar disturbances put ethnic cohesiveness on the shelf and concentrated on politics and economics when the times demanded. Some Swedes who had not voted Populist in the previous election evidently supported the Bryan ticket in 1896, and a shift away from their normal Republican average in 1900 as compared with 1898 may indicate an antiimperialist or anti-war sentiment. Thus, while the general run of the Swedish group was firmly Republican throughout the period, there were pockets of strong dissent.[16]

[16] Waldron, op. cit., pp. 26–32; Emory Kempton Lindquist, "The Scandinavian Element in Kansas," in Kansas: The First Century, ed. John D. Bright, I, 307–8; King, op. cit., pp. 16–17; C. Terence Pihlblad, "The Kansas Swedes," Southwestern Social Science Quarterly [Austin], XIII (June, 1932), 43; Swedish Evangelical Lutheran Church, Augustana Synod, Referat ofwer forhandlingarna wid Kansas-konferensens af Skand. Ev. Luth. Augustana-Synoden . . . 1890 (Rock Island, Ill.: Lutheran Augustana Book Concern, 1890), pp. 7–8; P. Lovene, History of the Swedish Baptist Churches of Kansas and Missouri, 1869–1927 (n.p., n.d.), pp. 13–66 and passim; Covenant Memories; Golden Jubilee, Swedish Evangelical Mission Covenant, 1885–1935 (Chicago: Covenant Book Concern, [1935?]), pp. 380–82; Alfred Bergin, "The Swedish Settlement in Central Kansas," CKSHS, XI (1909–10), 34–35; Emory K. Lindquist, Smoky Valley People: A History of Lindsborg, Kansas (Lindsborg: Bethany College, 1953), pp. 200–202; Lindsborg News, October 12, November 2, 1888; McPherson Republican, October 5, 1888; McPherson Democrat, October 12, 1888. For indications of Swedish immigrant support of the Farmers' Alliance and Populism in other states and of their support of the North Dakota and Minnesota Non-Partisan League of 1916–24 more strongly than the native stock, see the notice of a paper read by T. C. Blegen, in the American Historical Review, XXVII (April, 1922), 417–18; and a study by G. Lundberg

Danes and Norwegians were relatively scarce in Kansas, but some few settled in the eastern and central parts of the state in the seventies and eighties, and a Danish socialist colony had a six-week existence near Hays in 1877. Some of its leaders later became successful land agents and free silver lecturers. The Norwegians tended toward the Republican party, but the Danes were noticeably Democratic and Populist. French and French-Canadian settlers came to various parts of Kansas largely in the late seventies and eighties, and their political behavior varied greatly. Logan township in Rooks county and Aurora township in Cloud county were usually Republican, perhaps in the latter case because of the usual Republicanism of small towns, but South Shirley precinct in Cloud county was heavily French and heavily Populist. It is an open question, therefore, which district represented French political feeling in general.[17]

Bohemians settled in Kansas in the seventies, most notably in Ellsworth county and subsequently in Rawlins county near the northwestern corner of the state. Both settlements were strongly Populist. Bryan did not seem to catch their fancy, to judge by the voting returns, but their Populism perdured nonetheless, and after 1900 they moved somewhat decidedly toward the Democrats. Another Bohemian group in Republican county was considerably more Republican. In any case, the Bohemians were "not enthusiastic" about women's suffrage or prohibition, the two issues that blackened the banner of any kind of reformism in the sight of many immigrants.[18]

Political activity marked every one of these groups. It was an easy matter for aliens to vote, since the Kansas law that obtained at that time (and until it was changed constitutionally in 1918) allowed any person of twenty-one years or over to vote if he had lived in the state for six months and in his town-

in the *American Journal of Sociology*, XXXII (March, 1927), 719–32, cited in *Discontent at the Polls: A Study of Farmer and Labor Parties, 1827–1948*, by Murray S. Stedman and Susan W. Stedman (New York: Columbia University Press, 1950), p. 66.

[17] King, *op. cit.*, pp. 7, 25; Thomas P. Christensen, "The Danish Settlements in Kansas," *CKSHS*, XVII (1926–28), 300–305; Waldron, *op. cit.*, pp. 73–81; Carman, "Continental Europeans . . . ," pp. 171–72.

[18] Waldron, *op. cit.*, pp. 44–45; interview with J. Neale Carman in Lawrence, Kan., August 31, 1960; King, *op. cit.*, p. 46; Francis J. Swehla, "Bohemians in Central Kansas," *CKSHS*, XIII (1913–14), 487, 489, 495.

ship or ward for thirty days and if he was a citizen or had formally declared his intention to become one. This formal declaration of intention could be made as soon as the immigrant arrived in the state. Many had already made it in other states before they came to Kansas, and if an alien had neglected the matter, campaign workers for all political parties very civic-mindedly assisted him on or just before election day to get it done and get to the polls. Immigrants had commonly run for office or held party posts almost from their arrival, and though this happened most often among the Democrats, less frequently with the Populists, and apparently least of all with the Republicans, every party had some active foreign-born party workers and candidates and a great deal of alien-voter support under the laws permitting alien suffrage.[19]

2. Prohibition and Political Futility

While this immigrant influx was taking place, the reform and third party movements then boiling through American politics were quietly simmering in Kansas. The immigrants there were never the objects of their neighbors' reforming wrath, partly because the new land was plentiful enough for everybody, partly because of their active interest in politics, and partly because many of them had arrived as early as the native Americans.

Until the political explosion of 1890, practically no third-party candidate managed to win state-wide or congressional office, save when fusion occurred; yet reformers variously called Greenbackers, Anti-Monopolists, or Union Laborites got as much as 10 or 11 per cent of the total vote and made Kansas one of the leading reform-voting states. Third-party voting was heavy in some counties before 1890, and contrary to expectations, there was evidently no special concentration of radicalism in native-born counties as opposed to heavily foreign-born ones or in labor counties as opposed to agricultural ones. Im-

[19] Interview with Lloyd Ruppenthal in McPherson, Kan., September 15, 1960; Thomas I. Willard, "A History of the Amendments to the Kansas Constitution from 1861 to 1930," (Master's thesis, Kansas State Teachers College [Pittsburg], 1948), p. 24; *Constitution of the State of Kansas* (Topeka: Kansas State Printing Plant, 1931), p. cxlii; *Admire's Political and Legislative Hand-Book for Kansas, 1891* (Topeka: Geo. W. Crane & Co., Publishers, 1891), pp. 97–99.

migrant counties such as McPherson and Osage, Crawford county with its few immigrants but heavy labor concentration, and the native-born agricultural counties of Linn and Rice were above the average in third-party voting. Yet Ellis and Ellsworth counties, which were heavily foreign-born and agricultural, Leavenworth, both heavily immigrant and heavily labor, and Jefferson, a native-born agricultural county, showed only slight third-party tendencies. During the Greenback period, about 1878–84, the money question was of course the primary and overriding issue. Although these earlier reformers were more interested in paper currency, they objected also to the federal government's contraction policy and urged unlimited silver coinage on the same footing as gold in much the same manner as the Populists would do later. Silver was second only to paper in the national Greenback platform of 1880, for example.[20]

There were no Greenback planks directed at immigration in general, although the Greenbackers often demanded an end to the immigration of contract laborers and Chinese coolies. With the passage of the Chinese exclusion act in 1882, this issue faded, and perhaps the Arkansas Greenbackers' declaration that "we are in favor of immigration . . ." was the Kansas sentiment as well. These early platforms also regularly included a demand for land occupancy by "actual settlers only," a shaft aimed at native or foreign syndicates and speculators.[21]

Kansas politics in this period was chiefly notable for the successful fight led by a Republican governor, John P. St. John, to make Kansas as devoid of alcohol as its detractors often claimed it was of water. Constitutional prohibition of alcoholic beverages in 1881 started a drought that was to last nearly

[20] Stedman and Stedman, op. cit., pp. 51–52, 55; William F. Zornow, Kansas: A History of the Jayhawk State (Norman: University of Oklahoma Press, 1957), chap. x; official election returns, in KSHS; Edward McPherson, A Handbook of Politics (Washington, D.C. [publisher varies], 1878), p. 78; ibid. (1880), p. 196; Karl Arthur Svenson, "The Effect of Popular Discontent on Political Parties in Kansas" (Ph.D. dissertation, Department of Political Science, State University of Iowa, 1948), p. 29; Elizabeth N. Barr [Arthur], "The Populist Uprising," in A Standard History of Kansas and Kansans ed. William E. Connelley (Chicago: Lewis Publishing Co., 1918), II, 1126–27, 1131.

[21] McPherson, op. cit. (1878), pp. 163–68; ibid. (1880), p. 196; ibid. (1882), p. 156.

seventy years, and it brought with it the long and futile attempts of Germans, Democrats, and others to achieve resubmission of the constitutional amendment to the people. Part of their argument was that prohibition repelled the valuable and industrious immigrants who were sorely needed in Kansas agriculture.[22]

In 1882 George Glick became the first Democratic governor in Kansas history. Although this lonesome pioneer was not re-elected in 1884, he may have been helped when the third-party vote declined in that year nearly by half. In 1886 the Democrats apparently benefited slightly by the absence of a third-party ticket. Reform elements had little difficulty supporting the Democracy, because in Kansas it was hardly more respectable than they were: a permanent minority, poor, despairing, lackluster, and looked upon as the party of rebellion. As one Republican put it:

The Democracy, led by a devotion to the ham sandwich, the libidinous pretzel, and the bachanalian [sic] schooner, is essentially a lunch counter party. Let the Republican leaders continue to declare for a "good square meal" at every convention. . . .[23]

Both the Democrats and Republicans inveighed against land tenure not in accord with the homestead principle and against "undesirable" immigrant labor. The Democratic platform of 1886 called for "stringent legislation" against convict and pauper labor and wanted all land, alien-owned or otherwise, opened to homestead entry, while the Republicans committed themselves officially to opposing "cheap labor of foreign countries" and "pauper labor" and protested landownership by "alien landlords to the exclusion of the native born or naturalized settler." How an alien who had only gone so far as to declare his intention to become a citizen would have fared under such legislation was not made clear. The radical press was therefore not actually so very radical—although somewhat less

[22] I. O. Pickering, "The Administrations of John P. St. John," *TKSHS*, IX (1905–6), 378–94; *The Commonwealth* (Topeka), July 16, 1881; Marko L. Haggard, "Prohibition, a Political Factor in Kansas" (Master's thesis, Department of Political Science, University of Kansas, 1947), chap. ii and *passim*.

[23] *Manhattan Republican*, April 27, 1888; Raymond C. Miller, "The Populist Party in Kansas" (Ph.D. dissertation, Department of History, University of Chicago, 1928), pp. 38–42; Zornow, *op. cit.*, pp. 192–96.

generous—when it denounced foreign landlords, particularly "the infernal, inhuman Scully," an Irish absentee landlord who owned large tracts in Kansas and other states, and when it demanded the retrocession of all land titles held by foreigners or unnaturalized residents.[24] No one seemed to object to the foreign landholder if he showed signs of settling down and becoming a citizen.

Most of the great individual and syndicated properties were British, a fact that combined with British railroad interests and financial hegemony to produce in the reform press an intense dislike of the British ruling classes, who seemed on the verge of ruling the United States as well as their own country. But at the same time that the reformers poured their vitriol on English landlords, they found Jay Gould and Rothschild equally oppressive. The fact that the most splenetic denunciations of English capitalists and cattle barons were verbatim copies of squibs and articles that had appeared previously in the New York *Irish World* bespoke an easy alliance of American radical and Irish nationalist against a common enemy.[25]

Meanwhile, both major parties wooed the Irish vote in 1886. The Republicans slated an Irishman for state auditor in an attempt to offset what they felt was the Irish predilection for saloons and Democracy, which were then political synonyms. If the Irish were presumably very wet, the more vocal Germans, stolid and single-minded, brewed a sudsy tidal wave of antiprohibition editorials in an effort to drown the Republicans and their subversion of "personal freedom." The Democratic candidate for governor, Thomas Moonlight, ironically a Presbyterian born in Forfar, Scotland, received the vigorous support of most of the German press, and for a few German papers, prohibition was the only issue of the campaign, although other papers also supported the Democrats as the antimonopoly party. The *Nonconformist*, the leading radical paper, also op-

[24] *Evening Standard* (Leavenworth), August 5, 1886; circular letter from the Republican State Central Committee to "Republican Voters of Kansas," Topeka, October 29, 1886; speech by J. B. Johnson in *Topeka Capital*, September 17, 1886; Fourth Congressional District platform in *Topeka Capital*, June 18, 1886; *The American Nonconformist and Kansas Industrial Liberator* (Winfield), October 7, 14, 21, November 25, December 16, 1886 [hereinafter cited as *Nonconformist*].

[25] *Nonconformist*, October 7, 21, November 18, December 16, 1886.

posed prohibition as well as monopolies. When the despised and desiccated Republicans swept all offices, the *Wichita Herold* lamented that immigrant caravans were no longer stopping in Kansas, now known as "No Man's Land."[26]

No one would have been more astonished by a successful campaign than the *Nonconformist*, and it took the 1886 defeat in stride. During the political lull following the election, it enlivened its columns with an extended series of articles attacking the influence of churches in politics and the narrow-mindedness of the pious regarding liquor and churches not their own. It was especially wrathful about prohibition and Protestant intolerance for Catholics, who unlike some Protestants had never said "a single unkind word" about the *Nonconformist*. On humanitarian grounds, it denounced clerical interference and applauded the social if not the theological views of Colonel Robert Ingersoll and Father Edward McGlynn, the New York priest whose single tax views had recently got him excommunicated. This series was penned by the editors' father, James Vincent, Sr., a Congregational minister who was born and had lived in England "until of mature age, long enough . . . to see . . . the effects of a monarchical and aristocratic government."[27] In 1886 the senior Vincent had turned the paper over to two of his sons, who moved it from Iowa to Winfield, Kansas, where it was a powerful reform voice until the brothers pulled up stakes for Indianapolis in 1891. The younger Vincents figured prominently in the Southern Alliance and had much to do with its expansion into Kansas. Interestingly—in view of their English origins—the Vincents regularly ranted about what they viewed as the plunder of Ireland, Turkey, India, Australia, and other victims by England and her tyranny over her working classes. They had nothing against small businessmen who worked for what they

[26] Letter of John Madden, Cottonwood Falls, in the *Topeka Weekly Capital and Farmers Journal*, September 30, 1886; "Democratic Party Clippings," in KSHS, I, 239 and *passim; Kansas Staats Anzeiger* (Wichita), September 2 and September–November, 1886; *Kansas Staats Zeitung* (Fort Scott), October 21, 1886; *Kansas Telegraph* (Topeka), October 14, 1886; *Marysville Post*, September 15, October 20, 27, 1886; *Nonconformist*, December 2, 1886; *Germania* (Lawrence), October 21, 28, 1886; *Wichita Herold*, October 7, 28, November 4, 1886.

[27] *Nonconformist*, December 9, 23, 30, 1886; February 2, 1887.

earned and in a humanitarian vein blasted the trial of the Chicago Haymarket riot anarchists as judicial murder.[28]

To the Vincent brothers the political clouds of early 1887 were not without their silver linings. The Knights of Labor, extremely weak in the 1886 campaign, leaped ahead from December on, and several Knights such as John W. Breidenthal, B. E. Kies, Christian Hoffman, M. Senn, and J. N. Limbocker, who were later to become key Populists, accompanied the Vincents to what many reformers hoped would be 1887's political Pool of Bethsaida, the Union Labor convention at Cincinnati. When the March, 1887, convention produced a platform that reaffirmed Chinese exclusion, demanded an end to "foreign pauper labor," and denounced corporate speculative landholding, the Kansans must have gone home happy. The landholding plank, however, was hardly radical, since the United States Congress enacted a law in 1887 prohibiting nondeclarant aliens from owning land in the territories of the United States, and later that year, the relatively moderate National Farmers' Alliance (the "Northern Alliance") included in its new constitution a plank demanding "the prohibition of alien cattle and land syndicates."[29] At least as important as the platform, however, was the fact that the Cincinnati convention had been able to keep very vague a plank favoring women's suffrage and had avoided any statement whatever on prohibition. The reformers, threatened by splits over these questions even at this early date, were not to have such easy sailing in the future. Nonetheless, as they began their preparations for the campaign of 1888, they believed their usual eager optimism to be more solidly based than ever before.

A bevy of diffuse reform elements marched beneath the umbrella of the Union Labor party in 1888, searching for relief from the everlasting plutocratic drizzle. There were old

[28] W. F. Rightmire, "The Alliance Movement in Kansas—Origin of the People's Party," *TKSHS*, IX (1905–6), 1–8; Theodore Saloutos, *Farmer Movements in the South, 1865–1933* (Berkeley: University of California Press, 1960), p. 122; *Nonconformist*, October 14, 1886, April 7, 1887, and 1887 *passim*.

[29] *Nonconformist*, October 7, November 25, December 23, 1886, January 13, 1887; McPherson, *op. cit.* (1888), p. 189; John Higham, *Strangers in the Land: Patterns of American Nativism, 1860–1925* (New Brunswick, N.J.: Rutgers University Press, 1955), p. 42; N. B. Ashby, *The Riddle of the Sphinx* (Des Moines, Iowa: Industrial Publishing Co., 1890), p. 418.

Greenbackers, advocates of freer coinage, Haymarket sympathizers, antimonopolists, Christians, village atheists, Yankee zealots, Irish land reformers, pro-fusionists, anti-fusionists, drys and wets, suffragists and "defenders of the home," farmers, Knights of Labor, the shrewd and the obstinate, the sanguine and the sour. Parts of the Union Labor platform favored homesteads in Oklahoma, stay laws, state publication of school textbooks, women's suffrage, and an expression of sympathy to Charles Stewart Parnell coupled with the hope that he and his associates would "redeem the soil of Ireland from the tyranous [sic] rule of the English money power," while other parts opposed subsidies to corporations, interest on loans, Pinkertons, and Senator John J. Ingalls. (The Republicans also had a pro-Irish, anti-English plank that year.) On immigration matters, the platform, like the national Union Labor platform of 1888, opposed Chinese and contract labor competition with American workers. Such statements were common political currency that year, however, as Sedgwick county Democrats applauded the Cleveland administration's "laws and treaties under which the hordes of China and the paupers and criminals of Europe are excluded from competition with American workmen," and the Republican state platform called for "stringent laws to protect our workingmen against contract, pauper or Chinese immigrants." Union Laborite writers sometimes thought it inconsistent that labor was unprotected by restriction laws while manufacturers basked in the cool shade of high protective tariff walls.[30]

Both Republicans and Union Laborites favored an alien land law of the type passed by several states at that time, which was aimed at speculators and landlords who rented with no intention of ever selling to small landholders. In Kansas the Republican legislature outreformed the reformers by sending

[30] Fred E. Haynes, *Third Party Movements since the Civil War* (Iowa City: State Historical Society of Iowa, 1916), p. 141; *Council Grove Anti-Monopolist*, October 4, 1888; *McPherson Republican*, October 5, 12, 1888; *Ottawa Journal and Triumph*, November 8, 15, 1888; James Culverwell, *A History of the National Army of Rescue* (Dentonia, Kan., 1888); *Kansas Farmer* (Topeka), September 20, 1888; *Topeka Capital*, May 13, July 27, 1888; Republican State Central Committee (Kansas), "Political Platform of 1888" (n.p.); *Minneapolis Messenger*, November 22, 1888; McPherson, *op. cit.* (1888), p. 189; Porter Sherman, *Current Politics* ([n.p.], April 6, 1888), p. 7.

to the electors a constitutional amendment permitting such a law, and with the support even of Germans who preferred homesteads to tenancy and who agreed that landholding brought the duty of American citizenship, it passed overwhelmingly.[31]

All three parties made appeals to the foreign vote. The Republicans renominated their Irish state auditor, Union Labor tickets had their foreign-born Mohrbachers, Fleiners, and Durkins, and if an immigrant's English was not yet up to snuff he could hear or read any party's arguments in his own language. Some Democratic and Union Labor fusion took place for congressmen and for county offices, although not always successfully.[32]

If the foreign-language press is any indication, however, the Republicans were the beneficiaries both of Irish rage over Cleveland's endorsement by Sir Lionel Sackville-West (the English minister) and of German horror at the Union Labor advocacy of women's suffrage. With the exception of German papers in the Mennonite area, where liquor was anathema, and of the Swedish *Framat* of Lindsborg, all of which were Republican, the foreign press was not overly friendly to either the Republicans or the Union Laborites and backed the Democrats on the basis of their stand on the tariff and liquor. The *Leavenworth Post*, for example, took this line, and also announced that for fifty years the Republican party had been the home of the Know-Nothing movement and that in it "Prohibition, Sunday-squeezing, monopoly and hatred of foreigners found their warmest defenders."[33]

Yet in spite of the fact that the Germans called them a sink-

[31] Paul Wallace Gates, *Fifty Million Acres: Conflicts over Kansas Land Policy, 1854–1890* (Ithaca, N.Y.: Cornell University Press, 1954), pp. 288–89; Thomas I. Willard, *op. cit.*, pp. 39–40; *Constitution of the State of Kansas*, p. cxxx; *Marion County Anzeiger* (Hillsboro), October 5, November 16, 1888.

[32] *Atchison Times*, September 1, 22, 1888, September 4, 1890; *Courier-Democrat* (Seneca), November 2, 1888; *Marshall County Democrat* (Marysville), October 11, 25, 1888; *Census of 1895*, Vol. X, p. 5, Vol. XI, pp. 9–19, Vol. CCIX, p. 21, in KSHS; Raymond C. Miller, *op. cit.*, p. 58.

[33] *Kansas Herald* (Hutchinson), October 13, November 3, 10, 1888; *Atchison Times*, September 22, 1888; *Marion County Anzeiger* (Hillsboro), September 7, 14, 21, October 5, November 2, 1888; *Newton Anzeiger*, October 5, 12, November 9, 1888; *McPherson Anzeiger*, August 31, September 5, 12, 26,

ing ship full of prohibitionists and nativists, the Republicans routed the combined opposition. It was still true, as a leading Republican said, that when a man took four newspaper columns to accept a Democratic congressional nomination, it was "like putting four loads of fertilizer around a jimson weed." The strong Union Labor sympathy for the Haymarket anarchists had no more added to their respectability than it would to the Populists' in subsequent years when it became one of the new party's minor marks. Indeed, although no county gave the Union Labor party a lighter vote than earlier third parties had received, the areas of reform strength were very scattered. Among the heavily immigrant counties, for example, McPherson shifted abruptly toward the third party, but Leavenworth and Ellis supported it only moderately, and Ellsworth imperceptibly. The same was true for native-born counties, and furthermore, whether a county had some labor strength or was almost wholly agricultural seemed to affect its Union Labor voting only very slightly. When the third party took less than 12 per cent of the vote, surprise was general and the reformers' disappointment keen.

To the shrewder of them, the lesson was clear. The Union Labor party, in spite of its success in attracting more voters and more diffuse groups of voters than any previous third party of the eighties, had been too obviously a mere reprise of two decades of Greenbackery. New, pressing questions, not stale tales of the "Crime of '73," cried out for attention. The year 1888 taught them this: 12 per cent of the vote was a valuable thing to have, but neither it nor the appeals and organization producing it would ever really accomplish anything. Gloomily they asked themselves what could be done about these new, hard problems? By what means could the political base of reform be broadened further to solve them?[34]

1888; *Wichita Herold*, October 31, 1888; *Kansas Staats Anzeiger* (Wichita), October 31, 1888; *Germania* (Lawrence), September–November, 1888; *Leavenworth Post*, October 2, November 5, 1888.

[34] *Leavenworth Post*, October 24, 1888; *LaCrosse Chieftain*, November 8, 1888; Kirke Mechem (ed.), *The Annals of Kansas, 1886–1925* (Topeka: Kansas State Historical Society [1954]), I, 63; "The Plot Unfolded! or, A History of the Famous Coffeyville Dynamite Outrage, October 18, 1888"

3. Economic Boom and Bust

Answers to both these questions came within a few months. But while the political campaign swept the headlines, the economy of Kansas had been plunging toward a depression level. The buying power of farm commodities dived dramatically to its lowest level in generations, money was becoming an archeological curiosity, and Kansas found itself buried under mountains of ominous mortgages.

The state had undergone a rapid and apparently healthy growth in the early and middle eighties. Land was available for farms and towns, corn and wheat prices were favorable, railroads shot across the state, and improved farming methods made every acre increasingly productive. People poured into Kansas, and land values made a "slow and long continued . . . natural and entirely normal" rise.[35] Since their income appeared not only safe but destined inevitably to go up, farmers borrowed on the security of their land in order to buy more land, to equip their farms, and sometimes to speculate. Townspeople, and doubtless farmers too, snapped up town lots in crossroads hamlets in the expectation that town plats extending through acres of open countryside would soon be teeming with people, houses, churches, and stores. While the population of the thirty-one counties west of the 100th meridian soared from almost nothing to 139,000, "boomerism" also pervaded the central part of the state, with its headstart in population and high ambitions. Dozens of country towns, eyeing the marvelous surges of Chicago, Cincinnati, and Kansas City, and hoping to attract railroads and industries, issued millions of dollars in bonds funded mainly on hope and good cheer.[36] By the mid-eighties the buying, mortgaging, and bond-

---

(Winfield, Kan.: American Nonconformist, 1889) ; Raymond C. Miller, *op. cit.*, p. 62; *Council Grove Anti-Monopolist*, November 15, 1888; *Independence Star and Kansan*, November 16, 1888.

[35] Raymond C. Miller, *op. cit.*, p. 14. For much of what follows, I am indebted to the very capable discussion of the Kansas economic situation in the first two chapters of Miller's dissertation. For the mortgage problem in particular, I have found "Financing the Boom in Kansas, 1879 to 1888, with Special Reference to Municipal Indebtedness and to Real Estate Mortgages," by Glenn Harold Miller, Jr. (Master's thesis, Department of Economics and Business, University of Kansas, 1954), very helpful.

[36] Glenn Harold Miller, Jr., *op. cit.*, pp. 80–81, 201–3.

issuing was happening so fast that Kansas no longer had on its hands a healthy, vigorous growth, but a rickety, top-heavy boom.

The end of several years' abnormally high rainfall in the western counties, together with a long-term deflation of crop prices, brought a decisive and disastrous end to the boom after 1887. Three successive years of failures or near-failures in corn and wheat had quietly corroded its foundations, and much of the new population of western Kansas fled, leaving behind hopeless public and private debts and the wreckage of their own and their creditors' hopes. Most people in the better entrenched and older counties in the central third of the state remained, barely solvent, but only to face a future in the shadow of towering mortgage indebtedness.

Dozens of country communities declined and fell—like Ravanna, where the least unsuccessful of Kansas' Jewish agricultural colonies had been located. The *Ravanna Record* began its short, sad run in 1887 crowded with headlines, comments, and advertisements of the "boomer" and "razzooper" variety, predicting the town's imminent conversion into a prairie paradise. In early 1888, however, world-beating confidence gave way to warnings and nervous assurances about how promising the future was and how silly to leave just then. And after the failure of the crucial crop season of 1888, the *Record* gave itself over in rapid succession that autumn and into 1889 to notices of tax delinquency sales, then mortgage foreclosures, and a final, pitiful listing of sundry private debts.

This was the era when a wintry schoolhouse debate on the proposition that Kansas was remarkably prosperous was won by the negative speaker when, without saying a word, he rose and threw a few more shovelfuls of corncobs into the potbellied stove. It was little wonder that farmers despised the railroads since they got less for their corn than the close to thirty-five cents they had to pay to ship a bushel of it to Chicago. Little wonder, too, that many of them longed for silver or paper money when American production of gold, the basis of the elusive currency, was at its lowest point since 1849. Available currency declined from 1870 to 1900 in per capita amount, and the squeeze in circulating medium was painfully real. It became brutally obvious that contraction was still the government policy. Farmers could not understand why the law of supply and demand was apparently inoperative, since the population of the United States expanded while crop prices plunged. Though they worked as hard as ever, their income dwindled, and their mortgages, once investments in prosperity, if not compounded in an attempt to avert final ruin, remained heavily, hopelessly high.[37]

They were hardly unaware, as some said they were, that in good times mortgages were a useful means of improving their farms, buying equipment and supplies, or acquiring more land, and even by the desperate year of 1890, the "calamity class" of mortgages, those contracted to provide money for payment of current family and farm expenses, never exceeded 6 per cent of the total mortgages in force. Almost four out of five mortgages had been for land improvement or purchase in times when crop prices made repayment a very reasonable prospect. During the boom, national bankers, state and private banks, and private mortgage investment companies scoured the Kansas countryside for farmers willing to invest in prosperity. These mortgage companies, which were sometimes corporations issuing debenture bonds backed by mortgages and sometimes individual brokers working under a company name, loaned money for what was then a rather cheap 8 or 9 per cent on good security, or higher rates on poorer security, and found eager buyers for their paper among private individuals, insurance companies, and others with investment capital. Very often these buyers lived in the East, and some of them, such as the British Land and Mortgage Company, Ltd., and the Lombard Investment Company, were English. Some of these companies

[37] Raymond C. Miller, *op. cit.*, pp. 2–4, 7, 9, chap. ii *passim*; Gearld K. Aistrup, "An Investigation of the Relationship between Climatic Conditions and Population Changes in Western Kansas, 1885–1900" (Master's thesis, Fort Hays Kansas State College, 1956), p. 88; James C. Malin, *Winter Wheat in the Golden Belt of Kansas* (Lawrence: University of Kansas Press, 1944), pp. 143–46; figures for weather, precipitation, acreage, crops, and population are given in the *Biennial Report* of the Kansas Board of Agriculture (Topeka: [pub. varies], Vol. X (1885–1886) and later volumes; Chester W. Wright, *Economic History of the United States* (New York: McGraw-Hill Book Co., Inc., 1941), p. 821; Allan G. Bogue, *Money at Interest: The Farm Mortgage on the Middle Border* (Ithaca, N.Y.: Cornell University Press, 1955), pp. 263–67.

loaned more money than was asked and on security that in less competitive times would have been turned down, and many of them gave mortgages up to the full value of the land. With investors vying with each other for purchasable mortgage paper, with a "boom psychology" operating, a farmer would have been thought very unco-operative, very unpatriotic to Kansas, and a dull fellow indeed had he not taken advantage of the situation.[38]

Of course, this was no help after the boom collapsed. Even after thousands of western Kansas boomers left, Kansas led the country as the most mortgaged state, and in central Kansas, soon to become a Populist furnace, some counties had three mortgages for every four farms. Meanwhile, one hundred and fifty mortgage companies, by sale of stock or assets, came to be supervised by New York and New England bankers and public officials. Central Kansas, where actual farm failures were fewer than 10 per cent, was much better off than the west. "But the farmer who was struggling desperately to save his home could not know this; about him he saw the failure of people whose resources were only a little less than his." It hardly helped his peace of mind to hear that the Santa Fe was now in the hands of the Barings of London, that Englishmen singly and in companies owned large tracts of land in Kansas, and that London bankers had close ties both with the Eastern bankers who had bought up their mortgages at bargain-basement prices and with American statesmen, including John Sherman and Cleveland, to whom the contraction policy was economic dogma.[39]

Only the closeness of these connections can be a matter for argument. Some Kansans recognized that they had reached the nadir of a long agricultural decline, and with the sheriff just around the corner, it was hard to distinguish precisely

[38] Glenn Harold Miller, Jr., *op. cit.*, pp. 84–85, 109; W. F. Mappin, "Farm Mortgages and the Small Farmer," *Political Science Quarterly*, IV (1889), 436–41; Bogue, *op. cit.*, pp. 268–76.

[39] Wayne D. Angell, "A Century of Commercial Banking in Kansas, 1856 to 1956" (Ph.D. dissertation, Department of Economics, University of Kansas, 1957), pp. 206, 236, 239, 258; Raymond C. Miller, *op. cit.*, pp. 27, 31, 38; Glenn Harold Miller, Jr., *op. cit.*, pp. 32, 97; *Ottawa Journal and Triumph*, October 25, 1888.

between a long entrenched community of interest, a "well-organized effort," or a financial conspiracy.[40]

Under these conditions, the appeal of the Farmers' Alliance and the forthcoming People's Party was irresistible. To the woebegone native and foreign-born farmers, these movements were a messianic call to economic redemption.

[40] William A. Peffer, *The Farmer's Side: His Troubles and Their Remedy* (New York: D. Appleton & Co., 1891), pp. 28–29 and *passim*; Ashby, *op. cit.*, p. 388.

CHAPTER FOUR

"AGITATE, EDUCATE, ORGANIZE!"

1. The Birth of the Alliance

Before the boom had busted for very long, the Kansas farmer, caught in a three-way squeeze by mortgages, tight money, and high transportation rates, was ready for a change. While alone, his plight seemed hopeless. But in his calmer moments he remembered that there was one remedy that generations of American farmers before him had used with some success, and that remedy was organization. If he could in some way get together with his equally hard-hit neighbors, it might even happen that the agricultural producing class might find a way out. If the economic scene was in a shambles, his spirit was intact. If his reaction to affairs understandably bordered on the glandular, despair was beneath his scorn. As he pondered his problems through prairie winter nights, listening to his last year's corn crop pop nonchalantly up the stovepipe and wondering how much longer he could call the warm farmhouse his own, his utter disgust began to ebb before a fragile hope that his salvation might lie in the news just reaching him of a new farmers' organization.

The Farmers' Alliance had just begun to spread like a prairie fire across the state, turning the wobbling into warriors, respectability into revolt, and fear into faith. Farm organizations were nothing new in Kansas, but none of the older groups, including the Grange or the National Farmers' Alliance, which dated back to the seventies or the early eighties, had the nerve or the structural tightness or the economic viewpoints, as the case may be, to afford much promise. Ironically, the farmer of proud and puritan Kansas came to seek salvation not from these organizations but from the southern-oriented National Farmers' Alliance and Industrial Union, whose Kansas origins bore the stamp of anarchy and the once spat-upon Union Laborism.

The Alliance in Kansas was above all a grass-roots movement, and no one will ever know the full story of its beginnings. One of them was certainly the Vincent family of the Winfield *Nonconformist,* who had recently been stigmatized by their Republican competitors as the leaders of "A Secret Band of Conspirators" through whom "The Henious [*sic*] and Terrible Monster of Anarchy Rears Its Hydra Head." The conspiracy in question was the Southern Alliance, and the Union Laborite Vincent brothers had gone to Texas sometime in 1888, had had themselves initiated, and had returned to south-central Kansas to pour its message into the hope-starved ears of bewildered farmers. In other places, too, it seemed to spring up by some spontaneous combustion, and these diverse brush fires immediately fused a number of ideologically diverse people and ignited hundreds of schoolhouse meetings that dotted the state in those solemn months.[1]

Farmers interested not in ideologies but in practical explanations of agricultural depression in the midst of general prosperity and the lack of a relation between commodity prices and production costs—to them a "riddle of the sphinx" —began to believe that somewhere, somehow, the game was rigged. With no questions asked except "Can it help us out of this mess?" they flocked to this new organization open to those who "really worked" and closed to those who "lived off the labor of others." A farmer, farm laborer, mechanic, country doctor, preacher, or teacher could join the Farmers' Alliance, but bankers, lawyers, speculators, commission merchants, agents, and peddlers could not. The Alliance constitution also said that "there shall not be any political or religious bar for membership," and in practice a man's party, religion, or nationality was no bar. To their surprise, many townspeople shared their ideas and hopes, and the "Citizens' Alliance"

[1] *Winfield Daily Courier,* October 4, 18, 1888, accused the *Nonconformist* of leading an armed plot on the basis of a purported "secret ritual" that today resembles something in the genre, although, it is safe to say, not with the quality, of Lewis Carroll. *Marion County Anzeiger* (Hillsboro), October 26, 1888; W. F. Rightmire, "The Alliance Movement in Kansas," *TKSHS,* IX (1905–6), 2–4; Raymond C. Miller, "The Populist Party in Kansas" (Ph.D. dissertation, Department of History, University of Chicago, 1928), p. 94 n.; Hortense Marie Harrison, "The Populist Delegation in the Fifty-second Congress, 1891–1893" (Master's thesis, Department of History, University of Kansas, 1933), p. 6.

after early 1890 added the support of thousands who could not qualify for the parent body.[2]

This was a credit to the organizational shrewdness of its leaders. Shrewdly, too, they had linked the Kansas movement to the secret, more tightly organized, more radical National Farmers' Alliance and Industrial Union, or "Southern Alliance," rather than to the older, looser, less vigorous National Farmers' Alliance, the "Northern Alliance." The Northern Alliance had branches in Kansas as early as 1881 but after late 1888 was quickly subsumed into the younger body. In theory this southern affiliation committed Kansas Alliancemen to ideas such as the subtreasury plan to relieve the currency and warehousing problems, but as the movement broadened to include a consensus of Kansas agrarian thinking, the subtreasury was played down and more commonly held ideas such as free silver, laws against corporate and alien landholding, contract labor laws, laws against speculation in grain futures, creation of paper currency, the Australian ballot, direct election of Senators, and antimonopoly, became in practice the accepted program of the Kánsas Alliance.[3]

The Alliance, far from ostracizing the foreign-born farmer, hunted for his support. While a conservative critic of the Alliance movement lamented what he took to be the replacement of the native-born farmer by the foreigner, the *Advocate*, the chief Alliance organ, declared: "There is no race tinge neither any nationality [*sic*] to the angel which is troubling the waters of to-day." Farmers were facing an economic problem, and the

[2] Interview with Willard J. Breidenthal, Topeka, September 11, 1960; *Advocate*, January 16, April 16, 1890; N. B. Ashby, *The Riddle of the Sphinx* (Des Moines, Iowa: Industrial Publishing Co., 1890), pp. 52–54; W. P. Harrington, "The Populist Party in Kansas" (Master's thesis, Department of History, University of Kansas, 1924), pp. 15–16; Farmers' Alliance and Industrial Union of Kansas, *Constitution for Subordinate Alliances* (Hutchison: The News, Printers and Binders, 1890), esp. Art. IV, sec. 4; "Declaration of Principles, Platform, Constitution and By-Laws of the National Citizens' Industrial Alliance" (Topeka: Alliance Tribune Job Print, 1891), p. 13; W. F. Rightmire, "Organization of the National People's Party," *CKSHS*, XVII (1926–28), 730.

[3] Raymond C. Miller, *op. cit.*, pp. 81–82, 86, 103; Herman C. Nixon, "The Cleavage within the Farmers' Alliance Movement," *Mississippi Valley Historical Review*, XV (June, 1928), 23–33; Ashby, *op. cit.*, pp. 418–19; *Advocate*, January 30, 1890.

Alliance used foreign-language as well as English-speaking organizers to bring to the fold the German, Pennsylvania Dutch, Bohemian, or other immigrant who shared his economic anguish with his native stock neighbor. S. M. Scott, the "champion organizer of the Northwest" (of Kansas), was one of these able salesmen and may have been typical in his acceptance of ethnic stereotypes but not prejudices. Scott traveled from township to township preaching to native-born and immigrant farmers alike a solution to their common economic woes, and he could put in print a dialect story that would be thought offensive today side by side with compliments to such receptive groups as the Pennsylvania Dutch, of whom he said: "A more intelligent set of men I have never met."[4]

Diversity of background marked the national, state, and local leaders of the Alliance movement. For its northern and southern patriarchs, such as James Baird Weaver of Iowa and Leonidas L. Polk of North Carolina, humanitarian idealism dug the grave of Civil War hatreds. Dr. C. W. Macune, who guided the destinies of the Southern Alliance from his base in Texas, was a thirty-nine year old Wisconsin-born son of recent Canadian immigrants. H. L. Loucks, a one-time president of the Northern Alliance and later the vice-president of the Southern, had been born in the southern part of Ontario forty-four years before. A contemporary of his, also an Ontario man, was Isaac McCracken, president of the Arkansas-centered National Wheel, a major founding group in the Southern Alliance. The volatile Ignatius Donnelly of Minnesota, born in Philadelphia of prosperous Irish immigrants, was closing out his long and tempestuous reform career by some on-again, off-again leadership in his state Alliance, while during this same period opposing the American Protective Association, the leading nativist organization of the time. Donnelly's outstanding character traits were sincerity, earnestness, and lack of balance.[5]

[4] *Advocate*, January 9, March 6, April 16, 1890; S. M. Scott, *The Champion Organizer of the Northwest, or, My First Sixty Days as an Organizer* (n.p., 1890), pp. 68–70, 121–22, 124.

[5] W. Scott Morgan, *History of the Wheel and Alliance* (St. Louis: C. B. Woodward Co., 1891), pp. 298, 306, 330; Annie L. Diggs, "The Farmers' Alliance and Some of Its Leaders," *Arena*, V (April, 1892), 596; John D. Hicks, "The Political Career of Ignatius Donnelly," *Mississippi Valley Historical Review*, VIII (June, 1921), 80, 116–31, 132; Humphrey J. Desmond,

These men had little directly to do with the Alliance leaders in Kansas. Of the latter, one of the most curious figures was the Ohio-born Ben H. Clover, twice president of the state Alliance, twice vice-president of the national body, and a Populist congressman from 1891 to 1893. His "flop" to the Republicans in 1893 and 1894 cost him a Populist renomination to Congress, and though he "re-flopped" to the Populists in 1896, he never regained his former stature in the party. His final misanthropic years ended in suicide. Another Kansas leader was Stephen McLallin, a fifty-two-year-old physician and Civil War veteran from Pennsylvania and the editor of the *Advocate*.[6]

Another more famous editor, William Alfred Peffer, was born of Dutch or Dutch-descended parents in Cumberland county, Pennsylvania, and rose from farm to editorial chair to the United States Senate. Peffer had been variously an anti-slavery and antiliquor reformer, and his sedate, logical, fact-crammed, humorless speeches and editorials justify better the description of single-minded and dedicated rather than fanatical. He was much less important in Kansas after he went to the Senate than he had been in the 1890 campaign, and he fought unsuccessfully for a renomination in 1896. A former Greenbacker, he voted for prohibition and free silver in that year, but in 1898 was the Prohibition party's choice for governor and in 1900 stumped the state for the Republicans. In the Senate, influenced by pauper labor arguments, Peffer offered an immigration restriction bill, but it contrasted with the position of contemporary eastern literacy-test restrictionists in that he wanted, sympathetically, to save "all unfit persons [paupers, idiots, *et al.*] . . . the trouble and expense of a voyage across the Atlantic," since under existing law they would only have to be refused admittance. This method of restriction was called "consular inspection."[7]

The A.P.A. Movement, (Washington, D.C.: New Century Press, 1912), p. 56; Donald L. Kinzer, "The American Protective Association" (Ph.D. dissertation, Department of History, University of Washington, 1954), p. 266.

[6] Rightmire, "The Alliance Movement in Kansas," p. 4; Harrington, *op. cit.*, p. 77; Harrison, *op. cit.*, p. 23; Raymond C. Miller, *op. cit.*, p. 216; *Census of 1885*, Vol. CXV, Meriden city, p. 1, in KSHS.

[7] Harrison, *op. cit.*, p. 11; Donald H. Ecroyd, "An Analysis and Evaluation of Populist Political Campaign Speech-Making in Kansas 1890-1894" (Ph.D. dissertation, Department of Speech, State University of Iowa, 1949), pp. 86–

These and an army of other men soon found that they were guiding a mass organization with a membership numbering in the tens of thousands. Not only this, but they had a legislative program of ambitious dimensions, and although their original plan had been to endorse major party candidates who would commit themselves to the Alliance program, this raised some very knotty problems. The Alliance, even as early as the county elections of 1889, included natives and foreigners, Protestants and Catholics, whites and Negroes, Republicans and Democrats. Even today the branding iron of party affiliation sears more deeply and permanently in Kansas than among often mugwumpish city people, and in the politics of seventy years ago, independency was an aberration. What if, in a two-man race for an office, the Democrat went along with the Alliance program? Would the Republican Alliancemen support him or their own party's candidate? Or would an Allianceman who for decades had seen his Democratic party kicked and hated as the party of rebellion suddenly support a Republican who promised in a campaign to support Alliance measures? While it would have been painful for old party leaders to adjust their platforms to meet the Alliance halfway, it might very well have split the Alliance fatally when it was at the zenith of its power to have endorsed a Democrat here, a Republican there, or neither or both candidates somewhere else. Even if by some miracle the Alliance-endorsed winners added up to a majority of the legislature, it was not likely that the Alliance strength, dissipated across both sides of the aisle, would have proved stronger than the familiar call of party loyalty. Even if the members of a single subordinate Alliance could agree among themselves on a supportable slate from among the old party candidates, the agreement of over twenty-seven hundred of these local groups on a state or even congressional ticket was out of the question. For the Alliance to have functioned as a pressure group by making independent endorsements would have been of dubious efficacy for the farmers and at the same time would have created deadly fissures within the organization.

87, 92–93; "Ruppenthal Scrapbooks," IX: 155, in KSHS; *Downs Times,* October 13, 1898; *McPherson Republican,* October 12, 1900; *People's Party Advocate* (McPherson), January 1, 1892; *Topeka Cooperator and Press,* November 9, 1896.

It was natural, then, that the movement to develop a political party based on Alliance strength rapidly gathered momentum. The idea attracted most of the old third-party men, and a respectable number of subordinate Alliances had already entered full slates in the county elections of 1889. Many of the shrewder politicians and editors in the movement, such as McLallin of the *Advocate*, saw it as a solution to the problem of old party loyalty. Although more cautious souls, including Peffer, then editor of the *Kansas Farmer*, were afraid that the danger of the Alliance's going the way of previous third parties was greater than the likelihood of dissipation by helter-skelter endorsements, the majority of the membership through either obstinacy, astuteness, or fervor believed that the benefits outweighed the risks. By the middle of 1890 the 2,735 subordinate Alliances, reinforced by a possible four thousand members of Citizens' Alliances, were a crusading force with great political potential.[8]

Several distinct elements made up this crusade. One was the older farm protest groups, such as the Grange, which had declined in Kansas during the eighties but which retained a faithful following. The Grange never merged with the Farmers' Alliance, as it felt committed to its older, more conservative program, but in 1889 and 1890, at least, it condescended to co-operate with the squalling, giant infant, and when the chips were down the Grangers voted the Alliance ticket.[9]

Single-taxers also joined, and although they were never numerous enough even to threaten to carry the ideas of Henry George into the Alliance platform, their presence added to the solid reform front. It may be, too, that they helped win for the Alliance the votes of people, Irish or otherwise, who were sympathetic to Irish land reform, as Henry George is said to have done in his famous New York mayoralty campaign in 1886. The New York *Irish World*, perhaps the most raucous Irish-American organ, supported George in that campaign and was also often quoted locally by the *Nonconformist* on land ques-

---

[8] Raymond C. Miller, *op. cit.*, pp. 98, 99–101; George Barcus, "The People's Party" (Master's thesis, Department of Sociology, University of Kansas, 1902), pp. 4–5; Morgan, *op. cit.*, p. 353; *Advocate*, July 30, 1890.

[9] Harold Smith, "History of the Grange in Kansas" (Master's thesis, Department of History, University of Kansas, 1940), pp. 39, 86–97, 121–23; *Ottawa Journal and Triumph*, October 30, November 6, 1890.

tions. Edward Bellamy, who had propounded a kind of socialism which he called "nationalism" in his novel, *Looking Backward, 2000–1887*, also had a few Kansas followers. Like others
at that time who saw no real incompatibility between the methods of state socialism and the aims of Jeffersonian laissez faire,
the Bellamyite agrarians found at least a temporary home in
the Alliance, and Bellamy's ideas as well as George's appeared
in Alliance speeches.[10]

A far more important contributor of men and ideas, however, was the Knights of Labor. This organization had enjoyed
a healthy growth especially among Kansas miners and railroad
men in the late eighties partly as a device to offset direct competition with imported Italian contract laborers and also as a
result of wage disputes and needless mine disasters.[11] Like the
farmers, the Knights believed that producers of goods, whether
agricultural or mechanical, had common interests. Both were
traditionally antimonopoly, both favored land reform, both had
inflationist money ideas, and in Kansas and elsewhere the rural
membership of the Knights was always considerable.

The Knights were not so easily convinced that a high protective tariff was harmful, but since a major Alliance tactic in
1890 was to downgrade the old parties' emphasis on this issue,
this disagreement posed no great problem. Although both of
them felt a bond of fellowship for producers the world over, en-
abling an agrarian shocked by German labor conditions to cry
"Verily, the iron heel of the plutocrat is causing infinite woe
and vice throughout the whole world," native and naturalized
Knights were forced into a rather practical antipathy to the
competition of uncomplaining "four-dollar-a-month" Hungarians and Italians. For the warm and humanitarian Terence V.
Powderly, the General Master Workman of the Knights, the
situation was thoroughly regrettable, and though like previous
labor leaders he was an immigration restrictionist, he carefully
dissociated himself from racist arguments that then prevailed

[10] Nathan Fine, *Labor and Farmer Parties in the United States, 1828–
1928* (New York: Rand School of Social Science, 1928), pp. 42, 49; Ashby,
op. cit., pp. 263–65, 342–43 [Part II, chap. i, of this book is a very favorable
exposition of Bellamyism by a Northern Alliance spokesman]; *Kansas
Workman* (El Dorado), August 22, 1890; Ecroyd, *op. cit.*, pp. 174–75.

[11] Kirke Mechem (ed.), *The Annals of Kansas, 1886–1925* (Topeka: Kansas State Historical Society [1954]), I, 5, 6, 66, 110.

among such eastern patricians as Henry Cabot Lodge and Edward W. Bemis.[12]

Racism was a new idea, and the evidence indicates that both the Populists and the Knights of Labor held an ideology taken from the antimonopoly past and not, like Samuel Gompers' fledgling American Federation of Labor, from the industrial future.[13] In all probability, the contract labor and "undesirable immigration" planks in many Populist platforms were there because the Knights demanded them, together with eight-hour day and anti-Pinkerton laws.

Although the religious denominations seldom spoke directly about the Farmers' Alliance, many were quite clear about the apparently unrelated questions of prohibition and Sunday observance. These convictions had political significance, since the Republicans generally favored such things, the Democrats were usually opposed, and the Populists were to face continually a distinct internal division of opinion, since the strong if not always dominant pro-fusion wing had to stay at least somewhat moist to keep the Democrats interested.

The Roman Catholics did take an official stand on the Alliance, and it was distinctly favorable. The most prominent bishop was Louis M. Fink, of Leavenworth, a former prior of the then heavily Bavarian Benedictine monastery at Atchison and a thoroughgoing exponent of immigrant agricultural colonies and of the virtues of rural life in general. In the boom of the eighties Bishop Fink had written an immigration blurb atypical only in that it was especially aimed at attracting Catholic immigrants, and in an 1896 pastoral letter he uttered the rather Bryanesque sentiment that

The stalls of our merchants lie idle if the country has no crops; the railroads are carrying neither merchandise into the country, nor freights from the country to seaboard cities or foreign countries, if the country produces nothing. . . . Are not the country

[12] Gerald N. Grob, "The Knights of Labor, Politics and Populism," *Mid-America*, N.S. XXIX (January, 1958), 14–15, 18–19; S. S. King, *Bond-Holders and Bread-Winners* (privately printed, 1892), pp. 21, 54–55; "Ruppenthal Scrapbooks," III: 97; article by Powderly in the *Atchison Times*, October 6, 1888; John Higham, *Strangers in the Land* (New Brunswick, N.J.: Rutgers University Press, 1955), pp. 45, 101.

[13] Grob, *op. cit.*, p. 21.

population and country occupation the very foundations of general prosperity?

But apparently as a backwash of the controversy about secret societies in the American Catholic church in the late eighties, Fink was initially fearful that the Kansas Alliance, with its oath and ritual like the rest of the Southern Alliance, might be a primrose path to freemasonry, and he forbade Catholic participation. In less than a month, however, the bishop and a committee of the state Alliance worked things out agreeably, and Fink promptly published a pastoral letter in which he said: "I wish [the Alliance] 'God speed' in its honest aims. . . . The sympathies of the reverend clergy of the Catholic church are with the laboring men and with the farmers in their present distress." The priests tending their largely Irish and German flocks were delighted as well as relieved to be rid of a thorny pastoral problem, and the *Advocate* proudly reprinted Fink's letter as well as details of the Alliance's part in the negotiations.[14]

Unfortunately for present purposes, each of the denominations whose membership was of a single nationality apparently restrained itself from such direct expressions, although most of them were less reticent about liquor and related questions. The Swedes in the Augustana Synod of the Lutheran Church and the Germans of the Evangelical Association (German Methodists) and the Evangelical Lutheran Synod, Kansas Conference, which were English-speaking, were bone dry, as were the Mennonites, while the United Lutheran Church of America, Midwest Synod, and the Lutheran Church Missouri Synod, which were German-speaking, were somewhat opposed to liquor but not in favor of legal restrictions.[15]

[14] Peter Beckman, *The Catholic Church on the Kansas Frontier, 1850–1877* (Washington, D.C.: Catholic University of America, 1932), pp. 134–41; Louis M. Fink, *Kansas, Its Resources, Capabilities, Etc.* (Leavenworth, 1883); pastoral letter from Fink to the clergy and the laity of the Leavenworth diocese, January 6, 1896, and circular notices to the clergy, December 31, 1894, and to the clergy and laity of the diocese, March 9, 1890, in St. Benedict's College Archives; *Kansas Catholic* (Leavenworth), February 13, 20, March 13, 1890; *Advocate*, March 13, 20, 1890.

[15] H. A. Ott, *A History of the Evangelical Lutheran Synod of Kansas (General Synod), together with a Sketch of the Augustana Synod Churches* (Topeka: Press of F. M. Steves & Sons, 1907), pp. 227–28; Evangelical Lutheran Synod of Kansas, *Minutes of the 23rd Annual Convention of the*

The views of these churches were politically important in another way; often, as establishments in Europe, their religious and national viewpoints had become practically inseparable over several hundred years, and this amalgam was not quickly broken down among the recent immigrants. Some of the foreign-born tried to maintain their ethnic unity in other ways as well—when they mixed a rampant spread-eagle Americanism with a sort of anti-anti-foreigner feeling and an undisguised ethnic chauvinism. German newspapers boasted that foreign immigration had kept the Caucasian race in America from being overrun by the more prolific Negroes and that immigrants' farms were better kept up than the "Yankees's."[16] Most of these papers were strongly Democratic, and such leading ones as the *Leavenworth Post* frequently reminded their readers that nativism, whose home was in the Republican party, was a constant threat to their group.

To one editor, the "basis of the Anglo-American character is hypocrisy," stemming from a joyless Puritanism, as typified by Americans who ruin their families while endowing church schools or who starve their employees while giving a million for a public library. If a candidate was not, in the eyes of these editors, an advocate of "das Deutschtum" or at least a "friend of the Germans," he was a pariah; yet the same people could urge big crowds to hear German and English speeches about "this free and beautiful country of ours" on July 4.[17]

National and religious unity could sometimes become a political weapon, as when a paper in the Mennonite area alleged that a Catholic priest in Detroit asked for Catholic support of the Democracy as the party most favorable to his church, and commented that although they couldn't say whether the Catholics were going to bring the Pope to America, Rome lays her

Evangelical Lutheran Synod of Kansas . . . (Philadelphia: Lutheran Publication Society, 1890), pp. 16–17; Evangelical Association, Kansas Conference, *Proceedings* (publisher varies, 1888), pp. 16, 22; *ibid.*, 1890, p. 16; *ibid.*, 1896, p. 27; *Story of the Midwest Synod U. L. C. A.* (Published by Committee of Executive Board of Midwest Synod [1950?]), p. 64; Lutheran Church Missouri Synod, *Synodal-Bericht . . . 1889:* (St. Louis: Concordia-Verlag, 1889), pp. 42, 66; *Synodal-Bericht . . . 1891*, p. 33.

[16] *Kansas Staats Zeitung* (Kansas City), November 17, 1898; *Marysville Post*, September 8, 1886.

[17] *Leavenworth Post*, October 27, 1892; *Newton Anzeiger*, November 2, 1888; *Hillsboro Anzeiger*, June 13, 1890.

hands on what she can, and Protestant Germans would do well to keep their eyes open. It was the same paper that weirdly combined Teutonism, the G. O. P., and the American spread eagle when, arguing for high tariffs, it demanded, "Amerikanische Markt für Amerikanischer Produkte!"[18]

A great many of the foreign-born of Kansas nevertheless made the Democratic party their political home, as a result either of misty tradition, as with the Irish, or of more recent factors, such as the attitude of many Germans toward prohibition. Although the agrarian politicians would come to see it much more clearly in later campaigns, one of the most delicate political questions of 1890 was the possibility of winning the support of the foreign groups through fusion with the Democrats. The alternative to fusion was a less promising appeal to other parties strictly on the grounds of common economic distress. The third parties of the recent past had been too narrow, perhaps too pugnacious toward the old parties, to have gained widespread immigrant support, and throughout 1890 it was an astute Republican tactic to harp on the supposed Greenback and Union Labor origins of the People's party ticket. The Populists had always to be careful not to alienate either the Union Labor 12 per cent of 1888 or the newer elements whose votes were absolutely essential for victory.

2. Goodbye, My Party, Goodbye

There was no denying the fact that the Union Labor people and the Greenback element went lock, stock, and barrel into the new movement, even before it showed signs of becoming a political vehicle. W. H. T. Wakefield, the 1888 vice-presidential candidate on the United Labor ticket, W. F. Rightmire, the Union Labor candidate for state attorney-general, and Union Labor presidential electors John Davis, Cyrus Corning, J. L. Shinn, and P. B. Maxson, to name only a few, soon became prominent Alliance editors or candidates. This did not mean, however, as a Republican paper claimed, that the delegation at the Populist convention that August "was about the same crowd which has been attending union labor, greenback and other opposition political gatherings in Kansas for the past ten years."

[18] *Hillsboro Anzeiger*, December 2, 1892; *Marion County Anzeiger* (Hillsboro), October 12, 1888.

Nor, if the Alliance had been only a revamped Greenbackery, would Republicans have been so piqued at the frequent and feasible county-level fusion it effected with the Democrats.[19]

Nevertheless, the front echelon of the Alliance had strong Union Labor representation as it moved toward political action in the spring of 1890. After some consultation, Ben Clover, the state president of the Alliance, publicly called for a convention of Alliance, Grange, Farmers' Mutual Benefit Association, Knights of Labor, and single-tax groups to meet in Topeka on June 12. The response was excellent, and the convention, about half of its ninety delegates Alliancemen, resolved to put a full "People's Party" slate in the field and to convene a large convention for that purpose on August 13. They endorsed the St. Louis platform adopted in December, 1889, by the national Alliance, which included the abolition of national banks and substitution of legal tender notes, an end to grain futures speculation, "free and unlimited coinage of silver," alien and railroad land restriction, equal taxation, fractional paper currency, and government ownership of "communication and transportation."[20]

The foreign-language press observed all this with fascination, but angry as they were at the Republicans for their "prohibition craze" and "robber tariff," even though they knew the Democrats had no more hope than ever of a solo victory, they gave at first tentative and later only lukewarm support to the agrarian politicians. It would be ideal, they said, if the Alliance would endorse the Democratic ticket. Even without such an endorsement the People's party might be worth supporting for economic reasons. Nevertheless, the influence of dependable German farmers was essential if the People's party was to avoid fanatical Yankee ideas such as prohibition and the subtreasury.[21] On the last point many of the Alliancemen could not have

[19] *Lindsborg News*, June 20, August 14, 22, 1890; *La Crosse Chieftain*, October 10, 1890.
[20] John D. Hicks, *The Populist Revolt* (Minneapolis: University of Minnesota Press, 1931), pp. 427–28 [the subtreasury was not one of the seven demands of the St. Louis convention]. *Advocate*, May 14, June 18, 1890; Rightmire, "The Alliance Movement in Kansas," pp. 5–6. Of the ninety delegates, forty-one were Alliancemen, seven Grangers, twenty-eight Knights of Labor, and four single-taxers.
[21] *Pittsburg Herald*, June 5, 1890; *Leavenworth Post*, June 18, 1890; *Newton Anzeiger*, June 13, 1890; *Wichita Herald*, June 12, August 28, 1890.

agreed more. The June convention had side-stepped prohibition, and since it is likely that a majority or near-majority of the delegates personally favored it, the result was a considerable victory for astuteness and political realism.

This was the most that could be expected. Although no one could be sure that Alliance membership meant Populist votes, still the Alliance was two or three times the size of the Democratic party and could not very well endorse either the Democratic slate or its openly resubmissionist platform and expect to remain vigorous. It was remarkable that moderates urging either state liquor control and sales or complete silence on the whole question could overcome powerful prohibitionist voices such as Peffer's *Kansas Farmer.*

In spite of the fact that many German editors, as fanatical from their side as the Prohibition party was on the other, and a phalanx of Republicans who either were ardent drys or saw a chink in the Populist political armor, heaped scorn upon the Populists during the campaign for wholly ignoring this "most pressing" of issues, the agrarians had chosen the wisest course.[22] Sympathetic as the German press was on the mortgage, money, land, and antimonopoly questions, it was the liquor matter that kept them from full support of the Populist ticket. Although German Alliancemen and voters surely helped the new party considerably in November, the German press undoubtedly cost the Populists votes.

It was the action of the Democracy that gave the wringing wets a choice. Charles Robinson of Lawrence, first governor of Kansas and part of the state's folklore, in 1890 an Alliance-minded resubmission Democrat, had been ballyhooed by many non-Republican segments of the press from late spring onward as the obvious Populist candidate for governor. As the German-language *Kansas Herald* put it: "Had ex-Governor Robinson been nominated [by the Alliance], then the Democrats would without doubt have endorsed the nomination."[23] But when the Populists met in August to draw up a slate, the seesaw division

[22] *Advocate,* March 25, 1891; James H. Lathrop, *Voice of True Reform* (Topeka, October, 1891), I, 45; *Kansas Farmer* (Topeka), October 22, 1890; *Wichita Herald,* October 30, 1890; *Pittsburg Herald,* June 19, 1890; *Minneapolis Messenger,* October 30, 1890; *Topeka Capital,* August 14, 1890.

[23] *Kansas Herald* (Kansas City), August 15, 1890. See also *Germania* (Lawrence), June 12, 1890.

between the more radical prohibitionist, women's suffragist, non-fusion, Greenback-derived wing, on the one hand, and the almost equally large, more pragmatic and moderate group, on the other, made the convention less than harmonious. The moderates had generally prevailed on platform matters, but when the slate was drawn up they were stymied by a rigid interpretation of the Alliance doctrine that "the office must seek the man, not the man the office." Robinson had apparently done nothing for his candidacy except give benign indications that he would accept nomination if offered, but the very fact that he had been so prominently mentioned in the press was enough to defeat him. As the gubernatorial nomination of John F. Willits, a once-Republican farmer, rolled through, it crushed out the possibility of state-wide Democratic fusion and full German support.

The Democrats indignantly put up a slate of their own, with Robinson at the top; but although they had no qualms about endorsing previously selected Populist candidates for state attorney-general, a majority of the congressional seats, and scores of county jobs, the hope of success dimmed for both parties. Many Democratic papers plumped for Robinson and resubmission, described the Prohibition party as a horror surpassed only by the Know-Nothings, and were sympathetic to the Populists to the point of lamentation over the lost chance of fusion. The split in the Alliance and the People's party between prohibitionists, silent straddlers, and resubmissionists continued through 1890 and afterward, and the narrow margin by which the Republicans escaped from a fused opposition was underscored by the attitude of a number of Democratic papers in German areas. These papers had completely ignored the Union Labor ticket in 1888, but in 1890 they backed fusion tickets for county offices without a tremor and praised their Populist allies.[24]

Since the Republicans had drafted a platform nearly as radical as the Populists' on economic issues, the three platforms ap-

[24] *Alliance Tribune* (Topeka), August 21, 1890; *McPherson Democrat*, August 29, 1890; Raymond C. Miller, *op. cit.*, pp. 125–33; *Advocate*, August 20, 1890; *Wichita Herold*, September 4, 1890; *Le Roy Reporter*, September–November, 1890; *Topeka Capital*, October 18, 1890; *Dickinson County News* (Abilene), August 21, 1890; *Marysville Free Press*, October 6, 1890; *Seneca Courier-Democrat*, September–November, 1890.

parently left little to choose between. But everyone knew which was the radical party and which party was tied to the Harrison administration and the old guard. Both Republicans and straight Democrats publicly shrugged off the Populist effort, but in secret were aghast at its possibilities as well as unable, for fear of a backfire, to sound the tocsin of anarchy as they had with previous third parties. In a stodginess born of fear the Republicans fell back on the tariff and the bloody shirt in an attempt to split the opposition, while at the same time feebly echoing the straightforward Populist positions on land, money, and transportation. The Democrats favored cheaper money and a low tariff, mostly by force of habit, but it was the Populists who were making the campaign on the strength of their triple economic appeal.[25]

This was pure western Populism, with the subtreasury quietly passed by in favor of free coinage of silver and adequate issue of paper, with government ownership of railroads, antispeculator agitation, and mortgage relief laws in the van, and with the excision of the barnacle-like John J. Ingalls from the United States Senate and the Kansas ship of state a prime demand.[26]

None of the platforms bore any overt signs of nativism or anti-Semitism, unless the now customary alien land and contract labor planks, which were derived from the homestead principle and a competitive labor situation, can be construed as such. Some Populists were impressed with the reputed difficulties of the Knights of Labor with competitive labor imported under contract. While they sang such ditties as

> Railroads, also, must come under
> Wholesome, wise constraint;
> Syndicates and alien landlords
> Must yield to our complaint . . .

to the tune of "Hold the Fort," they made direct multilingual appeals to the foreign-language farmers with the same eco-

[25] William Allen White, "The Regeneration of Colonel Hucks," in *The Real Issue: A Book of Kansas Stories* (Chicago: Way and Williams, 1897), pp. 168–79; *Scandia Journal*, August 15, 1890; Ecroyd, *op. cit.*, p. 5; Raymond C. Miller, *op. cit.*, pp. 144–48; *Newton Journal*, November 7, 1890; *Lindsborg News*, October–November, 1890.

[26] Raymond C. Miller, *op. cit.*, pp. 161–62; Theodore Saloutos, *Farmer Movements in the South, 1865–1933* (Berkeley: University of California Press, 1960), p. 104.

nomic arguments they used with English-speaking crowds.[27]
Even though the foreign blocs had traditional affiliations with
either the Republicans or Democrats, so did the native-born,
and had it not been for complicating issues such as the liquor
question, the Populists would doubtless have made their strictly
economic appeals more widely felt. As it was, they gradually,
steadily came to a recognition of the immigrants' political importance.

Neither the more recently arrived nor the older stock Populists usually treated the immigrants in any special way except as
potential voters. The Kansas situation in the nineties does not
support the belief of a prominent historian of American immigration, Marcus Lee Hansen, that the mass of Populists, and
their leaders, were old-family, native stock Americans who had
made their trans-Atlantic trek no more recently than two or
three centuries earlier.[28] Hansen believed that although immigrants had been highly active and influential in middle western
politics since the Civil War, they excepted themselves in the
case of Populism, partly because, he said, they were customar-
ily conservative, and partly because their churchmen were un-
accustomed to American secular patterns and unwilling to let
their flocks adjust rapidly to it. But even the one-time state
churches, at least in Kansas, took no formal anti-Populist stand,
and there seems to have been no great difference in participation between members of former state churches and members
of nonconforming bodies. While it was true that the foreign-
born were not as prominent on the state level of the party in
1890 as they would become later, the fact that they were abundant in the rear echelons from the very beginning indicates not
that they were discriminated against but that they had not yet
sufficiently come of age to exert extensive political leadership
when the movement began. Indicators of foreign participation
and appeals, including the party's position on prohibition,
women's suffrage, and Democratic fusion, showed that many

[27] William A. Peffer, *The Farmer's Side* (New York: D. Appleton & Co.,
1891), p. 53; Nell B. Waldron, "Colonization in Kansas from 1861 to 1890"
(Ph.D. dissertation, Northwestern University, 1931), pp. 99–100; William T.
Edgare, "Our Battle," *The Alliance and Labor Songster*, by L. Vincent (Winfield of Kan.: H. and L. Vincent, Printers, 1890), p. 40; Ashby, *op. cit.*,
p. 208; *Hays Free Press*, September 13, 1890.

[28] Marcus Lee Hansen, *The Immigrant in American History*, ed., and with
a foreword, by Arthur M. Schlesinger (Cambridge, Mass.: Harvard University Press, 1940), pp. 85, 91.

of the foreign-born were active Populists from the beginning and perhaps increased their participation as time went on.

Even in 1890 the outstanding Kansas Populists were by no means many generations removed from Europe. Their backgrounds were varied in every respect. The gubernatorial candidate, John F. Willits, was nearly a political unknown. His prior eminence had been as overseer of the state Grange and as a member of two legislatures, but he was a much more familiar figure in the neighborhood of his farm near McLouth, in Leavenworth county, than he was around the statehouse in Topeka. W. F. Rightmire, the candidate for chief justice of the state supreme court, had been the Union Labor candidate for attorney-general in 1888, and as a founder of the Alliance in Kansas, was usually considered part of the old *Nonconformist* group, which played a vigorous but relatively far less important role in 1890 than it had in 1888.

With the possible exception of Mary Elizabeth Lease, the most famous Kansas Populist was Jerry Simpson, who was born in 1842 in the heavily Scottish and Welsh Westmoreland county, New Brunswick. Simpson had risen from sailor to cook to captain during twenty-three years of sailing on the Great Lakes, tarried briefly in Indiana after the Civil War to marry a girl of English birth or parentage, and finally stopped his roving on a farm near Medicine Lodge in south-central Kansas.[29] His almost total innocence of formal education did not prevent him from quoting Carlyle, Dickens, Thackeray, and other authors with point and accuracy during his campaigns for office as a Greenbacker and Union Laborite in 1886 and 1888. By his own count, Simpson had been, starting in 1864, a Lincoln Republican, a Peter Cooper Greenbacker, a single-taxer, a Union Laborite, and finally a Populist; but the inconsistencies were mainly of title, since his views broadened rather than changed.

As William Allen White said, he was neither sockless nor a clown:

Error dies hard. The myth about Jerry Simpson pulling up his trousers and showing his sockless shanks still prevails, yet noth-

[29] *Burlington Independent,* August 22, 1890; Annie L. Diggs, *The Story of Jerry Simpson* (Wichita: Jane Simpson, Publisher, 1908), pp. 15, 16, 21, 36, 37, 42; Diggs, "The Women in the Alliance Movement," *Arena,* VI (July, 1892), 176; Charles K. Franks, "Jerry Simpson—A Kansas Populist" (Master's thesis, Northwestern University, 1940), p. 2.

ing like the act in question ever happened. The whole story is made of the fabric of a dream by Victor Murdock. There was not the slightest foundation for it.[30]

But Simpson made the "Sockless Jerry" label one of his greatest political stocks in trade, and even the slight, frothy, and overly ladylike sketch by Annie Diggs cannot disguise a personality reminiscent of Lincoln, as his clear, calm, witty, sometimes sarcastic, homespun, usually warm speeches evoke it. "The government is the *people* and *we* are the people" was a sentiment few farmers could resist, and with his lightning tongue he was a sure thing in Populist politics.[31]

Such awesome figures as Speaker Joseph G. Cannon of the United States House of Representatives were said to have maintained a healthy respect for Simpson, and perhaps some of Cannon's respect grew out of an incident during a House debate in 1899 on army appropriations. Simpson opposed appropriations that would be used to help put down the Philippine insurrection, and Congressman Cannon, a Republican from Illinois, retorted heatedly that had Simpson made his anti-army remarks in Manila, he "would have been arrested, tried by a drumhead courtmartial, and shot." Simpson rose to a point of personal privilege and drawled:

Mr. Chairman, that may be true and it may not be true. I do not know, in choosing between two difficulties of this kind, whether I would rather be court-martialed and shot in Manila or be shot with an old muzzle-loading brass Cannon like that I was shot with a few moments ago. (Great Laughter).[32]

As a first-rank ideologue as well as a very able politician, Simpson was a rarity. Although theoretically opposed to fusion in 1890 and 1891, he did nothing to reject a Democratic endorsement in 1890, and, with his scruples dissolved in 1892 by more fusion, he was so firmly entrenched politically by 1894 that he managed to get Democratic backing even after he came

[30] *Emporia Gazette*, April 15, 1898. Murdock was a Wichita newspaperman and later a Progressive party congressman.

[31] *The Autobiography of William Allen White* (New York: Macmillan Co., 1946), p. 217; Diggs, *The Story of Jerry Simpson*, pp. 43, 58, 118–19; Harrison, *op. cit.*, pp. 14, 17; Franks, *op. cit.*, p. 53; Ecroyd, *op. cit.*, pp. 102, 105–11, 378.

[32] *Congressional Record*, 55th Cong., 3d sess., February 25, 1899, XXXII, 2407–8.

out for women's suffrage. On another thorny issue, prohibition, he could again work both sides of the street by denouncing the liquor traffic at the same time he scorned national legislative prohibition because of the bad effects it would have on brewery workers and other laborers, finally declaring that intemperance could be cured only by curing poverty first, which the Populist economic program would do. Thus, a Populist vote could be a vote both for temperance without legal prohibition and against poverty.[33]

Labor elements liked his single-tax coloration, and during his three terms in Congress he expressed the labor viewpoint on immigration by entering in the *Record* petitions (though no bills or resolutions) for restriction, Chinese and otherwise. Like many Populists, he could praise the free trade of England, which resulted in high wages for English workingmen and at the same time be lauded for making

all the corporations tremble with fear, and to a certain extent across the briny waters in Threadneedle street, London, where the money sharks of the whole world are firmly entrenched. He is the Polaris of the legislative heavens. . . .[34]

The "Sockless Socrates" remained a Populist from beginning to end, regardless of women's suffrage, prohibition, fusion, snubs or favors by the party high command, peace, war, or imperialism, and died unreconstructed at Wichita in 1905.

Another prominent Populist of the 1890 campaign was W. H. Biddle, the candidate for state treasurer. A typical member of the slate of that year—people who were mostly raised from obscurity and for the most part soon returned to it—Biddle had been born forty-five years before in Brown county, Illinois, of parents who had emigrated from Wales and England.

William Baker, a native of Washington county, Pennsylvania, one of the few college graduates among the prominent Populists, emerged from Lincoln county in 1890 for the first of

[33] Speech at Wichita, September 15, 1891, quoted in Ecroyd, *op. cit.*, pp. 386, 390; speech at Wichita, September 2, 1894, quoted in *ibid.*, p. 390; Franks, *op. cit.*, p. 42.

[34] *Leavenworth Labor News*, November 18, 1892; Harrison, *op. cit.*, p. 58; *Congressional Record*, 52d Cong., 1st sess., XXIII, p. 1764; Speech at Wichita, September 15, 1891, quoted in Ecroyd, *op. cit.*, p. 385; *Kiowa Review*, October 17, 1894.

three successful campaigns as congressman from the sixth district.[35]

The fifth district congressman for two terms beginning in 1891 was an Illinois native, John Davis. Like Simpson, he married an English girl, had been a Republican, Greenbacker, and Union Labor supporter, and was a favorite of the Knights of Labor. Davis had been president of the state Grange in 1874 and a year later became editor and publisher of that vigorous voice of reform, the *Junction City Tribune*, and although like most labor-oriented Congressmen he entered petitions for restriction, his editorial position was favorable to immigration.[36]

In the fourth district a Vermont-born Quaker, John Grant Otis, won brief prominence with a single term as a Populist congressman. Otis typified a certain group within the People's party with his New England background, advocacy of prohibition and women's suffrage, Greenbackery, and the fact that as late as January, 1890, he was state lecturer of the Grange but not an Allianceman. He was a lawyer and graduate of Williams College, and had come to Kansas in 1859, when it had seemed elsewhere to be still bleeding and abolishing.[37]

Almost an exact opposite of Otis was a millionaire socialist who joined the movement equally early but remained a leader throughout its history. Christian B. Hoffman was born in Switzerland in 1854, a year before his father began a trek to Dickinson county to become the head of a large milling firm at Enterprise. During early forays into the antimonopoly and greenback movements, Hoffman edited the Enterprise *Anti-Monopolist*, was a member of the Kansas House, mayor of Enterprise, president of the Kansas Millers Association, an officer in two banks, and a partner in his father's business. With John W. Breidenthal and others, Hoffman directed the fortunes of the Kansas-Sinaloa Investment Company, which was the corporate form of a socialist colony lasting into the mid-nineties that included

[35] *Advocate*, August 20, 1890; *Kansas Workman* (El Dorado), September 26, 1890; Harrison, *op. cit.*, p. 23.

[36] Joseph Wilson, *John Davis, The People's Candidate for Congress in the Fifth District. The Next Congressman* (Marysville, Kan.: People's Advocate, [1890?]), *passim*; Harrison, *op. cit.*, pp. 18–19; *Junction City Democratic Sentinel*, August 21, 1890; Diggs, "The Women in the Alliance Movement," 178; *Junction City Tribune*, November 30, 1900; *Congressional Record*, 52d Cong., 1st sess., XXIII, 867, 3857, 3900, 5025.

[37] Harrison, *op. cit.*, p. 20; *Kansas Farmer* (Topeka), January 8, 1890.

native and foreign Kansans and others at Topolobampo, Mexico. After the Topolobampo episode he was not so close to Breidenthal, the Populist state chairman, who nonetheless instigated his nomination as temporary chairman of the 1900 Populist state convention by a Scottish Populist, Andrew Shearer, of Marshall county. In that year he closed his boisterous political career with election to a term in the Kansas Senate.[38]

An even more bizarre personality, with a more checkered career, was the "uncrowned queen" of the Kansas Populists, Mrs. Mary Elizabeth Lease (née Clyens). So powerful were her revivalistic speeches and so dominant was her personality that in the 1890 campaign and forever afterward she was an issue in herself. Never quite trusted by the party organization and never willing to compromise an iota from what her intuition told her she should do, this larger-than-life virago caused no end of revulsion among the Germans, for whom it was dogma that the *frau* belonged in the home. For the few years she was involved in Populist politics, she probably provoked nearly as much mortification among her own party leaders as she did among her whilom enemies, the Republicans. But it is too easy to be unkind to Mrs. Lease. Her erratic, intractable, tempestuous personality was an accident of birth.

Exactly where that decisive event took place has been a matter of disagreement, partly since the lady herself occasionally informed whomever was listening that she first saw daylight in County Monaghan, Ireland, but the consensus, herself included, was that she was born of Irish political exiles at Ridgway, Pennsylvania, a place about two-thirds of the way from Pittsburgh to Olean, New York, on September 11, 1853.[39] In any case, she

[38] Edward G. Nelson, *The Company and the Community* (Lawrence: University of Kansas Press, 1956), pp. 229, 251, 287–97, 312–14, 338, 380; John D. Bright (ed.), *Kansas: The First Century* (New York: Lewis Historical Publishing Co., Inc., 1956), IV, 327–39; *The Integral Co-operator* (Enterprise), September 17, 1891 ff. [this was the organ of the Kansas-Sinaloa Investment Company]; interview with Willard J. Breidenthal, Topeka, September 11, 1960; *Topeka State Journal*, July 25, 1900.

[39] Probably the only extant Lease manuscript is a letter by "James Arnold" attributed to her in the KSHS archives. It is a useful biographical sketch. Although the *Advocate* (January 21, 1891), Elizabeth Barr [Arthur] ("The Populist Uprising," in William E. Connelley's *A Standard History of Kansas and Kansans* [Chicago: Lewis Publishing Co., 1918], II, 1149), and Diggs ("The Women in the Alliance Movement," p. 166) put her birth in

had some direct knowledge of English "oppression and injustice," and the death of her father at Andersonville prison together with the loss of one brother at Fredericksburg, another at Lookout Mountain, and an uncle at Gettysburg may have had a searing and traumatic effect. These facts help explain why her hatred of the Democracy was far more virulent and permanent than her dislike of the Republicans. If this inference is correct, those were black days not only for the family of Mary Elizabeth Clyens but for Kansas Populism, because the "party of rebellion" became the great potential ally of Populism, her chosen instrument of reform, and if anyone benefited from the enmity that ensued, it was neither Mrs. Lease nor the Populist party.

She came to Kansas in her teens, about 1870, and in the score of years between then and the campaign of 1890 she did so much to make a crusade, she married a Wichita pharmacist, Charles L. Lease, bore him four children (Charles H., Eva L., Lena Grace, and Ben Hurr), spent a few stifling years with her new family on a lonely prairie homestead, became one of Kansas' first female lawyers, lectured for the Irish National League, spoke and edited a paper for the Union Laborites, ran for Sedgwick county superintendent of schools and was defeated by a record margin, and joined both the Knights of Labor and the Farmers' Alliance.[40]

The People's party campaign of 1890 was her glory road. She told astonished audiences what had to be done about land, money, and transportation, and was particularly explicit about where John J. Ingalls, that plutocratic traducer of the people's trust, ought to be consigned. Her enormous presence, together

Ireland, the Pennsylvania attribution, given by implication in the Arnold letter as well as in W. G. Clugston's *Rascals in Democracy* (New York: Richard R. Smith, 1940), p. 92; an interview of Lease by W. A. White, in the *Fort Scott Weekly Monitor*, January 18, 1894; and *Who Was Who in America* (Chicago: A. N. Marquis Company, 1942), I, 713, is probably correct.

[40] "Arnold letter," in KSHS; *Advocate*, July 27, 1892; *Who Was Who*, I, 713; *New York Herald Tribune*, October 30, 1933; *The Nation* (Wichita), September 24, 1886; *Attica Advocate*, October 5, 1888; Betty Lou Taylor, "Mary Elizabeth Lease: Kansas Populist" (Master's thesis, Department of History, Municipal University of Wichita, 1951), pp. 1–9; *Census of 1895*, Vol. CCCVIII, Wichita Ward 3, p. 82, in KSHS; *The Tenth Directory of the City of Wichita and Sedgwick County, for 1896* (Wichita: Leader Printing and Publishing Co., [1896]), p. 205.

with a speaking style that was undisciplined, emotional, sarcastic, magnetic, eloquent, torrential, fitted the task superbly. Many of her sentences were of a ululating kind that Vachel Lindsay would at least have taken under advisement if not actually used. The following one came from a debate with an unsung and browbeaten Republican named James Brumbaugh, who was never heard of again:

India rich with every fertility of soil and climate, centralization of wealth, the curse of the money power, the incubus of bonds was loaded on India, and India went down as Persia, and Spain, and Greece, and Rome, as Turkey and Ireland went down, from the incubus of bonds, the curse of the money power.[41]

Read this aloud, multiply by two hours, and a faint echo will be had of the hypnotic impact of a full-scale Lease calamity howl.

In later years William Allen White had this recollection of her from his old guard youth:

I have never heard a lovelier voice than Mrs. Lease's. It was a golden voice—a deep, rich contralto, a singing voice that had hypnotic qualities. She put into her oratory something which the printed copies of her speech did not reveal. . . . She stood nearly six feet tall, with no figure, a thick torso, and long legs. To me, she often looked like a kangaroo pyramided up to a comparatively small head. Her skin was a pasty white; her jowls were a little heavy; her eyes, the most expressive feature of her face, were of a nondescript color but capable of everything except spoken language. She wore her hair in a psyche knot, always neatly combed and topped by the most ungodly hats I ever saw a woman wear. She had no sex appeal—none! She was not so quick and intelligent as Jerry Simpson. She knew much less than he about the fundamental causes of the uprising; but she knew it was an uprising, and she rode the waves.[42]

And ride the waves she did. Believing that "all true reforms, says Mazzini, are religious," she did her best to make this one so, as she wrenched the tears from the eyes of tired, windburned farmers with her frightful tales of Andersonville, and

[41] *Joint Debate beween Mrs. M. E. Lease and J. M. Brumbaugh, at Concordia, Kansas, Monday Afternoon, July 20th, 1891, on the Land, Finance and Transportation Questions* (Concordia, Kan.: Times Print, T. A. Filson, [1891?]), p. 3.

[42] *The Autobiography of William Allen White*, pp. 218–19.

then, a female John the Baptist crying in the wilderness, promised them redemption from Ingalls, railroads, grasping landlords, and the vicious money power.

She hardly knew it when the campaign ended, and in 1891, with another state campaign a year away, she kept up her barrage for reform of land, money, and transportation. But by now, with Ingalls in political oblivion, some of her other ideas began to obtrude. It was not surprising that she was a prohibitionist, a suffragist, and at least half a socialist, but that she was also a fervid exponent of Anglo-Saxon superiority, a racist, was as exotic among the Populists as the chalk-dusted air of Professor Burgess's Columbia classrooms. She had already been responsible for far more than her share of references to Shylock, Rothschild, Jewish bankers, and British gold, and her prominence in the movement put their ugly onus on the mass of Populists who had never dreamt of such things.[43]

Yet it was not for these things but rather for possessing a gender unusual in the politics of those days that the Germans ground their teeth when she strode by. The *Leavenworth Post* called her a "man-wife," and said, "We are no idolizers of Ingalls. But such an opponent he doesn't deserve," while *Der Waechter* of Kansas City, fretting about her 1892 candidacy for the United States Senate, said that if such a scandal came about, the whole world would know Kansas was insane. The severing of her stormy connection with the Populist Lewelling administration came in 1894, and the Republican *Kansas City Star* predicted that "the election of Mrs. Mary E. Lease to Congress is about as likely to occur as her elevation to the office of Grand Master of the Masons of Kansas. . . ." Even the friendly Democratic *Council Grove Guard* poked fun:

"Mrs. Lease cannot be with us on the occasion of our big pop rally, but we will make a terrible effort to have him here if he can get some one to wash the dishes and take care of the children while he comes."[44]

[43] Speech by Lease in *The Great Quadrangular Debate* (Salina, Kan.: Press of Republican Job Rooms, 1894) ; *Ottawa Journal and Triumph*, October 9, 1890; Taylor, *op. cit.*, p. 13; Lease, *The Problem of Civilization Solved* (1895), quoted in Ecroyd, *op. cit.*, pp. 119–20.

[44] *Leavenworth Post*, October 20, 1892; *Der Waechter* (Kansas City), November 24, 1892; *Kansas City Star*, quoted in *Parsons Daily Eclipse*, June 15, 1894; *Council Grove Guard*, October 26, 1894.

Not able to make a clean break, she carried on a partially successful campaign of sabotage against the Populist state leadership and in 1896 broke with Jerry Simpson and denounced Bryan, fusion, and "the senile Democratic party . . . the party of slavery and secession." Although her great issues in 1892 had been land and transportation, and in 1894 those issues and woman's suffrage, by 1896 it was Andersonville again, and the one-time scourge of Ingalls stumped for McKinley that year and repeated the performance in 1900.

In 1897 the home in Wichita had been claimed by the sheriff for a $1,400 mortgage debt and shortly afterward her long deteriorating relations with her hapless pharmacist, who had confined his reform efforts to leading torchlight parades as president of the Bryan Flambeau Club of Wichita, ended in divorce. Mary Elizabeth Lease and the four children left a rather shaken Kansas for New York, there to spend the last thirty years of her life in relative obscurity as a writer for Pulitzer's New York *World*, a lecturer for the New York City Board of Education, and the president of national and international birth control societies.[45]

People like Mrs. Lease, Willits, Simpson, and the others were only the generals in the Populist army. Thousands of now forgotten men and women took part as candidates, editors, or local party workers, and a great many of them were of foreign birth or parentage. Some of them appear briefly here and in later chapters, and while this list is in no way exhaustive and emerged from a sample which could hardly have been more random, it does give some idea about the age, the property holdings, the ethnic origin, and other facts about a few foreign-born Populists.[46]

[45] Taylor, *op. cit.*, pp. 51–57; Clugston, *op. cit.*, p. 94; *Kansas Commoner* (Wichita), November 5, 1896; William B. Bracke, *Wheat Country* (New York: Duell, Sloan & Pierce, 1950), pp. 158–59; *Great Bend Beacon*, October 5, 1900; *New York Herald Tribune*, October 30, 1933; Mechem, *op. cit.*, I, 333; *Topeka Cooperator and Press*, December 4, 1896.

[46] The random sample was arrived at in this way: the *Advocate* and other newspapers provide county tickets, lists of township and county committeemen, and mentions of other party aides with some frequency. From these were selected at random a number of names that "sounded" German or Swedish or Irish or some other nationality, and a check of the *Census of 1895* (if the person could be found) provided some personal data. Out of the nearly three thousand Alliances, over a hundred counties, and twenty-five hundred or so townships, only a few score names were checked. Furthermore, since the names of Englishmen do not sound "foreign," such names

Nels Anderson, a thirty-four year old Swede who had come to Kansas by way of Indiana, lived in Topeka with his wife and three children. A statute line marker by trade, Anderson roamed the state for the People's Party Lecture Bureau expounding in Swedish the Populist viewpoints on the tariff, money, and other matters.[47]

The candidate for state representative from Saline county, Patrick H. Dolan, was a farmer making his first entry into politics. Dolan was born in County Roscommon, Ireland, came to western Massachusetts when he was a boy, and had been in Kansas for thirteen years. A former Democrat and a Catholic, he was fifty-one when he began his several terms in the legislature and was Populist county chairman in 1894 and 1896.[48]

A Swedish-born farmer, F. O. Ostenberg, had been a trustee of Smolan township in Saline county before he became the Populist candidate for clerk of the district court at thirty. The clerkship, for obvious reasons, was often filled by immigrants who were bilingual.

This was also the case in Republic county, where A. Ellingson, a thirty-four-year-old native of Christiania, Norway, who had homesteaded just after the Civil War, was the Populist candidate for the clerkship. He was elected and ran again in 1892.

In Pottawatomie county, J. M. Regnier, 31, was the candidate for the district court clerkship. An Illinois native himself, he lived in a somewhat French Canadian township and had a Canadian-born wife. The secretary of the Alliance in a nearby township was a Kansan, Louis Bothe, 24, who farmed 720 acres adjacent to the farm of his German-born parents.

A large Welsh community lived in the southern part of Osage county, and members of it were represented in the farmers' movement. Roger Jones, 47, Welsh-born, farmed 320 acres and was secretary of the Hill Side Farmers' Mutual Benefit Association, and other Welshmen were Alliancemen and candidates.

G. J. Melzer, 44, was president of the Mulberry Alliance in

---

were not checked, and since some Englishmen or Canadians appeared in spite of this, the relative absence of these groups is a result only of the method used.

[47] James H. Lathrop, *The Voice of True Reform* (Topeka, 1891), I, 83–84; *Census of 1895*, Vol. CCCXLVII, Topeka City, p. 240.

[48] *Salina Union*, September 26, 1890; W. W. Admire (comp.), *Admire's Political and Legislative Hand-Book for Kansas* (Topeka: Geo. W. Crane & Co., 1891), p. 424.

Neuchatel township, Nemaha county. Born in Germany, he lived on a 320-acre farm with his wife and eight children. Regardless of the doctrine propounded by the Reverend Dr. Carl Swensson, the leader of Lindsborg, that a good Swede was automatically a Republican, there was a constant and vocal Swedish Populist contingent in Lindsborg and other parts of McPherson county from 1890 onward. Carl Ferm and H. Helstrom were the Populist county committeemen from Smoky Hill and New Gottland townships; O. W. Esping was secretary of the Alliance at Lindsborg; and N. O. Sandberg, 46, of Gypsum Creek, was on the county committee and was a candidate for county commissioner.[49]

The Farmers' Alliance in Gove county, in western Kansas, was studded with foreign names among its organizers and officers, and of these Peter J. Heinz, 46, a German-born printer, Henry Homm, 24, a German farmer of a quarter section, and John Wahl, another German farmer, were foreign-born, and there were probably others as well.

A. J. Harwi, prominent among the Populists at Atchison, was described in a western Kansas paper as a "poor 'Pennsylvania Dutchman' " who had been in Kansas for several years.

In heavily native-born Elk county, the doorkeeper of the Alliance, German Zirn, 59, a German-born Civil War veteran, probably was not the only immigrant member.

The president of the Alliance at Concordia, and candidate for county attorney of Cloud county, was W. H. Savary, who, although born at Momence, Illinois, had studied at the Presbyterian Seminary in Montreal and sometimes addressed his Alliance in French. And in adjacent Clay county, the secretary of the Alliance was Frank Schoenkoenig, 47, a European who farmed 120 acres.[50]

[49] *Salina Union*, September 26, October 24, 1890; *Republic County Freeman* (Belleville), September 8, October 23, 1892; *St. Marys Star*, July 31, August 21, 1890; *Lyndon People's Herald*, October 17, 1890; *Advocate*, January 16, 1890; *McPherson Industrial Union*, June 26, August 7, 1890; *Census of 1885*, Vol. CCXL, Smolan twp., p. 9; *Census of 1895*, Vol. CCXIV, p. 25; *ibid.*, Vol. CCXVI, Gypsum Creek twp., pp. 14, 20; *ibid.*, Vol. CCLVIII, Neuchatel twp., p. 10; *ibid.*, CCLXXIV, Arvonia twp., p. 7; *ibid.*, Vol. CCXCII, Wamego twp., p. 31; *ibid.*, Vol. CCXCV, Mill Creek twp., p. 14.

[50] MS minutebook of Gove County Farmers' Alliance, in KSHS; *Hays Free Press*, October 11, 1890; *Industrial Free Press* (Winfield), August 22, 1890; *Concordia Alliant*, October 4, 1890; *Advocate*, February 27, 1890;

Anton Wempe, president in 1890 of the Capioma Alliance, Nemaha county, and Edward Rooney, the secretary, had left the area by the time of the 1895 census, but left behind a sizable contingent of Wempes from Germany and Rooneys from Ireland. Wempe ran a general store and the post office at Fidelity, across the Brown county line. In that county the Hiawatha Citizens' Alliance was run by two Englishmen, President A. J. Hill, 44, an implement dealer, and Vice-President T. T. Fisher, 56, a printer.

Barton county, at the bend in the Arkansas River, was heavily immigrant and heavily Populist. The county committee included Charles Rodenberg, 31, a recent German immigrant who farmed a quarter section; George Bauer, 49, another German; and John B. Unruh, 29, a German-Russian, who was on the Pawnee Rock township slate. Joseph F. Strothman of Logan township, married to a German, ran for county commissioner.

The heavily German-Russian township of Lincoln, in Russell county, had its subordinate Alliance in 1890, and Adam Dietz, 54, was its president. Dietz and his wife Elizabeth came to Kansas from their native Russia sometime between 1874 and 1878, to judge by the ages and birthplaces of their three children. His 240-acre farm was half in pasture, half in wheat and corn, with three hand wells and a quarter section completely fenced; it held five people, four horses, eight cows, a pig, a dog, and a number of chickens. In 1895 the assessor put the farm's value at $1,500 and the machinery at $40. Unfortunately, the Census did not list one economic statistic of this substantial farmer or others who were apparently well-off but who became prominent Populists: the amount of their mortgage indebtedness.

Populism in Walker township of Ellis county was heavily German and German-Russian, to judge from its 1890 ticket. Nathan Von Feldt, a thirty-five-year-old Russian-born farmer, ran for township treasurer. Adolph Leiker, 32, a Russian-born farmer, ran for township clerk. The two nominees for road overseer were German-born Theo Munk, 34, a farmer and carpenter, and John Wassinger, 25, a farmer born in Russia. A twenty-seven-year-old Kentucky native, Joseph Griesse, who

Census of 1895, Vol. XIII, Atchison City ward 5, p. 41; ibid., LX, Clay Center twp., p. 9; ibid., Vol. CXVI, Howard twp., p. 1; ibid., CXXXIV, Gove City, p. 2; ibid., Grinnell twp., p. 3; ibid., Jerome twp., p. 4.

farmed next door to his German parents, sought the post of township trustee.[51]

If the Populists had any hatreds toward immigrants in 1890, they must have kept them well hidden. All parties made appeals to immigrant groups, with Republicans, Populists, and Democrats in an ascending order of intensity. It is impossible to say, however, whether the Alliance ticket benefited more from immigrant former Republicans or former Democrats, and foreign slating and appeals depended on the local situation. In Ellis county, for example, the Republicans had not been very serious contenders at least since 1881, when prohibition began, and the Democrats, who had no fears about what the five-hundred-vote German-Russian Catholic bloc would do, made no great efforts to hold them. The hopeful Alliancemen used German and English speakers, but it may have been that they were more successful among the Reich Germans than among the Russians in the area.[52]

The German-language press showed shades of disagreement on most issues, but on the liquor question it presented nearly a solid front. Many editors pointed out the clear distinction between the openly dry Republican plank and the silence of the Populists, and most of them went on to mention the undeniable fact that John Willits was a prohibitionist in personal persuasion. If in August the Populists had nominated Charles Robinson instead, very likely the Germans would have supported this "beloved" man whom the Democrats had taken over. But as it was, they said, since the Populist and Democratic platforms were the same except on this point, Willits' election would be only a half-victory, and Germans should vote for Robinson.[53]

[51] *Advocate*, February 20, 1890, March 4, 1891; *Seneca Courier-Democrat*, August 15, 1890; *Alliance Globe* (Pawnee Rock), October 2, 1891; *Great Bend Beacon*, October 18, 1890; *Hays Alliance Pilot*, October 2, 1890; *Census of 1885*, Vol. XXIV, Hiawatha city, pp. 13, 63; *Census of 1895*, Vol. XIX, Independent twp., p. 5; *ibid.*, Logan twp., p. 12; *ibid.*, Vol. XX, Pawnee Rock twp., pp. 2, 7; *ibid.*, Vol. CXX, Walker twp., pp. 1, 3, 8, 13, 17; *ibid.*, CCLV, Capioma twp., *passim*; *ibid.*, Vol. CCCXXXIII, Lincoln twp., pp. 16, 37, 40, 44.

[52] *Hays Free Press*, June 7, September 13, 1890; *Hays Alliance Pilot*, September 25, October 9, 1890.

[53] *Kansas Telegraph* (Topeka), August 14, 1890; *Leavenworth Post*, November 3, 1890; *Germania* (Lawrence), November 13, 1890; *Marysville Post*, October 24, 1890; *Pittsburg Herald*, October 2, 1890; *Kansas Staats Anzeiger* (Wichita), October 30, 1890.

In some cases the German press betrayed an unspoken fear that many German Alliancemen would vote Populist. Yet, considering that the usual editorial of the time was rabidly partisan, the German editors were using kid gloves when they said the Populists ignored the liquor question because of a simple hunger for office or when they made sure their readers knew that the Populists had slated "a black preacher"—meaning a Negro—for state auditor and a woman for state superintendent of public instruction. Earlier in the year the *Newton Anzeiger* had praised the farmers' attempts to help themselves by filing slates of candidates for county offices, but after the Democrats named a separate ticket, the paper quickly found itself disappointed that "so noble an organization as the Farmers' Alliance would become so heavily laden with political wire-pullers." The *Kansas Herold* of Kansas City had nothing against the Alliance's objectives but told its readers that the Alliance ticket was thoroughly unsafe on the liquor question. For these papers, economic questions were important, but the overriding interest was resubmission, first, last, and always.[54]

Only one German paper, the *Hillsboro Anzeiger* in the Marion county Mennonite area, was Republican. It claimed to be sympathetic to economic distress (although it suspected that much of the mortgage and money trouble was the farmers' own fault) but declared that the farmers would be better advised to exert their pressure through the Republican party than by bootless devices of their own. And its abstemious audience probably shared its disgust with the Populists because they did not *endorse* prohibition. Vehemently, if anachronistically, it capped its Republicanism by running a German translation of "Uncle Tom's Cabin" in serial form.[55]

Nevertheless it was without doubt mainly their rigidity on the prohibition question that kept the majority of the German press from Populism. Had Robinson been the Populist instead of the Democratic candidate, they very likely would have supported him as they showed signs of doing before Willits' selec-

[54] *Newton Anzeiger*, June 13, September 19, 1890; *Kansas Herold* (Kansas City), October 17, 31, 1890; *Kansas Staats Anzeiger* (Wichita), October 30, 1890; *Wichita Herold*, September 11, 18, 25, 1890.

[55] *Hillsboro Anzeiger*, September 5, 26, October 3, 1890, and *passim; ibid.*, September–November, 1890, for " 'Onkel Tom's Hütte,' von Harriet Beecher Stowe."

tion. Their main enemy was the Republican party. To many of them, that party was the permanent home of nativism, prohibition, Sunday regulation, and unfavorable school laws. "It has everywhere sympathized with fanatics and nativists. All these freedom-killing statutes exist in Republican states. . . ." They felt, moreover, that "every vote given to the Republicans is a vote for prohibition, for monopoly, for trusts—it is a vote for the benefit of the rich and the detriment of the poor and the middleman." From such views, fusion was only a step away.[56]

Among Germans other than the somewhat single-minded German-language editors, the call to Populism was strong and clear. Banks and railroads were ethnically impartial, and since even in the miraculous eventuality of a Democratic victory, resubmission was unlikely, the "foreign brothers" and "friends of foreign birth" found Populism the one realistic position.[57]

So, then, the questions that the gloomy experience of 1888 had raised were being answered. For the ugly problems of the Kansas economic catastrophe, new answers were being shouted, and to the problem of broadening the political base of reform, the twenty-nine hundred active subordinate Alliances at the end of 1890,[58] with their tens of thousands of native Americans, immigrants, ex-Republicans, ex-Democrats, Catholics, Protestants, Knights of Labor, single-taxers, and plain farmers of every description, were a devastating answer.

The Populist knights of Kansas, Galahads and Quixotes together, vigorous, hopeful, lances in hand, rode resolutely to the polls.

[56] *Kansas Staats Anzeiger* (Wichita), October 30, 1890; *Leavenworth Post*, October 4, 1890; *Kansas Herold* (Kansas City), October 31, 1890.

[57] *Seneca Courier-Democrat*, October 24, 1890; *Great Bend Beacon*, October 16, 30, 1890; L Vincent, *The Alliance and Labor Songster*, pp. 58–60, 69, for Irish appeals; *St. Marys Star*, October 23, 1890.

[58] *Lincoln County Farmer* (Lincoln), December 12, 1890.

CHAPTER FIVE

THE PEOPLE'S PARTY AND OTHER PEOPLE

1. Fruits of Victory

It was a nightmare for the Republicans. The Populists actually became the other major party in Kansas, nearly matching the Republican vote and overwhelming the Democrats two to one. This was no Union Labor or Greenback protest vote. The Populists swept the house of representatives, guaranteeing Senator Ingalls' imminent retirement, and elected five of the seven congressmen.

Beyond this, however, the result was unsatisfactory. For the first forty-eight hours after the election Willits looked safe, but when late returns trickled in from the western counties the balance slowly swung to give the governorship to Republican Lyman Humphrey by about eight thousand votes. The single Populist endorsed also by the Democrats on the state level, J. N. Ives for attorney-general, was the only state-wide Populist winner.

It is interesting to speculate what would have happened had the Populists nominated Robinson, subsequently the Democratic candidate, whom many Populists had favored before their August convention. Robinson ran ahead of the other Democrats by over fifteen thousand; Willits ran about nine thousand behind his party and about eight thousand behind Humphrey. Apparently, about six thousand resubmission Republicans voted for Robinson rather than Humphrey. But about nine thousand otherwise Populist voters chose Robinson over Willits. It must remain pure conjecture, and quite possibly Robinson would have repelled more dry Populists than Willits did wet ones, but a strong case can be made that had Robinson, well liked among the Germans and much better known across the state than Willits, been nominated by the Populists, they would have taken the governorship, especially since the Democrats would not likely have put up a separate ticket. Many jubilant Populists saw only that the Republican 1888 majority of eighty thousand had shrunk to a sixty-three thousand vote deficit against the combined opposition, and with the Populists behind the Republicans by only 3 per cent of the total vote, they thought they needed only to fight a little harder. As the smoke cleared, however, fusion beckoned seductively toward an even more buxom margin. Furthermore, the congressional experience was that fusion candidates won while the Republicans got pluralities in the three-ticket districts. Even though the hold-over Senate, elected in 1888 for four years, was heavily Republican, the Populist sweep in the lower house was so great that Ingalls had no chance. There was some speculation, even among Republicans, that Willits had been "counted out."

The laboring counties in the southeast corner of the state and elsewhere backed the Populists heavily, but the massive Populist strength was in the central counties, where mortgage pressure and Alliance activity were greatest. The counties that shifted most abruptly to Populism were very often the ones with high immigrant populations and with large numbers of people occupied in industry or mining. Counties such as Crawford (heavily labor-mining but about average in foreign-born), Linn (heavily agricultural and heavily native-born), and McPherson (agricultural and heavily immigrant) had supported the Union Labor ticket relatively well in 1888, and in 1890 went Populist more decidedly still. But counties such as Ellis and Ellsworth (agricultural and immigrant) and Osage (agricultural-mining and immigrant), which had not paid much attention to Union Laborism, suddenly became Populist strongholds, along with native-born agricultural counties such as Jefferson and Rice. There was evidently a definite trend in the southeast, northeast, and north-central counties, where immigrants (farmer or laborer) and native laborers lived of a Republican vote well below the average of the native-born agricultural counties. This trend was not universal. And although one may not say that Populist votes came even primarily from immigrant areas, one certainly cannot say that they came only, or even in large part, from native-born areas.[1]

Since Alliance membership and the Populist vote had been practically identical, the old bloody shirt and the tariff were

---

[1] Official voting returns, in KSHS. On the method of their use here, see chap. iv, p. 38, n. 5, in this book.

moribund as campaign issues, and bread-and-butter economic issues seemed likely to dominate Kansas politics for the foreseeable future. The Democrats had no real quarrel with the hard core Populist economic program, and both the English and German wings of the Democratic press hoisted their victory roosters to the mastheads of their papers to crow over the Republican legislative and congressional defeats. Some German editors were delighted to see the Republicans bite the dust, looked forward to bigger and better fusion, and convinced themselves that there was a real likelihood of resubmission of prohibition to the people by the Alliance legislature.[2] Ingalls was going, the Republicans were about gone, and antiplutocracy had won a moral victory.

This absence of an ideological disagreement with the Democratic party came to be one of Populism's great electoral virtues, but in many ways it was a weakness as well. The undoubted fact that at least half, perhaps "the great majority," of the Populists had recently been Republicans gave the party the only numerical means for breaking Republican control, but it also built into Populism, through the everpresent threat of "flops" to the old party, a permanent threat of instability. By shouts of anarchy and socialism, appeals to status, and waving the bloody shirt, the Republicans with constancy and effect urged the return of their vagrant brethren, and it was the Republican argument from that day nearly to this that Populism was no more than "the group that for twenty years had been the laughing-stock of the countryside for its visionary nonsense."[3]

2. A Populist Profile

Yet the very number of former Republicans in the People's party was an unanswerable argument. Whether it came from

[2] Raymond C. Miller, "The Populist Party in Kansas" (Ph.D. dissertation, University of Chicago, 1928), p. 142; *Downs Chief*, November, 1890; *Pittsburg Herold*, November 6, 1890; *Leavenworth Post*, November 5, 1890; *Kansas Herold* (Kansas City), November 7, 14, 1890.

[3] *The Autobiography of William Allen White*, (New York: Macmillan Co., 1946), p. 182; see also p. 216, for an accusation of Populist Marxism. On the bloody shirt, see White's story, "The Regeneration of Colonel Hucks," *ibid.*, and an interview with J. C. Ruppenthal, Russell, Kan., September 16, 1960; but cf. W. P. Harrington, "The Populist Party in Kansas" (Master's thesis, University of Kansas, 1924), p. 33.

their lately jilted Republican respectability, or the puritanism that Carl Becker and others have sniffed in the Kansas air, or their preachments of agrarian virtue, the Populists had a moral tone, an evangelical armor, a dedication, and a simplicity that infused their country schoolhouse meetings. One of their editors claimed that the Populists

average with their Republican neighbors. No better, no worse, but just as good. . . . Republican farmers who look on so complacently while the neighbors of their younger days are assailed have but to show a sign of wavering from the g.o.p. to be assailed in just as ferocious a manner.

They may have been naïve, or quixotic, or economically one-sided, but they were neither the failures or the ne'er-do-wells[4] nor a vicious, rag, tag and bobtail mob.

Their farms were about the same size as their neighbors', their mortgages only slightly larger. Some were first-time voters in their twenties; some were septuagenarians. They probably had a lower percentage of foreign-born among them than the Democrats did but a higher percentage than the Republicans. Over certain non-economic questions that were not connected with their original program or early, rapid spread, but that always had profound political implications, such as prohibition, women's suffrage, and fusion, they coalesced into several shifting, vaguely cohesive groups. A vocal minority, overemotional on two issues, land tenure and money, used arguments and imagery neurotically critical of English and American landlords and bankers and Jewish bankers of both countries, but the mass of Populists were remarkably unimpressed by arguments not strictly economic.[5]

For the mass of the party, however, political reality came not only from grim economic facts but from deep democratic faith as well. Far from being idle, sullen, or fear-ridden, Populists

[4] *Republic County Freeman* (Belleville), October 13, 1892; interview with J. C. Ruppenthal, Russell, Kan., September 16, 1960; interview with W. J. Breidenthal, Topeka, September 11, 1960; Annie L. Diggs, *The Story of Jerry Simpson* (Wichita: Hobson Printing Co., 1908), pp. 64, 84; Donald H. Ecroyd, "An Analysis and Evaluation of Populist Political Campaign Speech Making in Kansas 1890–1894" (Ph. D. dissertation, State University of Iowa, 1949), p. 59; *Downs Chief*, August 28, 1890; Paul W. Gates, *Fifty Million Acres* (Ithaca, N.Y.: Cornell University Press, 1954), p. 244.

[5] Raymond C. Miller has assessed this, I think, correctly in *op. cit.*, p. 36.

agreed overwhelmingly that "one who can work and won't work ought to starve" and had no use either for people who were paupers on purpose or for those who lived "on the labor of others."[6] This latter class, unfortunately, was too often extended to include contemporary representatives of what was to become the mass-producing, mass-consuming, mass-communicating, managerial future, but the western farmer in his honest naïveté, isolation, and rural nineteenth-century experience found it easy to consider these people sybaritic thieves. As social and political philosophers the Populists, like the Knights of Labor, with whom they shared many values, and unlike either the A. F. of L. or the progressives of a few years later, sought not the promise of the American twentieth-century future but the standards of their nineteenth-century past and present.

From the American Revolution and the War of 1812 they took their egalitarianism and their nationalism, and from the past of the pre-industrial mechanic and the independent farmer they took their idea of producers as the fulcrum of society. They were quite aware of the necessity of distributors, merchants, and bankers, but these occupations were thought to be secondary in logic, justice, and profits to the farming or laboring producer.[7]

What really irked them was not commerce but the abuse of commerce, not loans and interest but usury, not banking but special privilege, not enterprise but speculation. They had the balance and common sense not to reaffirm the Union Labor party's overzealous plank for the abolition of all interest on loans, and their outlook was quite understandable in view of the very real conflict between harsh economic facts and an agrarian worldview, no matter how progressive. But if the middle of a wheat field was a poor vantage point for looking inside a steel mill or a stock market, and may have given the farmer short

[6] *McPherson Republican*, November 20, 1896; "Ruppenthal Scrapbooks," III: 52, 441, 457, in KSHS.

[7] See *McPherson Industrial Union*, July 31, 1890, which reproduces an open letter from the leaders of the June 12 Populist formation convention at Topeka under the headline, "Echoes of 1776 and the American Revolution." See also N. B. Ashby, *The Riddle of the Sphinx* (Des Moines, Iowa: Industrial Publishing Co., 1890), pp. 26–28 and *passim*; William A. Peffer, *The Farmer's Side* (New York: D. Appleton & Co., 1891), pp. 6–9, 43–44, 226, 243.

sight, it does not follow that it gave him a narrow mind as well.[8]

Only the more radical among them believed entirely that "labor is capital," and the men they elected to the United States Senate either in the movement's early, raucous days or in later years when it became more politically adept were well adjusted to industrial society. Senator Peffer, at about the time he was sent to Washington to replace Ingalls by the calamity-howling legislature elected in 1890, raised rhetorically the idea of abolishing modern transportation, factories, and other industrial artifacts, and replied to the implied question himself:

But does anybody believe such things either desirable or practicable? . . . It is folly to talk about farmers going back to conditions from which they emerged by reason of influences that moved all other classes of men.

Peffer certainly disliked the looks of existing industrialism, but to him the situation called for progressive adjustment, not reaction:

To give the employer all the profits is to make slaves of the men, and we have about got through with slavery in this country. If capitalists are not satisfied with this forecast let them scatter their money to the four winds of heaven; let the large establishments melt away, and men and women will open up their little shops again. But nobody wants that. All we demand is a just measure of the profits realized over our labor in connection with capital.

Another Populist, a former Democrat and Confederate officer, W. A. Harris, who was elected to the Senate in Peffer's place by the Populist legislature of 1897, faced up to industrialization and spelled out the Populist doctrine on the matter:

We would like to see in every little country village the old time mechanic with his journeymen, manufacturing wagons, agricultural implements of all sorts, harness, tinware, etc., and building up busy little hives, which were the support and pride of their respective communities all over the country, but it is impossible to turn the hands of the clock back, and the question now is, "How shall individual rights and freedom be preserved, in spite of the enormous capital and the monopolization of every field of industry?" How shall our legislatures be freed from the influ-

[8] Diggs, *op. cit.*, pp. 62, 79; *Kansas Commoner* (Wichita), October 13, 1892.

ences which control and affect from one end of the country to the other, every form of legislation? We can not go back to the old ways, and the trusts themselves, by teaching the possibility of perfect organization, are also pointing clearly to the only possible remedy. The power which is concentrated in the hands of a few people can only be met and defeated by concentrating and utilizing the power of all the people. . . . In order to do all of these things essential to the general welfare, it is necessary to take it out of the grasp of the powers that have no thought for the welfare of the people.[9]

It may have been idealistic, this certainty about the supreme worth of the individual, but it was an ideal the Populists shared with Revolutionary War soldiers, Jacksonian Democrats, and Lincoln Republicans. They placed upon this ideal their own stamp, the stamp of optimism, past progress and expected success, and made the first widely accepted response to the overwhelming problem of reconciling democratic values with industrial society. They then transmitted the ideal, together with their own timely amendments, to others in the twentieth century who employed it to produce newer programs, to attack more widespread evils, and to provoke more apt solutions. Of course they were sorry to see the old order disappear; what group likes to see its primacy pass? But if the Populist did not play Lear in the first act, neither did he play him in the second. Power gone was power not lamented; power intact was power to improve. If the long-term trend against the farmer was irreversible, no such inevitability lay in present extremities or in the tendency of corporate enterprise to reduce individual opportunity. Would-be reformers of the future would remember that American democratic values made their first strong stand against the evils that lay in the industrial revolution under the banner of Populism, and through those blue-shirted, coveralled regulars they met the enemy not with a whimper but a bang.

The Populists instinctively knew that it was not the ideals that should change, but the system that oppressed them. To achieve this, there was only the government. Here they found themselves at a philosophical crossroads from which many men

[9] *F. A.* and *I. U.* and *Helping Hand* (Topeka), October, 1894; Peffer, *op. cit.*, pp. 46–47, 64; *Advocate*, April 19, 1899.

of good will, then and later, have proceeded only to descend into a quagmire that not only stopped their progress but discouraged them into sinking toward reaction. The Populists avoided this path. They moved unchecked down the road of reform (the bogged-down called it socialism) by the simple assertion that although in undemocratic countries the government is an oppressive soulless force, in the free republic of America the government

is not a foreign entity, governed by some outside power with which we have no connection. It is not, as some imagine, a great father sent to us to take care of our interests without any action upon our own part, but is simply the agent of the people. It is just what the people themselves have made it. It is an instrument to express and to interpret and to execute their will.

They scoffed at charges of paternalism, saying that

they only demand[ed] that public functions shall be exercised by public agents, and that sovereign powers shall not be delegated to private persons or corporations having only private interests to serve.[10]

Such views were not respectful of minority opinions, and since these ideas were self-evident to the Populists as to the signers of the Declaration of Independence, they might have tolerated no dissent. Nevertheless, it was the humanitarian rather than the potentially oppressive strain that prevailed. The Populists indeed worried very little about limiting governmental action, and a government without limits may lead easily to the oppression of minorities or to the "socialism" their opponents so often accused them of. To put the main stress on this unconcern, however, would be to take Populism out of its context; it would be stressing a "might-have-been," not the existent facts. After all, in the nineties a lack of limits on governmental action was hardly the main danger. Whatever may have been the case at a later time, the real problem when Populism was alive was the presence, not the absence, of limits—limits that Eric Goldman has called "conservatism's steel chain of ideas," limits that

[10] Diggs, *op. cit.*, pp. 167–69; Peffer, *op. cit.*, p. 132 [for Republican agreement, see *The Great Quadrangular Debate* (Salina, Kan.: Press of Republican Job Rooms, 1894), p. 5]; Peffer, "The Mission of the Populist Party," *North American Review*, CLVII (December, 1893), 666.

meant in practice unresponsive government. The Populists sought governmental action not to oppress but to accomplish. Both logic and sentiment led them to a humanitarian regard for minorities, including ethnic minorities, and if they preferred the welfare of the labor minority already here to that of an ethnic minority yet to come, their basic position was the traditional one of that time that America was not only the new experiment in democracy that made a social lie of a decadent, cruel, reactionary Europe but a sympathetic haven for Europe's pleading masses.

It was this traditional combination of American egalitarian democracy and American national superiority to Europe—a kind of affable belligerence—that checked the personal and intellectual antagonism the Populists might have felt, and also provoked the few specific antagonisms they did hold. Friendly to the immigrants with whom they had personal contact, including the Jews, laudatory of many institutions of European and other foreign countries, the Populists (or rather some of them—they were no more intellectual carbon copies of each other than any other group of over a hundred thousand people) had three specific foreign resentments: pauper or contract laboring immigrants, aristocratic English landlords, and Anglo-Jewish bankers. These resentments must be carefully explained, compared, and qualified.

Although Populist editorials and pamphlets often declaimed the need for preserving American liberties, many of them at the same time praised progressive institutions in foreign countries. Switzerland was a favorite example of enlightened government and social institutions for the Populists as it had been for colonial constitutional theorists just before the American Revolution. In one fictional dialogue a Harvard man, reproachful of Populist "radicalism," was converted when a Populist informed him that Swiss institutions included government ownership of transportation and communication, a government liquor monopoly, initiative and referendum, proportional representation, and high inheritance and income taxes. Another Populist praised Swiss legal tender and mortgage laws and the government bank.[11]

[11] Carl S. Vrooman, "A Kansas Populist Abroad," *Advocate Quarterly* (Topeka), I (July, 1900), p. 57; *Marion Times*, October 13, 1892.

The hero of Ignatius Donnelly's *Caesar's Column* is a Swiss living in Uganda, and he is treated sympathetically by Donnelly, as is another character of Irish origin. Donnelly was entranced by the masterly virtues of the Swedes, included among the oppressed and needy masses of the world the French, Germans, Irish, English, Hungarians, Italians, Russians, Jews, Christians, Chinese, Japanese, and others, and remarked about "illiterate immigrants" from Europe that the percentage of illiteracy was lower in some European despotisms than in the United States.[12]

Other Populists sympathized with South Americans under English financial pressure, cited the British and French greenback experiences as an argument for fiat money, and praised the resourcefulness of French farmers since the end of landlordism in 1789. One even wanted his republic to emulate European nations that had surpassed the United States in political and economic democracy in the nineteenth century.[13]

In spite of a consistent antipathy to English aristocracy and bankers, Populists were clearly favorable to the English people in general, such English institutions as the Rochdale co-operatives, public control of transportation, the judicial system, and short political campaigns.[14]

Seldom did a Populist express any antipathy to European immigrants as individuals, and when they did, it was clearly an opposition either to paupers, shared by practically all Americans of that period, or to southern and eastern Europeans because of their "unfair" labor competition. In direct contrast with eastern racist restrictionists of the period, the

[12] At that time a common eastern form of restrictionism was literacy testing. See *Caesar's Column: A Story of the Twentieth Century*, ed. Walter B. Rideout (Cambridge, Mass.: Belknap Press of Harvard University Press, 1960), pp. 57, 102–3, 237, 238.

[13] Ashby, *op. cit.*, pp. 41–43; G. Campbell, *Island Home: An Old Man's Story of the Rise and Fall of "Island Home" Government* (Parsons, Kan.: Foley Printing Company, 1894), p. 27; Erasmus R. Baker, *The Subject of Money . . ."* (Winfield, Kan.: H. and L. Vincent, Printers, 1887), pp. 36, 39–40; Carl S. Vrooman, "Twentieth Century Democracy," *Advocate Quarterly*, I (July, 1900), 59–75.

[14] W. Scott Morgan, *History of the Wheel and Alliance* (St. Louis: C. B. Woodward Co., 1891), pp. 516, 660–61, 707, 709; Ashby, *op. cit.*, pp. 142, 355; Henry E. Allen, *In Hell and the Way Out, A Non-Partisan Political Hand-book* (Chicago: Direct Legislation Publishing Company, 1896), pp. 47–48.

Populists had as yet only a faint idea of the distinction between the "older" and "newer" immigration and restricted their concern to a strictly economic level. Only a handful of writers had even a vague awareness of any remarkable change in the pattern of immigration. In this investigation only one Populist writer was found who made a distinction between "old" and "new" immigrants on race grounds by speaking of the alleged inability of eastern European immigrants to assimilate, and that author never showed the slightest sign of antipathy of a personal kind.[15]

The fact of the matter was that the Republican party was the home of immigration restriction on racist grounds at that time, whether in the East or in Kansas. One of the more liberal Kansas Republican dailies, commenting on the Chicago trial of Prendergast, the assassin of Mayor Carter Harrison, said: "What could you expect of a foreign murderer, before foreign judges, with a foreign police force? Chicago citizens who are disgusted with the Prendergast case should move to the United States." And it would have taken a rare Populist to endorse the statement made to a friend by one young Kansas Republican of the nineties: "What would you do, go west—and grow up with the country or stay in New York or some other Eastern seaport and take chances with the european rifraf [sic] and cholera microbes?" German editors shared the Populist demands to cut off anarchist and other radical immigration, and all parties and nationalities opposed "pauper labor immigration."[16]

[15] S. N. Wood, *Wood's Manifesto: An Address to the People of Kansas* (Topeka: Hamilton Printing Company, 1891), pp. 21–22; W. A. Tilton, *The Way Out: A Few Thoughts Relative to the Condition of the Labor and Producing Classes* . . . (Winfield, Kan.: H. and L. Vincent, Printers, 1890), pp. 3, 15; Baker, *op. cit.*, pp. 6–7; letter of John Davis, to a Philadelphia newspaper, May 7, 1891, in "Davis Scrapbooks," IX: 29–31, in KSHS; "Davis Scrapbooks," I: 3; *Luray Herald*, October 20, 1905, in "Ruppenthal Scrapbooks," IX: 89, and a few Ruppenthal columns of 1893 and 1894, in KSHS; but compare *Luray Herald*, June 16, 1905, in "Ruppenthal Scrapbooks," IX: ix; H. B. Kelly, *Between Millstones* (Lawrence, Kan.: Jeffersonian Publishing Co., [1896]), pp. 7–9; *Ellsworth Populist*, September 5, 1896; *Parsons Daily Eclipse*, October 16, November 3, 1890; *St. Marys Star*, November 20, 1890.

[16] John Higham, *Strangers in the Land* (New Brunswick, N.J.: Rutgers University Press, 1955), pp. 98–101; *Wichita Morning Eagle*, June 13, 1894; letter of George McQuaid to George Angle, Washington, D.C., February 12, 1893, in Angle MSS, University of Kansas; *Newton Anzeiger*, November 16, 1890.

On neither racist nor economic grounds did the Populist farmers find anything objectionable about immigrants, and as political and philosophical allies of the Knights of Labor, they apparently endorsed the desire of T. V. Powderly, the Knights' General Master Workman, for restriction of eastern and southern European competitors in the labor market; but neither for Powderly nor for the farmers did race or nationality have anything to do with the problem. A Populist pamphleteer of the party's most doctrinaire and least politically-minded faction talked of the pitiful condition of European labor, the result not of any innate viciousness but of a system of wage slavery worse than ante bellum Negro slavery in the United States. And Powderly minced no words in a series of articles he wrote for a Union Labor paper in 1888, in which he excoriated Hungarian and Italian immigrant workers for their filthy living conditions, their willingness to accept absurdly low wages, and their lack of civic sense; however, he said:

If I had found the same number of Irish, Welsh, English or Germans huddled together as I have found Hungarians and Italians, I would have written exactly the same. It is the infamous practice of taking advantage of the ignorance and necessities of these men that I oppose. . . . What do I care whether they are Sclavacks, Polacks [sic], Italians, Irish, English or native Americans so long as they live, eat, sleep and work like slaves.[17]

3. Money Question or "Money Power"?

The Populists, then, lacked any consistent antipathy either to foreign countries or to immigrants, with the single exception of labor competition. But when they dealt with the deceptively innocent-looking problems of money and banking and land tenure, problems which lay at the very heart of their program, they laid themselves open to the double charge of Anglophobia and anti-Semitism; and it is on their expressions about these two specific problems that the whole case for Populist nativism must rest.

The money question, to Populist thinking, lay at the root of many evils. They blamed much on a lack of sufficient circulating medium: low commodity prices; the oppressiveness of in-

[17] Erasmus R. Baker, *The Money Monopoly* (Winfield, Kan.: H. and L. Vincent, Printers, 1890), pp. 9 ff.; *Atchison Times*, October 20, 27, 1888.

terest rates on loans contracted when more money could be had for a given amount of labor and produce; a lowered ability to buy equipment, improvements, or consumer goods; and the greater ease with which banking and finance could be controlled by small groups of specially interested men. As solutions, they continually advocated a return to the policy of the United States prior to 1873, either by the issuance of legal tender paper money, or by the remonetization of silver, freely coined and as legal as gold.[18]

From 1865 to 1879 the United States had unquestionably followed a definite policy of contracting the currency, and in spite of the Bland-Allison Act of 1878 and the Sherman Silver Purchase Act of 1890, which allowed limited purchases of silver by the Treasury, this policy had not been effectively altered. This policy did not go down well with the western farmers, who laid many of their own most serious problems at the door of the tightly closed Treasury.

They also saw certain other obvious conditions. First, in spite of a stable or dwindling amount of currency, population and trade were constantly increasing. Second, more and more wealth of all kinds was concentrating in fewer and fewer hands. Third, powerful statesmen, including John Sherman, William McKinley, and Grover Cleveland, suggested laws and policies that speeded this concentration. Fourth, the primary beneficiary of concentration, as well as of the national banking system endorsed by the same statesmen, was the Wall Street financial community, which controlled the assets or stock of many smaller banks, important corporations and trusts, and mortgage loan agencies. And fifth, either through actual agency, as in the case of the Belmont firm, or simply because of the position of the United States as a debtor nation in the international balance of payments, Wall Street was also in part economically tributary to the larger and richer financial com-

[18] A source for the Kansas Populist platforms that demonstrate the generally equal importance given to silver and paper is the *Advocate* during the summer months of even-numbered years, when state conventions took place. See also Morgan, *op. cit.*, Book II, chap. iv; "The Farmers' Defensive Movement," *Forum*, VIII (December, 1889), 464–73; Peffer, "The Mission of the Populist Party," p. 666 and *passim*; Peffer, *The Farmer's Side*, pp. 126–28, 239, and the final chapter *passim*; Peffer, "The Cure for a Vicious Monetary System," *Forum*, XXII (February, 1897), 722–30.

munity on Lombard and Threadneedle streets, London, where the old Anglo-Jewish Rothschild family played an influential part. Under these circumstances, the western farmers with their crashing prices and crushing mortgages reacted with a remarkable lack of deviation from the facts.

Of course, this is a generalization, and Populism like any other American reform movement of large proportions had many voices and comprised a broad spectrum of groups and individuals. Even so, only a tiny, narrow band let their rhetoric get the better of them. Most of them were puzzled and angry but not irrational. They listened attentively when the unsentimental Senator Peffer told them drily that the percentage of national wealth owned by farmers had declined from over 70 per cent to less than 25 per cent since 1850, that crop prices had gone down while labor was costing the same and purchased items were costing more, and that "if a farmer had given a mortgage for $1,000 in 1870, he could have paid it with 1,050 bushels of corn. Ten to seventeen years later it would have taken, without interest, 2,702 bushels to have paid it." This may have been exhortation, but it was not rabble-rousing. A farmer need not have been a hopeless neurotic to have taken a look at corporations, grain markets, finance capitalism, and the leaders of Congress and mistaken a common non-agrarian outlook for positive co-operation. He agreed easily with the author of *The Riddle of the Sphinx* that "well-disciplined organizations of capital and handlers have forced the farmer to sell his products to them at prices fixed by themselves, and to buy his commodities of them at prices again fixed by themselves."[19]

It is certainly true that if farmers had been more worldly-wise, if they had traveled to New York, Washington, Chicago, and London and seen at first hand what cities, industry, and finance were actually like, they would have realized that dogged competition, not class conspiracy, were more the hallmarks of urban, industrial life in the late nineteenth century. Yet no educational excursion would have rid them of the certain conviction that whatever may have been the regard of these groups for one another, they were united in a way of life, a common economic viewpoint, that left farmers and laborers out of account except as factors in production and, very often,

[19] Peffer, *The Farmer's Side*, p. 29; Ashby, *op. cit.*, p. 388.

as subjects for exploitation. Populism was shot through with naïveté and oversimplification. But at the same time, it had its roots and its being in a realistic conflict of economic interest.

In its salad days the party that had sprung from high mortgages, currency stringency, and high railroad freight rates settled upon reforming land, money, and transportation as its foremost aims, a trident for puncturing a bloated plutocracy. Even in 1890, the central prong, money reform, was a little longer than the others, and as time passed, it became by far the longest and sharpest of the three. The Populists were guilty of oversimplification and one-sidedness, and they have been accused of treating silver coinage as a panacea and of demonstrating a lack of principle by emphasizing the money question almost to the exclusion of the others, especially in the Bryan-McKinley campaign of 1896, but there are some plausible reasons for this concentration.

In a political campaign a single issue that subsumes other objectives is a valuable thing; leading Populists, like other political battlers before and since, believed that he who started on a campaign trip with least baggage traveled farthest. Both in Kansas and throughout the rest of the country, the money question seemed to have the broadest appeal among potential reform voters. Furthermore, currency expansion as a nearly exclusive issue was a long tradition with post-Civil War reformers. Most of all, it seemed solidly rooted in economic logic, which relieved fretful Populists of any worry that stressing it heavily would indicate a lack of principle. If money were more plentiful, buyers of farm commodities would have a greater supply of it relative to their demand for the available corn, wheat, and other crops, and commodity prices would rise. The farmer would receive more cash; he would be loosed from the vise of low crop returns and high prices on his purchases. He could buy more. He would have more cash to pay mortgages, and the debts that had seemed insignificant when he contracted them in prosperous times would become trifling again. In addition, with greater cash returns for crops, railroad rates would eat up a smaller percentage of the return. Laws passed in state legislatures to stay foreclosures or to set maximum freight rates would be helpful, but, essentially, they would operate only as stop-gap or supplementary measures while the farmers awaited a more plentiful supply of money. As for those "well-disciplined organizations of capital," bankers agreed with farmers that a small amount of circulating medium was easier to control than a large amount; a greater money supply would even alleviate the worst effects of economic combinations and monopolies.

The money question, then, was not only an issue in itself, but as more and more Populists viewed it, it underlay political success, reform traditions, mortgage problems, freight rates, improvement of (or speculation in) land, and the reduction of monopoly power. They did not notice, they were not in a position to understand, that such knotty problems as trust formation, urban slums, inequitable wealth distribution, and unresponsiveness of governments were not ultimately soluble by money reform alone or even in large part. The few of them to whom such problems were real could convince themselves that money reform would go some way toward solving them. Meanwhile, they believed firmly that far more than any other single reform, or even combination of reforms, it would relieve them of the immediate distress that had pushed them into political action in the first place.

Frequent discussion of the money question took place in Populist pamphlets, books, newspapers, speeches, and so it seems, street corner and convention shoptalk everywhere. When they talked about the money question practically all Populists, including recent immigrants, had four things in common. First came actual, imminent, or proximate financial distress. Second, they professed a certain creed about America, which included a scorn for manipulators of wealth in contrast to producers of wealth, a strong dislike of any kind of "English oppression," which invoked patriotic "memories" of 1776 and 1812, a distrust of European decadence, and a humanitarian welcome for downtrodden Europeans who sought a breath of free and fresh American air. Third, they perceived a connection between United States Treasury contractionists, eastern financiers, and London-centered magnates of world finance. Fourth, they agreed that free coinage of silver, the issuance of legal tender paper money, and the abolition of the national banking system were the chief solutions to financial distress.

Many, perhaps most, Populists restricted their expressions on the money question to an exposition of the economic situation and an advocacy of free silver, legal tender paper money, and the end of the national banks in order to put an end to this rule by special interests. Many others, however, by a personalization of the combined facts, substituted for "money question" the term "money power." After this, the next question was, of course, Who controls this power?

The answer, embedded in the facts, was Wall Street and Lombard Street, Cleveland and Sherman, Gould and Vanderbilt, the Belmonts and the Rothschilds. Perhaps the facts strictly construed proved only that these groups had common interests and agreed on financial theory and policies. With very slight extrapolation, however, this agreement became a collective self-interest—in a word, a conspiracy. Even here, the conspiracy involved in equal parts American bankers, English and Anglo-Jewish bankers, and members of the American government.

When it became specific, as it sometimes did, the conspiracy harked back to the Civil War, when by a "Hazzard Circular" of 1862 European capitalists were supposed to have warned American capitalists that together they had to keep the control of money in the hands of the international capitalist class when the war was over. As the story went, the London financiers sent a certain Ernest Seyd to Washington with one hundred thousand English pounds put up by themselves and (less important) some German bankers. This scheme, with the connivance of certain American financiers and political bigwigs, successfully brought about the demonetization of silver in 1873. The spreaders of the story were often at great pains to prove it by affidavits, witnesses, and the like. Silver Republicans along with Populists swallowed it. It has all the earmarks of fantasy, yet financial historians ignore it rather than explode it and place the cause of the demonetization of silver on the gold-silver ratio in 1873, the disappearance of silver coin from circulation, and inadvertence. If the story was true, the "conspiracy" was a fact. If it was false, it was nonetheless propagated with documentation and not gullibly or frantically. One Populist congressman, John Davis, called this particular story a tall tale that his fellow Populists should never swallow, but he not only knew of Seyd's existence but defended him as a bimetallist, a real friend of silver, who had been incautiously maligned.[20]

Aside from the "Hazzard Circular"–Ernest Seyd story, different writers gave the money power or conspiracy argument different forms and textures. Mrs. Lease, as usual, violently erupted with it:

The capitalistic press rejoiced in the power of Grover Cleveland, the American agent of Jewish bankers and British gold. . . . [The Populists are] the only political party in existence that says to robber England "Hands off our money; American finance for Americans!"

But more often it appeared something like this:

The demonetization of silver was the result of a carefully laid conspiracy between capitalists of the loaning classes against the business and debtor classes. The United States government, as a debtor, and also as the chief silver country, allowed the European Rothschilds and their American allies, millionaire bankers, to overreach her in dealing with the money question.[21]

Again, it is worth stressing that the "conspiracy," whatever its particulars, was international. Censure fell on bankers, whether American or English, Jewish or Gentile. This was the consensus of those Populists who dealt with the money question in terms of a "money power," and it indicates that even among these people, who were by no means the whole party or its ideologues, it was bankers, not Jews, bankers, not England, who were the conspirators. When the Populists talked of an "international money power," they meant just that: not a foreign power but a foreign and domestic power that cared nothing for national boundaries or ethnic origins. To a Populist it was indeed remarkable that there were dozens of millionaires in New

[20] John Davis to the editor of the *Advocate*, January 27, 1897, in "Davis Scrapbooks," II:18–24, in KSHS; *Advocate*, January 4, July 12, 1893; *Atchison Times*, September 4, 1890; Morgan, *op. cit.*, pp. 420, 456; Campbell, *op. cit.*, pp. 37–39 (including affidavits), 47, 51, 58; *Hays Free Press*, summer of 1892 *passim*; *Advocate*, June 4, 1890; and finally, with a title more extreme than its contents, Sarah E. V. Emery, *Seven Financial Conspiracies Which Have Enslaved the American People* (Lansing, Mich.: Robert Smith & Co., Printers and Binders, 1891), p. 57.

[21] Mary E. Lease, in *The Great Quadrangular Debate*, pp. 76, 81; Ashby, *op. cit.*, p. 166.

York, but not remarkable that there were among them a handful of Jews.[22]

There were exceptions who unambiguously proclaimed that American policy was dictated by England and that "monarchy . . . continues to suck the life's blood from the Nation while the Republic sleeps," but these statements were more than balanced by more frequent and equally unambiguous statements blaming everything on Wall Street.[23]

The preceding argument can be summed up briefly, along with many of the newspapers, speeches, pamphlets, and books of the 1890 campaign and afterward. Most Populists talked about the money question. A large portion never referred to England or to Jews. Some talked about the money question in terms of a "money power," and they referred frequently to England or Jews. This group was almost always equally severe with Wall Street capitalism and its putative congressional allies.

4. Englishmen and Jews

From their treatment of the "money power" this group of Populists derived their only two consistent antagonisms to foreign groups. The first antagonism was to Jews, or more properly, Jewish bankers. The second antagonism, evoked by land tenure questions as well as money, was to English bankers and landlords.

First, the Jews. A distinction is in order between two forms of anti-Semitism: social discrimination and ideological hatred. The connection between the two is more logical than historical, and in many cases, one exists in the absence of the other. The use of the word "anti-Semitism" involves an assumption that there is a connection between what may be unrelated anti-Jewish acts; but for present purposes it will be assumed that it is more than a catchword. As for the distinction between ideo-

[22] Mrs. Lease quoted in *Topeka Capital*, August 14, 1890; S. S. King, *Bond-Holders and Bread-Winners* (privately printed, 1892), p. 41; *Advocate*, December 6, 1889; W. V. Marshall, *Aids to the Study of a Cumulative Tax* . . . (Winfield, Kan.: H. and L. Vincent, Printers, 1890), p. 41; *Newton Journal*, October 24, 1890; *Topeka Alliance Tribune*, November 6, 1890; D. C. Zercher, *Stubborn Facts in a Nutshell* (Topeka: Advocate Publishing Co., 1894), pp. 60–78.

[23] *Advocate*, June 25, 1890; *Jennings Alliance Times*, October 3, 1890; H. B. Kelly, *op. cit.*, p. 2.

logical hatred and social discrimination, it has been said that "Anglophobia, a political ideology, was as harmless to English immigrants as ideological anti-Semitism was to Jews," but both aspects are still worth looking at.[24]

Social discrimination can be disposed of quickly: it was not a Populist trait. There were few Jews in Kansas, fewer still on farms, and as far as is known, they were well treated by Populists, Republicans, and Democrats alike. The relative absence of Jews in Kansas has been used to support the idea of Populist ill feeling, apparently on the ground that what one does not know, one is suspicious of. There is no denying that personal contact with minorities can often decrease suspicions and antagonistic attributions. But this "absence theory" fails to distinguish between personal and ideological antipathy; it fails to explain why Jews were so much more discriminated against in large cities and in the East, where they lived and were known in large numbers; it fails to explain why the Populists bore no resentment against other absent minorities; it fails to note that foreign groups or countries, whether represented in Kansas or not (as, for example, the English certainly were), were unfavorably regarded if they were significantly connected to gold standard finances and favorably regarded if they were pro-silver. Merchants with strongly Jewish names were mentioned favorably in the local press. Others, singly or in groups, were well regarded in their communities. Jewish mayors administered, at various times, the Kansas towns of Rosedale, Wichita, and Dodge City, and probably others; Populists supported a Jew for postmaster of Salina, and the son of the Populist state chairman told me of his fond remembrance of the only Jew in his home town of Chetopa, one Sig Lehman, who was elected mayor "year after year."[25]

Out of hundreds of Populist newspapers and pamphlets, there were only a few references to large noses, nearly all in

[24] Shlomo Bergman, "Some Methodological Errors in the Study of Anti-Semitism," *Jewish Social Studies*, V (January, 1943), 47; John Higham, "Social Discrimination Against Jews in America, 1830–1930," *Publication of the American Jewish Historical Society*, XLVII (September, 1957), 27 n.

[25] "Trail Blazers of the Trans-Mississippi West," *American Jewish Archives*, VIII: 93; interview with W. J. Breidenthal, Topeka, September 11, 1960; *Topeka Press*, April 11, 1894; interview with J. C. Ruppenthal, Russell, Kan., September 16, 1960. Unfortunately for present purposes, the *Census* did not identify Jews, since they had no common country of origin.

boiler-plate cartoons of "Rothschild"; there were two or three sentences of dialect writing, such as Thomas Bailey Aldrich or Finley Peter Dunne were using for other minorities; there were no references at all to ritual murder or other vicious libels that were getting some mention, if not acceptance, in the large city press of the time. Even the more radical segments of the Populist press, when they mentioned Jewish immigrants, showed a sympathetic attitude to them as when the *Topeka Alliance Tribune* related the story of a thrifty, industrious, but unavoidably out of work Jewish immigrant family in New York which was driven to suicide to escape sure starvation, while a few blocks away "live[d] the Goulds, Vanderbilts, and dozens of other millionaires, with their $10,000 a year cooks."[26] As individuals, Jews were simply another welcome group of immigrants.

Ideological anti-Semitism is a more complex problem. Populist discussions of the money question were by no means studded with possibly anti-Jewish references, but two words— "Rothschild" and "Shylock"—recur frequently and demand attention. Other anti-Jewish references are conspicuous by their great rarity, and even when they do occur they lack a tone of irrational opprobriousness. Leaving Shylock and Rothschild aside for the moment, a search of several thousand Populist newspapers, pamphlets, and books yielded only nine antagonistic references, all of which can be mitigated in small or large part by reasonable analysis. For example, a series of fictitious letters in the *Advocate* in 1894 between "K. Gold Isaacs," a Wall Street banker, and his nephew, "W. M. Naut, Boomtown, Kansas," contained, other than the name, not a single implication of anti-Semitism unless mentions of Lombard Street are to be construed as such. The choice of name meant nothing more than the use of a stereotype of a harmless kind in order to achieve economic ends, if "Isaacs's" advice to play up the appointment of Edward White, a Roman Catholic, to the United States Supreme Court because "bloodshed over difference of creed would be much more agreeable than conflicts between the rich and poor" means anything.[27]

[26] *Topeka Alliance Tribune*, October 2, 1890.
[27] For the series of "K. Gold Isaacs" letters, see *Advocate*, April, 9, 1890, and April–July, 1894; *Kansas Workman* (El Dorado), June 18, 1890;

Another example is Ignatius Donnelly's *Caesar's Column,* which probably sold well enough in Kansas and which has been given as clinching proof of "Populist anti-Semitism." Unlike Bellamy's *Looking Backward,* in which the problems of industrialism in the 1880's came to a happy solution, *Caesar's Column* was anti-utopian. Its world of the future drew out the worst aspects of industrial society to a "logical" conclusion, in which a submerged mass of slaves existed in a world in the grip of an oligarchy of malefactors who possessed all wealth worth having. A secret revolutionary group rose gradually, however, and with the help of the oligarchy's jet air force, destroyed the oligarchy in a bloody purge and set up a popular dictatorship in its place. The good elements fled both. There are three important "anti-Semitic" aspects: the most powerful malefactor was Jacob Isaacs, alias "Prince Cabano"; the oligarchy was nearly all Jewish; the Jewish nation was reborn in the chaos of the revolutionary upheaval.

As for Jacob Isaacs, Donnelly portrayed him as an outcast, "driven from his synagogue"; and furthermore, the second in command of the opposing revolutionary forces was a Russian Jew, like his colleagues driven to violent rebellion by a traumatic personal incident produced by a vicious economic system beyond his control. This has been interpreted to mean that Donnelly thought Jews to be radicals on both sides of the fence, "working toward hidden Jewish ends," but it is just as likely, since the revolutionary forces are portrayed as Jewish-inspired but justice-seeking, that the evil Jew, Isaacs, is cancelled out by the good, if not always well-advised, Jew of the revolution. If the oligarchy was nearly all Jewish and was extremely powerful, this was because, Donnelly explained carefully, any weak Jews had long since been purged by Christian persecution, and not unnaturally they had become "as merciless to the Christian as the Christian had been to them." If the Jews were powerful, it was because Christians had started a fight they were

Kansas Agriculturalist (Winfield), October 13, 1894; letter to the editor, *Advocate,* January 4, 1893, May 30, 1894; advertisement for "The Great Red Dragon, or London Money Power" in book with missing cover and title page, and p. 6 of the same books in "People's Party Pamphlets," VII, in KSHS; two or three items listed in People's Party State Central Committee, "Agitate, Educate, Organize; Price Catalogue of Books, Documents, and Periodicals" ([n.p.] 1896?) ; Ignatius Donnelly, *Caesar's Column.*

too weak to finish. The idea that the Jewish nation was reborn out of the revolution's chaos may indicate a fear of Zionism, but it more likely showed Donnelly's admiration for the ancient chosen people, whom he praised in another novel of fantasy, *The Golden Bottle*.[28]

Donnelly, the "K. Gold Isaacs" series, and references in other writings may be "ambiguous" in their attitude toward the Jew, but that is the worst that can legitimately be said, and it is probably too much. Even if they should receive the harshest interpretation, they would still remain nothing more than scattered references. Not slips of the pen, they nonetheless occurred so rarely that no pattern can be drawn from them except perhaps that they were an incidental part of the ideological baggage of a few Populists on the extreme left wing of the movement, people who in many cases were neither pure nor constant in their Populist affiliation.

In the more important Populist financial treatises such references are missing. N. B. Ashby, for example, mentioned Shylocks once in connection with control of the money market and Rothschilds once as part of "the interests which profit by a shrunken volume of money," in neither case making any explicitly Jewish reference. In his opening sketch of agriculture in world history, he described the biblical Jews as a group with a high respect for, and skill at, agriculture. W. S. Morgan used the word "Shylock" about a dozen and a half times but never made it specifically Jewish, and in his concluding list of the major aims of reform did not, of course, include elimination or confinement in ghettos of the Jews as one of them. Furthermore, his references to Shylock were balanced by many references to Vanderbilts, Goulds, Huntington, and monopolists in general. N. A. Dunning's 742-page *Farmers' Alliance History* hardly used the word "Shylock." W. A. Peffer, in *The Farmer's Side*, came down hard on Wall Street but avoided Shylock, Rothschild, London, and the Jews. These books were the lengthiest and most involved expositions of Populist financial doctrine, and if it be objected that there is no way of

---

[28] Ignatius Donnelly, *op. cit.*, pp. xxvi, 32, 130, and *passim;* Oscar Handlin, "American Views of the Jew at the Opening of the Twentieth Century," *Publication of the American Jewish Historical Society*, XL (June, 1951), 340; Handlin, *Adventure in Freedom, op. cit.*, p. 188.

knowing how widely they circulated in Kansas, we may note that newspapers certainly circulated, and they are at least equally chaste on the subject. In fact, a radical Jewish publicist had heard so little about Populist anti-Semitism that he sent the Populist governor, L. D. Lewelling, a pamphlet beginning, "Moses, the Populist Law-Giver."[29]

It should be needless to say that discriminatory laws, exclusion, mob action, and overt agitation were not a part of Populism.

The use of "Shylock," although frequent, fell far short of anti-Semitism. Even a critic of Populism has said that "the American stereotype [of Shylock] involved no hostility, no negative judgment"; and another analyst pointed out that it was never vicious until combined with the new stereotype of the "quintessential parvenu" in areas, particularly the East, where discriminatory patterns were taking shape. The mass of evidence supports this. Very infrequently is there an identification of Shylock and Rothschild, and in any case Shylock was not a symbol or collective title for Jews but rather for Wall Street or English moneylenders.[30]

The Rothschild reference, less common than Shylock but a favorite subject of cartoons, needs two comments. The first is that it indicates a specific person who was in fact one of the world's leading bankers. Like Gould, Morgan, and Vanderbilt,

[29] Ashby, op. cit., pp. 328, 330; Morgan, op. cit., passim; N. A. Dunning (ed.), The Farmers' Alliance History (Washington: Alliance Publishing Company, 1891), passim; Peffer, op. cit., passim; Naphthali Herz Imber to Lewelling, Indianapolis, Ind., in Lewelling MSS., in KSHS.

[30] Handlin, "American Views of the Jew . . . ," p. 328; Higham, "Social Discrimination . . . ," pp. 6, 9; People's Herald (Lyndon), October 20, 1892. Typical references to Shylock, which made no specific Jewish reference, include Kansas Workman (El Dorado), June 6, September 26, 1890; L. Vincent (comp.), Alliance and Labor Songster (Winfield, Kan.: H. and L. Vincent, Printers, 1890), pp. 17, 49, 52, 56, 64, 67; "Campaign Songs, as sung by the National Quartette, Topeka, Kansas" (n.p., n.d.), pp. 3–4, 6, in "People's Party Pamphlets," VII, in KSHS; Morgan, op. cit., passim, but cf. pp. 439, 446, 743, 752. The only item wholly concerned with Shylock was Colfax B. Harman's "Shylock's Judgment" (Valley Falls, Kan.: George Harman, 1893), a thirteen-page poem in the manner of Poe's "The Raven" in which Shylock, a Wall Street banker, was denied entry into heaven. But the author was hardly a typical Populist, since his family published not only a Populist sheet but Lucifer, the Light Bearer, a free love paper. See also John Higham, "Anti-Semitism in the Gilded Age: A Reinterpretation," Mississippi Valley Historical Review, XLIII (March, 1957), 574.

who are mentioned at least as often, Rothschild was a flesh-and-blood person, and if he symbolized anything, it was the power of selfish finance not the power of world Jewry. The second is that Rothschild's Englishness is more significant than his Jewishness; for example, concerning the national banking laws and contraction—"Bunker Hill, Trenton, Yorktown, and a hundred victories of a brave people avenged by the success of this hellish plot; the victory of New Orleans wiped out by the money of the Rothschilds."[31] Rothschild is recognized as a Jew, but the significant facts are that he is an English banker Jew and that his interests are representative of other bankers, whether in London or New York, whether Jew or Gentile. In the "Hazzard Circular"–Ernest Seyd tale, bankers were sometimes labelled Shylocks, but neither Seyd nor any of the others involved were labelled as Jews.

Shock waves from the Dreyfus case, perhaps the world's most severe anti-Semitic explosion in the nineties, hardly made a ripple in Kansas, but when it did the local press took the Jewish captain's part very decidedly. The Republican *Wichita Eagle* cursed the "anti-Semite prejudices" that brought France to persecute the great Emile Zola just because he had come to Dreyfus' defense, and the Populist *Kinsley Graphic* decided that Dreyfus' unpopularity sprang from three sources: he was a Jew; he was Hebrew; he was Semitic. The *Graphic* summarized the case and concluded: "One may wonder which is more curious and typical of France, the story of the Iron Mask, the murder of the Duc d'Engheim [*sic*], or the torquemada trial and torture of this hapless Jew." Meanwhile, in Boston, hardly a Populist stronghold, Henry Adams could hardly believe that he, the French military establishment, and the descendants of his "Norman ancestors" had been wrong about Dreyfus and that perhaps a Jew, this Jew, could have been innocent after all.[32]

A much better case can be made for Populist Anglophobia

[31] Morgan, *op. cit.*, p. 428. Other references, fairly typical, are in Walter Vrooman's "The New Democracy," *Volunteers Quarterly* (St. Louis, Mo.), I (June, 1897), 113; *Seneca News*, October 4, 1894; and a cartoon in *Hill City Peoples Advocate*, October 20, 1892.

[32] *Wichita Eagle*, February 9, 1898; *Kinsley Graphic*, December 2, 1898; Edward N. Saveth, "Henry Adams' Norman Ancestors," *Contemporary Jewish Record* (June, 1945), 258.

than for anti-Semitism, because although this attitude was mainly another case of umbrage at misused financial power, and although the English people in England or as immigrants were regularly excepted from the charges, there was some overflow of antagonism from strictly economic to more generally national characteristics. Revolutionary fervor helped to create this antagonism, as well as the plain man's disgust with what seemed to him aristocratic dudism, for which there may have been empirical grounds in Kansas. In the seventies, colonies of dissipated and refractory younger sons of the English gentry were established in Kansas by their worried fathers in the hope that the fresh air, distance from saloons, and tough sod would make men out of them. They failed, both in their purpose and in their financing, with great rapidity. Maybe, as one writer has suggested, the Runnymede colony left such a bad name in Harper county that the local citizenry were unusually receptive to any reviling of the English.[33]

Some Populist criticism of England was more than financial, however. They heatedly recalled Sir Lionel Sackville-West's alleged interference in domestic politics in 1888. They chauvinistically raised "American language . . . literature . . . education . . . inventions . . . advancement in the arts and sciences" above Britain's. They reviled many Americans for agreeing with Andrew Carnegie that England should "accept the headship of the race" in a unification of England and America. Too many Americans, they thought, "do nothing but ape the English aristocracy." England was supposed to have subsidized Hinton Rowan Helper's 1857 book, *The Impending Crisis in the South,* in order to bring on the self-destructive American Civil War. Britain was said to have tried in two wars to take over the United States and now concentrated her efforts on financial control. And one said, "Queen Victoria has a pet dog named Cleveland."[34]

All the same, these were minority expressions. Others believed that the English labor system bore down on the English people harder than American pre-Civil War slavery bore

---

[33] Ecroyd, *op. cit.,* p. 46.

[34] *McPherson Republican,* November 2, 1888; Campbell, *op. cit.,* p. vii; *Advocate,* June 14, 1893, October 9, 1895; *ibid.,* February 13, 1890; Baker, *The Money Monopoly,* pp. 94–95; "Davis Scrapbooks," VII: 20, in KSHS.

upon the Negroes and admitted that British merchants were generally honest. The distinction between oppressors and oppressed was clearly made. English financial hegemony was unquestionably real, and there was plenty of English capital invested in Kansas.[35] The Populists were not simply baying at the moon.

One possible source of their Anglophobia lay in the curious and recurrent Populist references to Ireland, not, usually, in relation to the money question but to the problem of land tenure. Beginning with third-party and Alliance platforms in the late eighties and running through the nineties, agrarians frequently praised Parnell, Irish attempts to throw off the yoke of landlordism and rack-renting, and in general such putative Irish virtues as frugality, industriousness, bravery in battle, and fortitude in economic distress.[36] Could it be that the anti-English feelings of many Populists came in part from Irish-American nationalism? Mrs. Lease was not the only Populist with personal knowledge of Irish political exile. Furthermore, Irish-Americans in Kansas seem to have forsaken their usual Democratic affinities and voted Populist when three-ticket campaigns gave them the opportunity.

Whatever contribution Irish-American nationalism may have made to Populism, Irish experience with English landlords had much to do with the frequent Populist injunctions against alien ownership of land, probably for the most part by providing a topical issue by which to re-awaken ideas of Jeffersonian physiocracy and the natural goodness of the homestead principle.

Populist platform planks and other statements against alien

[35] C. Wood Davis, *Some New Views of 'Options,' 'Futures,' and 'Hedging'* . . . (n.p., n.d.), p. 4, in "People's Party Pamphlets," I, in KSHS; see also "Davis Scrapbooks," I: 73, in KSHS; Kirke Mechem (ed.), *The Annals of Kansas* (Topeka: Kansas State Historical Society, 1954), I, 76, 79.

[36] Morgan, *op. cit.*, p. 142; *Atchison Times*, September 8, 1888; "Davis Scrapbooks," VIII: 37, 45, in KSHS; S. N. Wood, *Wood's Manifesto: An Address to the People of Kansas* (Topeka: Hamilton Printing Co., 1891), pp. 24, 31; Ashby, *op. cit.*, pp. 38, 81, 83, 99, 257; W. R. Kent, *A Historical Review of the Causes and Issues That Led to the Overthrow of the Republican Party in Kansas in 1892* (Topeka: Topeka Daily Press, 1892), p. 4; *Points for Populists as to Organizing the House of Representatives* (n.p.; [1893]), p. 9; *Kansas Farmer* (Topeka), July 25, 1894; Jerry Simpson in the *Congressional Record*, 55th Cong., 1st sess., April 3, 1897, XXX, 568–69; *ibid.*, 55th Cong., 3d sess., XXXI, 1006.

land ownership comprise the only overt official references, except those against contract labor, to foreign countries or the foreign-born. Were they intended to be anti-immigrant? The platforms could leave that impression, except that they very often include a clause to the effect that land should be held "for actual settlers only" and often use the Irish situation to warn Americans. A typical and important formulation was the Kansas state Alliance plank of 1890:

We demand the passage of laws prohibiting alien ownership of land, and that congress take early steps to devise some plan to obtain all land now owned by aliens and foreign syndicates, and that all land now held by railroads and other corporations in excess of such as are actually used and needed by them be reclaimed by the government and held for actual settlers only.[37]

If one takes for granted, as the farmers did, that land should not be held for speculation or for renting when smallholders are readily available, then the alien land problem was certainly real. Cattle syndicates, some of them foreign-owned, had been common in Kansas and in other plains states for some years, and syndicated, corporate, or individual ownership by foreigners of large farming tracts was becoming more and more common. In Kansas the most prominent example was William Scully, an Irishman living in London, who held possibly over seventy thousand acres in Kansas, centered in Marion, Butler, Marshall, and Dickinson counties, and rented them without intent to sell, supposedly to Germans, Swedes, Danes, and others, generally excepting the more fractious Americans and Irish. Absentee landlordism was by no means peculiar to Kansas. Nebraska and Illinois were passing alien land acts at about this time, and bills dropped into the congressional hopper from California, Alabama, and Ohio representatives.[38]

[37] An early Alliance formulation was the following: "To secure the prohibition of alien cattle and land syndicates," quoted in *Topeka Capital-Commonwealth*, February 7, 1889. More ambiguous were the platform of the Jefferson county Alliance (*Advocate*, October 12, 1889) and the statements of speakers at the St. Louis convention in 1889 (*Advocate*, December 13, 1889). See also, *Advocate*, August 24, 1889; *Topeka Capital*, March 19, 1890.

[38] "Davis Scrapbooks," VIII: 39–44, in KSHS; King, *op. cit.*, p. 13; Mechem, *op. cit.*, I, 8; Gates, *op. cit.*, pp. 288–89; *Advocate*, February 13, 1890; Allen, *op. cit.*, p. 9; *Congressional Record*, 52d Cong., 1st sess., XXIII, 125, 731, 2071. For Scully operations, see Homer E. Socolofsky, "The Scully Land System in Marion County," *KHQ*, XVIII (November, 1950), esp. 337–48.

But aside from the fact that not only Populists but Republicans and Prohibitionists supported alien land legislation, the content of Populist statements on the question makes it virtually certain that they had nothing against the individual foreign settler and in fact welcomed him. The enemy, as with the money question, was the man who profited by other men's labor. The Homestead Act of 1862 was not only the great charter of the American rural freeholder, in the Populists' opinion, but made land available to any immigrant who had declared his intention to become a citizen. The Populists were very consistent adherents of the homestead principle, including this provision for yet-to-be-naturalized aliens.[39]

The eyes of the German press in Kansas, so balefully cast at the slightest glimmer of nativism on other questions, glanced very lightly over the alien land issue; and with immigrant small farmers, even Mennonites, unhesitatingly taking out citizenship papers in the eighties and nineties, either on their own responsibility or at the behest of politicians who wanted their votes, there was no local problem. German farmers complained about land syndicates too. Almost universally the Populists held that the small farmer, whether native or naturalized, should be the owner as well as the operator of his land and that titles of large syndicates or individual speculators should be extinguished.[40]

In the spring of 1891, Populist leader (later Supreme Court chief justice) Frank Doster and Republican (later governor) Ed Hoch debated their parties' positions. Neither one showed any antipathy to the immigrant smallholder, but Doster much more clearly denounced large landholders, whether foreign or domestic. Even in the middle of their 1890 crusade, the Populists were clear on all points:

[39] For Republican attitudes to alien land laws, see chaps. iii and v in this book; *The Great Quadrangular Debate*, p. 100. The homestead act of May 20, 1862, opened one quarter section of land to "a citizen of the United States, or who shall have filed his declaration of intention to become such, as required by the naturalization laws of the United States. . . ."

[40] Hortense M. Harrison, "The Populist Delegation in the Fifty-Second Congress, 1891–1893" (Master's thesis, University of Kansas, 1933), p. 31; Cornelius C. Janzen, "Americanization of the Russian Mennonites in Central Kansas" (Master's thesis, University of Kansas, 1914), pp. 112–13; Friedrich Strauss to Lewelling, Woodbine, August 24, 1893, in Lewelling MSS., in KSHS; "Farmer Alliance Clippings," I: 137d–137h, in KSHS (from *Marion Record*, May [?], 1891).

It makes the American blood boil to see with what cool audacity the alien landlords seek to obtain possession of our soil to the detriment of the American farmer. If the farmers alliance can overcome this they will have attained a great victory, and one that was begun when our forefathers threw the tea into Boston harbor. America for Americans, say we, both native and naturalized![41]

The Populists were also exercised about foreign industrial and mining syndicates, but this problem was distinctly secondary to either land tenure or the money question, and the real complaint was against landlords, railroads, and other corporations who removed Kansas assets from Kansas hands. Both of the Populist governors not only did not oppose but actively encouraged foreign investment so long as Kansans held a share in the ownership and management. Populist Governor Lewelling tried to help a Bristol, England, company find mining investments in Kansas, and Populist Governor Leedy kept in touch with foreign consulates on trade opportunities. Perhaps the two governors were crooked, but perhaps, too, the ogre of the British money power did not stalk every Populist household after all.[42]

The question of nativism in Kansas Populism, as just discussed, can perhaps be summed up as follows.

1. Antagonistic references to foreigners occurred on two issues only: money and land tenure.

2. Antagonistic references were limited to England and Jews, specifically to English landlords and bankers and to Anglo-Jewish bankers.

[41] Editorial of John Davis, in *Abilene Chronicle*, July 18, 1890, in "Davis Scrapbooks," VIII: 38, in KSHS; "Farmer Alliance Clippings," I: 137d–137h, in KSHS. Ashby (*op. cit.*, p. 266) seems to oppose alien landholders generally, but his opposition only to large holdings quickly appears in the context.

[42] Letters of Lewelling to Rowe Brothers & Co., of Bristol, England; Lewelling to W. F. Page of Galena, Kan.; Lewelling to Col. W. B. Stone of Galena; and Lewelling to W. F. Sapp of Galena—all from Topeka, March 15, 1894, in Lewelling MSS, in KSHS. Letters of Leedy to William Wyndham, British Consul at Chicago; and Leedy to Portuguese Consul, New York City—both December 2, 1897, in Leedy MSS, in KSHS. *Advocate*, June 14, 1899. See also *Hillsboro Anzeiger*, June 20, 1890; *Points for Populists* . . . , p. 10; *Kansas Farmer* (Topeka), November 30, 1892 [an editorial notice announcing a foreign investor seeking business opportunities and asking the readers for suggestions].

3. Such references emanated from a small minority, a wing that generally favored prohibition and women's suffrage, opposed fusion, and perhaps drew more of its strength from former Republicans than from former Democrats.

4. Even within this group, the unfavorable references were remarkably infrequent and the expressions of a tiny fringe.

5. Nearly all antagonistic references were based on factual situations; for example, it was true that English bankers, including Rothschild, were powerful, self-interested, and unsympathetic to the farmer-debtors.

6. Such Populist antagonism as there was was rooted in democratic ideals nourished by the American Revolution, the War of 1812, and pre-Civil War nineteenth-century experience, not on later racist theories.

7. Populists who dealt in these terms found Wall Street and Lombard Street, Gentile financiers and Jewish financiers, equally opprobrious, with if anything the greater stress on the American and Gentile financiers than on the English and Jewish ones.

8. Antagonism was seldom directed to Englishness, practically never to Jewishness; rather to the financial power and aims of certain classes of Englishmen, Jews, and Americans.

9. Republicans, especially silver Republicans, made similar references.

10. Populists often supported their arguments with laudatory references to successful instances of reform practices in foreign countries.

11. Populist antagonism did not exist on a personal, individual basis and almost never on a racial basis, as did the antagonism of contemporary eastern restrictionists; it can be considered an infrequent emotional or rhetorical overflow which resulted from membership drives, political campaigns, and bleak agricultural depression.

5. Alien Land

The actions and makeup of the Kansas legislature elected in 1890 lend further support to these points. Because the Republicans had squeaked into the governorship and because the quadrennially elected Senate remained heavily Republican, not a great deal was accomplished, even though ninety-two Populists overwhelmed twenty-six Republicans and seven Democrats in the House of Representatives. This was a large enough majority to dispose of Senator Ingalls in joint session, but only one other plank of the Populist program of 1890 became law, for the reason that it had the support of the Republican governor and senators. Interestingly, it was the only Populist proposal concerning a primarily state matter that made any reference to foreigners: the alien land question.

In his message to the legislature opening the 1891 session, Republican Governor Lyman Humphrey pointed out that in 1888 the voters gave an overwhelming mandate to "legislation restricting or forbidding the right of aliens to accumulate and hold large landed estates in Kansas." Several bills were introduced in one house or the other by both Populists and Republicans, but the one introduced by Senator H. E. Richter, Republican of Council Grove (later nominated by the Republicans for lieutenant-governor and publicized as a German although he was American-born), finally became law. In the Senate there were no dissenting votes, and the favorable House margin was 79 to 17. The dissenters included ten Republicans and a scattering of Democrats and Populists. Among the eleven foreign-born Populists in both houses, eight voted for, one voted against, and two did not vote.[43]

However careless some Populists might have been in aiming clearly at large landlords rather than small settlers, the wording of the law was precise enough. Any imputation of nativism emanating from the campaign literature evaporates completely on examining the text:

Be it enacted by the Legislature of the State of Kansas:
SECTION 1. That a *non-resident* alien, firm of aliens, or corporation incorporated under the laws of any foreign country, shall not be capable of acquiring title to . . . any land or real estate in the state . . . (Italics added).

Heirs of aliens had to sell or lose their lands in three years (five years for minors) unless the alien heirs became "actual residents"; aliens who became residents were assured full

[43] Richter's bill was S. 165; For the legislative process in the Senate, see Kansas, Senate, *Journal; Proceedings of the Senate of the State of Kansas; Seventh Biennial Session* . . . (Topeka: Kansas Publishing House, 1891), pp. 44, 120, 130, 134, 192, 200, 594, 619–20, 652, 768, 744; see also Kansas, House of Representatives, *Journal; Proceedings of the House of Representatives, Seventh Biennial Session* . . . (Topeka: Kansas Publishing House, 1891), pp. 237, 251, 260, 476, 620, 789, 882, 886, 925. Other bills, mainly stopped in committees, were S. 22, S. 62, and H.B. 41.

land rights as soon as they declared their intention to become citizens, and they were given plenty of time to do so. The law specifically denied any attempt to confiscate during their lifetime lands held by aliens. The clear intent of this act was the abolition of large estates owned by non-resident aliens and possibly the desire to bring resident alien landholders within the outlines of the homestead principle. Especially since most resident aliens were declaring their intentions of citizenship anyway, the law was not onerous; nor, obviously, was it nativistic, since it encouraged the alien landholders, resident or not, to become American citizens. In succeeding sessions Republicans and Populists entered various amendments, none of which became law, but which had the support, in so far as is recorded, of members of both parties and of natives and foreign-born alike. The law was repealed, again in a bipartisan manner, in 1901.[44]

With Republican support the Populist legislature also passed a banking law that, although not faultless, still relieved greatly the previous instability and confusion, and some labor legislation emerged as well. There was not much else. The Populist House passed a usury law limiting legal interest to 10 per cent and a redemption law making it possible to redeem a mortgage within two years after foreclosure and abolished many patronage sinecures, but these laws met immediate doom in the Republican Senate. The same fate met a bill requiring out-of-state railroads to incorporate in Kansas.[45]

Some idea of the Populists' lack of ideological unity and parliamentary immaturity can be had from the history of H. B. 279, "An act conferring upon women the right to vote and

[44] Kansas, *Session Laws of 1891* . . . (Topeka: Kansas Publishing House, 1891), chap. iii, pp. 7–10. The repeal act was S. 385, in *Senate Journal* . . . *1901*, pp. 309, 328, 475, 793, 819, 844, 1093, 1123, 1125; *House Journal* . . . *1901*, pp. 1160, 1161, 1195, 1310, 1512–13. Other bills (by date of entry only: *House Journal* . . . *1893*, p. 384; *Senate Journal* . . . *1893*, pp. 445, 578; *House Journal* . . . *1895*, pp. 147, 241; *Senate Journal* . . . *1895*, pp. 340, 424; *Senate Journal* . . . *1897*, p. 384.

[45] Section 2 of the alien land act, however, forbade corporations more than 20 per cent foreign-owned from holding land. *House Journal* . . . *1891*, p. 18; *Advocate*, March 25, 1891; "Ruppenthal Scrapbooks," I: 161, in KSHS; Wayne D. Angell, "A Century of Commercial Banking in Kansas, 1856 to 1956" (Ph.D. dissertation, University of Kansas, 1957), pp. 294–98; Karl Arthur Svenson, "The Effect of Popular Discontent on Political Parties in Kansas" (Ph.D. dissertation, State University of Iowa, 1948), pp. 89–90.

hold office." The farmer legislators passed this bill, 60–39 (of course it failed in the Senate), with some Populists for, some against. J. L. Soupene, of Manhattan, a Populist, entered the bill, but the Populist speaker, Parley P. Elder, of Ottawa, like Soupene an old third-party man, voted against it, explaining that he thought it was unconstitutional. Such was Populist party discipline. A Republican editor, summing up the session, was struck by the inexperience of the farmer legislators and by the ease with which these previously clear-thinking theorists became, under parliamentary pressure, the tools of a few lawyers and lobbyists. Rather than more democracy, the state got more efficient lobbying, he said, and although undoubtedly the railroad lobby, at least, was less influential, others had a field day.[46]

The foreign-born representation in the House, 13 of 125, matched closely the state ratio of 10.4 per cent in 1890. But the fact that of the thirteen, none were Republicans, two (a Canadian and an Englishman) were Democrats, and all the rest were Populists is itself a commentary on "Populist nativism." Furthermore, one other Populist member, A. H. Lupfer, of Pawnee, was a native of New Germantown, Pennsylvania, and may have been Pennsylvania Dutch. He was an ex-Republican, a teacher, and a Methodist. The "anglophobe" Populists had elected three Englishmen among their eleven foreign-born legislators.

Fred Jackson, representing McPherson county and city, was an English-born farmer who came early in life to New York state and then to Kansas by way of Iowa. He was 47, a former Republican, and a Union veteran. John T. Jones, of Cherokee county, came to Illinois from south Wales at the age of eighteen, had been an alderman at Collinsville, Illinois, and moved to Kansas in 1881. A former Republican, Greenbacker, and Union Laborite, this Presbyterian miner and farmer was elected by the Populists with Democratic endorsement by a ten to one margin.[47]

---

[46] Noble Prentis in the *Kansas City Star*, March 11, 1891, in "Ruppenthal Scrapbooks," I: 123, in KSHS; *House Journal . . . 1891*, pp. 76, 490, 494, 527.

[47] *Admire's Political and Legislative Hand-Book for Kansas, 1891* (Topeka: Geo. W. Crane & Co., Publishers, 1891), pp. 434–35. One of the eleven, Pat Dolan of Salina, from southern Ireland, is described in chap. iv in this book.

Another Welshman, Robert W. Lewis, represented part of Osage county. He was a farmer, an ex-Republican, a Congregationalist, and had held township office. He won in 1890 by a two to one margin.

A minister in the Christian church, Benjamin Matchett represented Osborn county. He was a native of Essex, England, had lived in Canada and several states, had been a spy for the Union, and was an ex-Republican.[48]

George McConkey, a farmer of Ottawa county, was an Irish Methodist and a former Republican.

A Populist endorsed by the Democrats, John Rehrig had left Germany in his thirties, before the American Civil War, to become a Kansas farmer, stock raiser, and feeder. He had been a Republican.[49]

Hugh M. Reid, of Crawford county, was an Irish Presbyterian who had been an inactive Republican. He was a farmer, married with seven children, and like some of his colleagues, self-educated.

Plymouth, England, was the birthplace of William Rogers of Washington county, who came to Illinois at the age of three and then to Kansas. He was also a Union veteran, a farmer and stock raiser, a former delegate to one or two Republican state conventions, and a former township and county official.[50]

M. Senn, of Dickinson county, was a Swiss. He had been a Republican until 1882 and then a very active third-party man. He was a farmer but as a first cousin of Chris Hoffman was closely tied to considerable wealth. He was a Union veteran.

Finally, D. S. Steele of Cloud county, was an Ontario man who had lived in Kansas since the territorial period. He was a Union veteran, a former Republican and Prohibitionist, a Methodist, and a farmer.[51]

In practically every respect, except for a brogue here or an *umlaut* there, these men resembled their native-born Populist colleagues. Their foreign birth was neither curious nor constricting.

Unfortunately, the Populist legislature adjourned with the state still unredeemed, and since the 1890 elections, although a

[48] *Ibid.*, pp. 436, 438.
[49] *Ibid.*, pp. 439, 445.
[50] *Ibid.*, pp. 445, 447.
[51] *Ibid.*, pp. 448–49.

tremendous step forward, had fallen short of complete success, the future was by no means certain. Pure crusading fervor had done wonders, but it was now over two years since the great organizing days of the Farmers' Alliance, and experience indicated that a greater admixture of smooth political organization had to come if Populism was to progress. The party had already shown a tendency, whenever such questions as prohibition, women's suffrage, and fusion arose, to coalesce into two opposing factions—shifting and amorphous, perhaps, but politically ominous too. Both factions, which could be called the pragmatic and the idealistic, had won successes in the convention and campaign of 1890. The results of the election and the work of the legislature somewhat strengthened the hand of the pragmatists, and although nothing very black and white occurred, nothing more than a slight shift in emphasis, Populism became a little less of a strictly economic crusade and a little more of a political party. Although this trend was still not strong, it showed a healthy appreciation of necessity and experience and a real gain in common sense.

The events of late 1891 accelerated this trend. In a simple factional fight the remnants of the *Nonconformist* group eased out Frank McGrath as state president of the Alliance.[52] Probably this sort of manoeuver was not new but only better publicized than other conflicts. Political factions had always existed in the Alliance and the People's party, although they seldom came to public view. They are a concomitant of any party, especially one out of office, and the Populists lacked a real degree of central control until the campaign of 1892. What does seep through the largely silent sources in 1891 is a sign here and there of a rusting away of some of the older factions, facilitating the trend to centralization in 1892.

The county elections of 1891 furnished a further pressure toward fusion and centralization: they flatly reversed the 1890 vote. In 1890 the Republicans took only 71 offices to the Populists' 324, but in 1891 the score was Republicans, 277, Populists, 127.[53] Many Populist voters of 1890 were reverting to the old party, either because of the lack of state-wide issues or a simple decline in zeal. Was Populism already dead?

[52] *Salina Republican*, October 23, 30, 1891; *Wellington Peoples Voice*, October 27, 1892; Raymond C. Miller, *op. cit.*, pp. 189–91.
[53] *Advocate*, December 9, 1891.

PART THREE

THE POLITICAL YEARS

KENT: That which ordinary men are fit for, I am
qualified in; and the best of me is diligence.
                                    —*King Lear*, Act I, scene 4

FUSION AND VICTORY

1. An Arm-in-Arm Campaign

Before 1892 was over, the "corpse" of late 1891 showed itself to be not that at all, but a sleeping giant that awoke, after a little intravenous feeding of Democracy, to stride thunderously to the polls and into office.

Powerful forces operated against fusion as the new year opened. Other states that had lagged behind Kansas in Populist strength in 1890 were now catching up, and partly through the stimulating aid of periodic national reformers' meetings in 1891, the current of independency flowed swiftly toward the Omaha convention in July and the nominations of Weaver and Field on a Populist national ticket. Within Kansas both parties strove to maintain their separate identities, the Democrats to avoid being subsumed permanently and the Populists (although in sheer numbers the other major party with the Republicans) to establish themselves as something more than a single-campaign oddity. With nothing terribly important at stake in 1891 these antifusion considerations had been very strong, and as 1892 opened, the press of each party frequently set up impossibly high and idealistic prices for the support of the other. As it happened, however, this was only the beginning of a process of mutual bargaining.

The handwriting had been on the wall since the election of 1890, and the doleful results of local campaigns in 1891 underscored it. Party leaders saw this more clearly than many of the rank and file, and it was much easier for slate-makers to select congressional candidates in closed-door parleys than for fusion to gain even a whisper at the less manageable Populist state convention.

The convention met at Wichita on June 15 with a dearth of either available candidates or fusion sentiment and an abundance of such Populist convention earmarks as the principle of "letting the office seek the man," crusading zeal, and lack of cohesion. The potentially disrupting questions of prohibition and women's suffrage were avoided, however, and the platform largely repeated the state and national reform planks, political and economic, that had been put forth by the 1890 convention and intervening national gatherings.

When the delegates arrived in Wichita they had no runaway contender in mind for the governorship, but after hearing a poignant address of welcome by the Sedgwick county chairman, a produce-dealer named Lorenzo D. Lewelling, they nominated him by acclamation. Lewelling had been born in Iowa in 1846, had a Quaker and abolitionist background, and was a college graduate who had done a number of things including farming, teaching, and heading the Iowa State Reform School before he came to Kansas in 1887. As a speaker he was not a spellbinder, but he had a natural warmth that convinced more gently. By 1890 he had become county chairman at Wichita and remained a Populist from the beginning of the movement to its end.[1]

The platform, the candidate for governor, and the rest of the slate made, to say the least, no concession to the Democrats. While this was mostly a result of the quixotism of the mass of the delegates rather than any strong feeling either way toward the Democrats, the political situation worked out advantageously for the Populists, because obviously the Democrats would lose much and gain nothing if they failed to endorse the Populist ticket. They had attempted to get some influence in naming the state ticket in return for endorsing the Weaver electors, knowing that Cleveland did not stand any chance in Kansas and hoping that, at least, Harrison would not get Kansas' ten electoral votes. Even though in state matters "they had been more than repelled, they had been insulted," they endorsed the Weaver electors anyway. Through the work of at least one powerful Democrat, John Martin, of Topeka, through the lack of a strong alternative such as they had had

[1] W. J. Costigan, "Lorenzo D. Lewelling," *TKSHS*, VII (1901–2), 121–26; Donald H. Ecroyd, "An Analysis and Evaluation of Populist Political Campaign Speech Making in Kansas 1890–1894" (Ph.D. dissertation, State University of Iowa, 1949), pp. 95–96, 100; Dawn Daniels, "Lorenzo D. Lewelling—A Leader of the Kansas Populists" (Master's thesis, Department of History, Northwestern University, 1931), p. 20; *The Autobiography of William Allen White* (New York: Macmillan Co., 1946), p. 228.

in Charlie Robinson in 1890, and through the impact of presidential politics, whatever personal disgruntlement the Democrats may have had was overcome. The two parties' rather similar platforms now supported a fused ticket. Democratic labor elements could look at the national Populist platform drawn up at Omaha that year and find planks opposing contract labor, other "undesirable immigration," and Pinkertons and others favoring boycotts and hour laws. Fusion had been missed in 1890 only by the Populists' wish to remain silent on the liquor question—thereby following a middle course between the Republicans and Democrats—together with many delegates' fears of nominating Robinson simply because many newspapers had backed his candidacy. In fact, one newspaper in the 1890 campaign had suggested that leaders of the Populist and Democratic parties had agreed long before November of that year on all of Willits' appointments to state offices should he have been elected.[2]

In many papers an open letter appeared in which Martin declared his agreement and presumably that of most Democrats with the Populists on all proposals except the subtreasury and government ownership of railway and telegraph facilities, which made the differences small indeed. The opposition of a sizable element of Populists, either former Republicans still worried about mixing with the party of rebellion or third-party men congenitally unable to coexist even a little with the old parties, was not enough to overcome the fact that fusion was both profitable and practicable. In fact, many Democrats must have felt much like W. A. Harris, the ex-Democrat who was the Populist candidate for congressman-at-large that year. When he was asked what the difference was between the Populist and Democratic parties, he said it was virtually nil; he had satisfied himself, he said, that the People's party followed Jefferson and Calhoun, especially the former, even better than the existing Democratic party. To be a Populist was to Harris to out-Jefferson the party Jefferson had founded. In 1892 there was no divisive clamor over the liquor question, and it did not

[2] Raymond C. Miller, "The Populist Party in Kansas" (Ph.D. dissertation, University of Chicago, 1928), p. 226; Gerald N. Grob, "The Knights of Labor, Politics and Populism," *Mid-America*, N.S. XXIX (January, 1958), 19; *Ravanna Chieftain*, September 11, 1890.

seriously threaten the Populists' equilibrium after Prohibitionist leader John P. St. John was given the cold shoulder at the Cincinnati meeting of May, 1891, which many Kansas men attended. Populist papers in immigrant and native settlements alike either opposed prohibition or kept quiet.[3] If not entirely cordial, an entente had nevertheless been created. The Populists, moreover, had made the Democrats come to them hat in hand.

For the most part, the campaign issues and appeals of 1892 followed the route charted in 1890. Crops had improved slightly but mortgages remained staggeringly high, transportation costs still ate up crop returns, and it was easier to shake loose a banker's teeth than his money. Populist speakers ranged as usual from cold statistics to boiling rage as they stressed the primacy of the money question and at times blamed England for silver demonetization. Shylock reared his head occasionally, and as Mrs. Lease seconded the presidential nomination of General Weaver at Omaha, she ranted, "Give him to us and we will drive from the American shores the English robbers with their stolen gold, and we will make plutocrats and monopolists cringe and tremble!" In 1892 Mrs. Lease was still incensed about money, land, and transportation and snarled that prohibition and women's suffrage were "absurd" as political issues. When the Populist chairman of McPherson county found two men to edit the *People's Party Advocate*, he touted them as "men whose forefathers helped to throw off the galling yoke of King George," and many a Populist heart thumped at the memory of Yorktown and bled for Irish tenants tethered with landlordism.[4]

[3] Kermit E. Opperman, "The Political Career of Senator William Alexander Harris" (Master's thesis, University of Kansas, 1938), p. 7; Hortense M. Harrison, "The Populist Delegation in the Fifty-Second Congress, 1891–1893" (Master's thesis, University of Kansas, 1933), p. 8; *Independence Star and Kansan*, October 7, 1892.

[4] L. D. Lewelling, "Problems before the Western Farmer," *North American Review*, CLX (January, 1895), *passim*; articles by W. A. Peffer cited above in chap. v, p. 103, n. 18; R. A. Sankey, *The Silver Question: Speech at Peoples Party League in Wichita, Delivered August 30, 1892* (Wichita: Kansas Commoner Print, [n.d.]), pp. 3, 9, 12; statements by Mrs. Lease from *Kansas Commoner* (Wichita), July 7, 1892, and from *Marion Times*, March 3, 1892, quoted in Betty Lou Taylor, "Mary Elizabeth Lease: Kansas Populist" (Master's thesis, Municipal University of Wichita, 1951), p. 26; *Peoples Party Advocate* (McPherson), January 8, 1892; *Kansas Commoner*

The alien land question was still alive, and although Populists now figured the American holdings of foreign noblemen, principally English, at twenty-one million acres or so, they often anathematized the domestic speculating landlord as well.[5]

All parties agreed that restriction of certain types of immigrants would be beneficial to labor, although the Democrats and Populists were perhaps more careful to limit themselves to strictly economic arguments. First District Congressman Case Broderick, a Republican, entered labor petitions for immigration restriction, as did others of all parties. The sole Kansas Populist restriction bill, Senator Peffer's S. 357, apparently provided for consular inspection of immigrants before they left Europe rather than after they had already arrived at American immigration depots. As Peffer put it:

I believe our immigration laws could be very much improved by requiring done on the other side of the ocean most of the work which is done on this side by the immigrant, to the end that all unfit persons may be saved the trouble and expense of a voyage across the Atlantic and our people here saved the annoyance of returning them. Besides that, no person ought to be permitted to come here under any circumstances to remain among us as a laborer unless in good faith he intends to become a good citizen and remain here permanently.

While a Populist claimed that tariff protection against foreign goods was useless if railroad freight rates stayed up, a Republican denounced the Democratic low tariff idea as a means for the protection of England.[6] Whatever else may be said about it, the Populist position was not a lonely one.

Another issue, one that nauseated Democrats in general and Germans in particular, was Mrs. Lease. Even those happiest with fusion would have been delighted to be rid of "agrarian

(Wichita), October 20, 1892; inaugural address, of Lewelling, quoted in Ecroyd, *op. cit.*, p. 359.

[5] *Labor News* (Leavenworth), October 7, 1892; *Advocate*, February 8, 1893.

[6] *Peoples Party Advocate* (McPherson), January 1, 1892; *Kansas Agriculturalist* (Winfield), November 18, 1893; *Congressional Record*, 52d Cong., 1st sess., XXIII, 29, 2856; Democratic National Platform of 1892, Sec. 12, in unidentified newspaper clipping, "Ruppenthal Scrapbooks," I: 171, in KSHS; Frank Oliphant, "Immigration," *New Kansas Magazine* (Atchison), V (September 23, 1893), 26; *Kansas Commoner* (Wichita), November 3, 1892; *Russell Journal*, October 13, 1892.

and paternal schemes of cranks like Mrs. Lease and her crazy followers," and Teutonic bile flowed like Kansas buttermilk at the slightest mention of Frau Lease's rumored candidacy for the United States Senate. Her endorsement of Jerry Simpson's re-election campaign had made even that pro-fusion realist suspect among the Germans. One German paper said that the two leading candidates for the Senatorship from Kansas were "ein Blaustrumpf und ein Ohnestrumpf—Frau Lease und Herr Jerry" (a blue-stocking and a no-stocking).[7] Even with fusion effected, the People's party obviously comprised many disparate personalities indeed, and such persons as Mrs. Lease, who was to the extreme left wing of the party the faith healer of reform, became not only to nervous Democrats but to many Populists as well a repulsive political leper.

With Jerry Simpson, Mrs. Lease, John Willits, John Davis, William Baker, and others actively participating, the Populist leadership in 1892 did not differ very much from what it had been in 1890. Some who were not widely noticed in the first campaign, however, became highly influential in the second, and of these, four demand special notice.

The difficulty and danger in trying to categorize individual Populists as left-wing or right-wing reformers, because of the peculiar combination of traits some of them possessed, is nowhere greater than in the cases of Annie L. Diggs, G. C. Clemens, William A. Harris, and John W. Breidenthal. On the one hand, all of them espoused radicalism by other routes than Populism, two personally favored women's suffrage, three favored prohibition, and all came from upper-middle- or middle-class origins. Yet at the same time, one of them became the political genius of Kansas Populism, the architect of fusion, and the other three were his close personal friends and advisers. One was an immigrant, another had close business and personal ties with immigrants throughout his life, another was a former Confederate officer, and the fourth actively supported the most execrated immigrants of their time, the Haymarket anarchists. If these four demonstrate some of the variety and divergent forces within Kansas Populism, they also show that

[7] *Oskaloosa Times*, December 1, 1892; *Pittsburger Volkszeitung*, November 25, December 1, 1892.

when dealing with politics it will not do to put all stress on ideologies and forget personal quirks.

Annie LaPorte Diggs, better known today as a suffragette than as a Populist, was born at London, Ontario, in 1853, moved as a child to New Jersey, and came to Lawrence, Kansas, in 1873. She soon married A. S. Diggs, bore him three children, and then turned to a mélange of reforms. In 1878 she was a temperance speaker; in 1880 an advocate of socialist silkworm colonies (there was one in the next county); in 1881 a light of the Free Religious Association; in the late eighties a supporter of Breidenthal's and Chris Hoffman's Kansas-Sinaloa Investment Company and its Topolobampo colony; a women's suffrage proponent throughout; and in 1890 a participant in the political dismemberment of John J. Ingalls. She remained an active Populist throughout the life of the party, although at times her suffrage convictions strained the chords of party harmony. The gentility and suppliant femininity of her speaking style, her physical diminutiveness, her dependence on blandishments rather than battle axes, and her good relations with the party leadership made her a total contrast to Mrs. Lease.[8] The two ladies had at least one public blow-up, from which neither emerged unscathed, but for Mrs. Diggs to have at least held her own, as she did, against the "uncrowned queen" showed that for all her mildness she was no pushover.

Probably closer to Governor Lewelling than to Mrs. Diggs or Breidenthal but still a friend of theirs, Gaspar Christopher Clemens included Populism in his reform portfolio for at least several years. Reputed to be a first cousin of Mark Twain, whom he resembled closely, Clemens was born in Ohio in 1849 of a Virginia and Kentucky family and was an eminent member of the Topeka bar for thirty years, often pleading in the Kansas Supreme Court and the United States District, Appeals, and Supreme courts. Prior to Populism, he defended by pamphlet and a memorial oration at Chicago's Waldheim

[8] Elizabeth Barr [Arthur], "The Populist Uprising," in *A Standard History of Kansas and Kansans* ed. William E. Connelley (Chicago: Lewis Publishing Co., 1918), p. 1152. For a pronounced example of her writing style, see Annie L. Diggs, *The Story of Jerry Simpson* (Wichita: Hobson Printing Co., 1908), pp. 33–34. Also, Ecroyd, *op. cit.*, pp. 111–16; interview with Willard J. Breidenthal, Topeka, September 11, 1960.

Cemetery the Haymarket anarchists; during its heyday, he praised Altgeld's pardon of the remaining rioters; and after Populism ceased to be, he ran for governor on the Socialist ticket. Clemens shared with the anarchists anticlericalist as well as social ideas, as had the important Kansas reform weekly, the *Nonconformist*, in the old Union Labor days. In spite of his earlier and later anarchism and socialism, however, he was a close adviser of Governor Lewelling and a steadfast Populist for several years. Although he was not a fusion advocate, he never bolted because of it during a campaign, as some did.[9]

Some Populists joined the movement in its earliest days, reaching prominence only with the passing of time, and William Alexander Harris was one of these. As an 1861 graduate of the Virginia Military Institute, Harris rose to become a colonel in the Confederate army before Appomattox ended his military career. He came to Kansas in 1865 as a civil engineer on the Kansas Pacific Railroad project, settled on a farm not far from Kansas City, and became a noted shorthorn breeder. An early and active Granger, he had also been a Democrat and belonged to the more conservative wing of the People's Party. This led to his being drafted for the nomination for congressman-at-large on the fusion ticket of 1892 because he was acceptable to all factions. Harris' Republican opponent was ex-Governor George T. Anthony, who a Populist paper rather underhandedly reported had urged the complete shutting-down of Castle Garden, the immigrant depot, and the return of many immigrants already in the United States: "If they don't go, I would open the gates of eternity and hurl them into hell at a rope's end." In the House of Representatives and later in the state Senate and the United States Senate, Harris constantly worked to weaken monopolies, especially railroad monopolies. With the support of a Nebraska congressman

---

[9] James L. King (ed. and comp.), *History of Shawnee County, Kansas, and Representative Citizens* (Chicago: Richmond & Arnold, 1905), p. 626; interview with Willard J. Breidenthal, Kansas City, September 12, 1960; G. C. Clemens, "Miscellaneous Briefs," in KSHS; Clemens, *A Common-Sense View of the Anarchist Case* (n.p., n.d.); *The Labor Problem* (Enterprise, Kan.: Anti-Monopolist Job Office, 1887); *Topeka Journal*, November 5, 1893; *Advocate*, December 27, 1893; Raymond C. Miller, *op. cit.*, pp. 300–302.

named Bryan, he advocated that the federal government take over the Pacific railroads that had defaulted on the debts they owed the United States on bonds issued for their construction in 1862 and 1864. Harris worked closely with Breidenthal throughout the Populist years. Before his death in 1909, he returned to the Democratic party and came very near defeating Republican Ed Hoch for the governorship in the 1906 campaign, so near that some have said he was "counted out."[10]

None of these, however, had the astuteness, staying power, political insight, or authority of John W. Breidenthal, whose personality Kansas Populism came to resemble probably more than that of any other single person. He was born in Sibley county, Minnesota, in 1857, and when eleven years old came with his Pennsylvania-born father and the other members of his family to a farm in Labette county, Kansas. When Breidenthal reached adulthood, he farmed for three years and then began a career in real estate, insurance, and politics. An early Greenbacker, he was the 1884 candidate of the Anti-Monopoly party for lieutenant-governor, was a delegate to the 1887 Union Labor convention at Cincinnati, and in 1887 and 1888 was state chairman of the Union Labor party.[11]

At about this time Breidenthal and Christian B. Hoffman formed the Kansas-Sinaloa Investment Company, the parent of a socialist colony on the west coast of Mexico. Populism naturally attracted him. As early as 1890 he was perhaps the functioning head of the party as well as a possibility, along with Peffer and Frank Doster, for the United States senatorship to replace Ingalls. By 1892 he was state chairman of the People's party and retained that post throughout most of the nineties. With his warmth, magnetism, astuteness, and high honesty, he set well with the Populists, and with the single notable exception of the state convention of 1894, accomplished the somewhat spectacular feat of having most of his plans and wishes accepted by the rank and file. So successful was he that the "middle-of-the-road Populists," a non-fusion, no compromise, and politically dangerous splinter group led by Mrs. Lease and others, could only wail that Breidenthal was "the most col-

[10] Opperman, op. cit., pp. 1–7, 9–10, 17–18; Topeka Daily Truth, November 8, 1892.

[11] Nonconformist, January 13, 1887; Atchison Times, September 1, 1888.

lossal [sic] aggregation of political cussedness on earth."[12] Although personally in favor of prohibition and women's suffrage, and once a fairly radical third-party thinker, he nonetheless had the political wisdom to realize the poisonous effects these ideas would have on the core of the reform program and the courage, furthermore, to lay his ideas aside in order to avoid repelling the Democrats and others whose support was essential.

The Breidenthal home at Sixth and Fillmore in Topeka was the unofficial party headquarters after late 1892 or early 1893, and Populists of all varieties—Mrs. Diggs, Jerry Simpson, Mrs. Lease, John Willits, G. C. Clemens, all of the congressmen and state officials—visited there along with not a few Democrats and Republicans. Breidenthal was appointed by the Populist governors to two four-year terms as state banking commissioner, a post established by the banking law of 1891, and during the banking panic of 1893 and 1894 and at other times, he did an able job. In 1900 he was the Democratic and Populist nominee for governor, and after he went down with the rest of the ticket, he was largely occupied until his death in 1910 in building the banking empire his family still controls.[13]

Polyglot participation was more than ever a Populist mark in 1892, as foreign-born persons continued to crowd conventions and tickets. Even in the generally Republican county of Cloud, several ethnic groups sent delegates to the county convention. From the heavily French townships of Aurora and South Shirley came Louis Letourneau, 48, a farmer of 800 acres, N. Asselin, 54, who farmed 235 acres, and A. M. Lafond, 55, another farmer, all born in Canada, as well as C. Guimond, 28, a farmer of a quarter section, born in Illinois and married to a Canadian. Sibley township sent Frits Youngberg, 47, a Swede, who lived with his brother on a quarter section, and A. Richardson, possibly a Scot. Two Danes,

[12] *Topeka New Era*, December 9, 1893; Taylor, *op. cit.*, p. 14.

[13] Wayne D. Angell, "A Century of Commercial Banking in Kansas, 1856 to 1956" (Ph.D. dissertation, University of Kansas, 1957), pp. 301–2; The foregoing depends largely on *Kansas: A Cyclopedia of State History . . .* (Chicago: Standard Publishing Company, 1912), III, 30–31; interviews with Willard J. Breidenthal, Topeka, September 11, Kansas City, September 12, 1960.

Lewis Hanson, 42, and Robert Hanson, 38, who together farmed 1,160 acres, and another French Canadian, M. Charbonneau, 45, represented Buffalo township; and Colfax township sent M. Malo, 39, and John Lapolice, 57, French Canadians, and P. J. McDonough, 59, an Irishman.[14]

The Populist candidate for state representative from southern Osage county, John Graham, was an Englishman who had worked in the West Cumberland coal mines and had become a minister before he emigrated to Kansas after the Civil War. The Republicans had to put up a Welshman against him, but despite this the Welsh mining settlement at Arvonia was largely Populist.[15]

In Barton county, Carl Voigt and Fred Reiche joined other Germans at the county convention, and in Jackson county, in spite of the sparse foreign population, a German named Lutz began several years as Populist county chairman. Lutz had been a Republican. One year he sold his wheat crop for $300, which he deposited in a bank before it closed on a Saturday afternoon. On Monday morning neither the bank nor the $300 were available for business, and Lutz, deciding a change was in order, left his old party permanently for Populism and then the Democracy.[16]

In mostly native-born Butler county, Thomas Ohlsen, 50, a German, ran as a Populist for County Commissioner, and in Graham county, a Swede, Oscar Gustafson, 42, an Irishman, John Monaghan, 49, and a German, J. A. Eichman, 42, represented Morelan township at the county convention.[17]

The German-Russians in Ellis county were looked after by the nomination of two of their group, Phil Jacobs, 26, for clerk of the district court, and Joe Rupp, "a successful and hard-

[14] *Concordia Alliant,* September 1, 1892; *Census of 1895,* Vol. LXV, Aurora twp., p. 20, and Buffalo twp., pp. 11, 19, 20, in KSHS; *ibid.,* Vol. LXVI, Colfax twp., pp. 13, 18, 24; *ibid.,* Vol. LXVII, S. Shirley twp., pp. 12, 25, 29; *ibid.,* Vol. LXVIII, Sibley twp., pp. 22, 23.

[15] *People's Herald* (Lyndon), November 3, 1892.

[16] Letter from H. W. Lutz to author, Holton, Kan., October 16, 1960; *Great Bend Beacon,* August 18, 1892; *Census of 1895,* Vol. XVIII, Homestead twp., p. 2; *ibid.,* Vol. XIX, Lakin twp., p. 13.

[17] *Industrial Advocate* (El Dorado), October 6, 1892; *Hill City People's Advocate,* October 6, 1892; *Census of 1895,* Vol. XXXVI, Murdock twp., p. 10: *ibid.,* Vol. CXXXVI, Morelan twp., pp. 2, 6, 8.

working farmer, . . . thoroughly competent to perform the duties of the office, and . . . understands English," for county commissioner.[18]

The thirteen northwest counties making up the thirty-ninth senatorial district elected John J. Griebel, a native of Wisconsin, who was billed as "a German and speaks the language" and whose parents had emigrated from Baden just before his birth. Griebel, 36, of Rooks county, was a carpenter and farmer with a wife and six children, and he won in spite of Republican criticisms of his big German feet. Griebel was an example of many second generation persons who were thought of by themselves and their neighbors as "Germans" or "Russians" in spite of their American birth. In Rawlins county he was joined on the ticket by Paul Haller, "an intelligent representative German," which was no doubt exactly what the Populists were looking for, running for probate judge.[19]

One township slate in Marshall county included Joseph Ellenbecker, 56, a German farmer of 260 acres, and William Harrigan, 49, an Irishman with a wife and seven children, for road overseers; and in McPherson county, H. Helstrom, 51, born in Sweden, was a delegate to the senatorial convention, committeeman of New Gottland township, and the candidate for state representative. Helstrom finally lost a contested election to another Swede in a district including the heaviest Swedish (and often Republican) townships in the state. Farther south in McPherson county, Gust Beyer, 39, a German, ran for county commissioner, and Joseph C. Goering, of Moundridge, a German-Russian merchant and farmer, ran for clerk of the district court.[20]

Populists in the senatorial district including Nemaha and Pottawatomie counties nominated Constantine Umscheid, 42, a German who lived with his wife Birgit and their seven chil-

[18] *Hays Free Press*, August 27, September 3, 1892; *Census of 1895*, Vol. CXVIII, Hays City, p. 10.

[19] *Stockton Alliance Signal*, June 16, November 3, 17, 1892; *Atwood Times*, November 3, 1892.

[20] *People's Advocate* (Marysville), October 14, 1892; *McPherson Democrat*, September 30, 1892; *Industrial Union* (McPherson), August 7, 1890; *McPherson County Advocate*, June 24, 1892; *Census of 1895*, Vol. CCXV, Mound twp., p. 4; *ibid.*, Vol. CCXVI, Groveland twp., p. 19; *ibid.*, Vol. CCXVIII, New Gottland twp., p. 9; *ibid.*, Vol. CCXXX, Marysville twp., pp. 9, 16.

dren on a 680-acre farm. Umscheid, who was an ex-Republican, spoke for his cause in German and English throughout his district. He was joined on the Nemaha county ticket by John Aeschlimann, 47, a Swiss farmer of a quarter section, and on the Pottawatomie county ticket by S. A. Eytchison, whom the Populists proclaimed to be of German descent, J. J. Brunner, a Swiss, and J. M. Regnier, American-born but possessing a knowledge of French that was important for the court clerkship he sought. Swiss, French, Irish, and German names studded the list of secretaries of the Pottawatomie county Alliances that year.[21]

About one out of four Atchison county delegates to the Populist congressional district convention and the state convention were immigrants. Arthur Leacy, 38 and Irish-born, went to the district convention. Leacy had a 373-acre farm that was assessed at $9,500, with enough cattle and hogs to make his 1894 livestock slaughter worth $40,000. Another Mount Pleasant township farmer, English-born J. E. Keats, 71, who had a quarter section mostly in cereals, grasses, and fruit trees, attended the district convention. Atchison city sent James G. Thayer, 44 and of Canadian birth, and Lancaster township sent another Canadian, James Andrews, 38, whose 182-acre farm of cereals, grasses, orchards, and a vineyard was assessed at $7,000. An 80-acre grain and dairy farmer named F. H. Kloepper, an Illinois native who lived with his German wife with or next door to his German-born brother and father, also went from Lancaster. W. M. Graham, 49, whose wife was Irish, went to the district convention. Delegates to the state convention included Julius Peterson, 42, a Norwegian of Benton township, and Kapioma township sent S. H. Allen, 63, who farmed a quarter section with his German-born wife.[22]

The Populists started the campaign by having the pastor of a German Reformed church in Wichita give the invocation at

---

[21] *Seneca News,* October 6, 13, 20, 1892; *St. Marys Star,* October 20, 27, 1892; *Westmoreland Alliance News,* September 2, October 7, November 4, 1892; *Census of 1895,* Vol. CCLV, Berwick twp., p. 27; *ibid.,* Vol. CCXCV, Mill Creek twp., pp. 3, 10, 13.

[22] *Advocate,* May 25, 1892; *Census of 1895,* Vol. IX, Benton twp., p. 41; *ibid.,* Vol. X, Benton twp., p. 41, Kapioma twp., p. 3, Lancaster twp., pp. 5, 48; and Mount Pleasant twp., pp. 3, 21; *ibid.,* Vol. XIII, Atchison City ward 5, p. 27.

the state convention, and from that time on, they vied continually with the Republicans for the foreign vote. Republicans supported and guided the editorial policy of German newspapers, harped on the issue that Democrats and Populists in the Congress had voted against an appropriation to relieve a famine in Russia, and employed German and English speakers to repeat the familiar chant about Populist financial irregularity.[23] The Populists replied with foreign language newspapers of their own, endorsements by well-known foreigners, compliments to ethnic groups for every conceivable putative virtue, rallies, and in one case an accusation of nativism directed toward the Republican county leaders as

lineal descendants of the witch burners of New England. These misguided people, finding it impossible to persecute anybody in England first emigrated to Holland, were not permitted to infringe upon the liberties of the people, and becoming dissatisfied they came to America, settled in the country which is now New England, where they varied the ceaseless round of their enjoyment of so called religious liberty by exterminating the Indians, hanging Quakers, banishing Baptists and Catholics, burning witches and other Godly diversions . . .

finally coming to Kansas to run the Republican party. In one case a Devonshire-born Populist county committeeman, one J. Browse Oldreive, affirmed his admiration for the Germans in reply to Republican accusations that he was a Germanophobe.[24]

Republican Swedes were particularly upset about threatened Populist inroads from Swedish speakers, newspapers, and personalities including Carl Ferm of McPherson, "the notorious leader" and "Weaver of the Swedish Populists." The Populists of McPherson county were quite pleased because

Mr. Goering and Mr. Byers are being loyally supported by their German friends on the south while Mr. Helstrom is winning

[23] *Advocate*, June 22, 1892; "Ruppenthal Scrapbooks," III: 61, in KSHS; *Hillsboro Anzeiger*, November 4, 1892; *Russell Journal*, October 27, 1892; *Lindsborg News*, October–November, 1892; *McPherson Republican*, October 21, 1892.

[24] Quotation from *Farmers Voice* (Clyde), October 6, 1892. See also *Peoples Party Advocate* (McPherson), January 8, 1892; *Kansas Staats Anzeiger* (Wichita), October 20, 1892; *Ellinwood Advocate*, October 27, 1892; *Larned Tiller and Toiler*, November 5, 1892; *People's Advocate* (Marysville), November 4, 1892; *Marion Times*, September 29, November 3, 1892.

friends every day on the north. The Populists have a winning ticket from top to bottom.

Bohemian speakers are not recorded, but Populist efforts among the group were publicized.[25]

Kansas Swedes had only one local newspaper during this campaign, but several others published throughout the Middle West were circulated. Although for the most part they were strongly Republican, their anxieties about a substantial Swedish Populist vote sometimes showed through.[26]

The German press, as usual, regarded prohibition as the chief issue. The Populists, who had to straddle the issue as weightlessly as possible because of the large contingents of dry former Republicans and wet former Democrats among them, gained German press support only through fusion, which many of the newspapers looked upon simply as a means to ending prohibition. The other horn of the Populist dilemma poked through the pages of a Prohibitionist paper that exulted over the Republican defeat on the grounds that the Populists were shaking people loose from their Republican moorings and would thus soon insure victory for "the true party of the people —the Prohibition Party." Most of the German press was still staunchly Democratic, but because of fusion the Populists were regarded favorably. They still backed Democratic candidates for local offices where there were three county tickets, but fusion was very widespread and got their ungrudging support.[27]

At least, they said, the Populists were not nativists, whereas a Republican victory would mean nativist, fanatic, monopolistic, prohibiting, foreign-hating leadership and (one said) the taking of the last step to a state church, national prohibition, and force bills. One German paper strongly criticized two others, in fact, for trying to pin the prohibition label on the

[25] Quotation from *McPherson Democrat*, November 30, 1892. See also *Scandia Journal*, October 14, 1892; *Lindsborg News*, November 4, 1892; *McPherson Republican*, November 4, 1892; *Advocate*, September 9, 1891, April 20, 27, May 25, 1892; *Kansas Commoner* (Wichita), October 20, 1892.

[26] O. Fritiof Ander, "The Swedish-American Press and the Election of 1892," *Mississippi Valley Historical Review*, XXIII (March, 1937), 536–40.

[27] *Pittsburg Advance*, November 18, 1892; *Leavenworth Post*, October 26, November 2, 1892; *Germania* (Lawrence), October 27, 1892; *Marysville Post*, October 14, 1892; *Marysville Post*, October 7, 1892 (clearest expression of fusion as a means toward resubmission); *Kansas Staats Anzeiger* (Wichita), October 13, 1892.

Populists. It reminded its readers that it had not been the Democrats and Populists who had started the dry business and advised that Germans, especially German farmers, would do themselves a favor by voting the Lewelling (Populist) ticket. This paper noted an item in the *Wichita Eagle* that claimed that Jerry Simpson had bragged that the German vote could be had for a stick of wurst, a glass of beer, and a bowlful of kraut, but denied the report and sputtered that things were just the opposite—that it was the Republican party that put kraut and wurst on the free list to entice German voters.[28]

Only two German papers were Republican, but one tried to convince its readers that the Populists were dry. Lewelling suddenly became the "Moses" of Iowa prohibition before his trek to Kansas, and Jerry Simpson was a secret tool of corporations. The other paper was honestly dry and loyal to the Republicans as the party of morality, law and order, and anti-socialism—and besides, the Republicans had voted to send money to the starving Russians. In the Mennonite area the Catholic criticism of the Harrison administration's Indian missions policy was a Republican asset.[29]

After the election the Germans growled in their beards at the defeat of a referendum on a constitutional convention (meaning possible repeal of prohibition) but on the whole, they were pleased. As a German punster put it, "Volks Stimme ist Gottes Stimme!"[30]

2. Storms in the State House

Although the Republicans saw little evidence of divine intervention, nobody could doubt that the people, at least, had spoken. The fusion ticket swept all state offices, the Senate, and seven of the eight congressional seats. The Democrats were happy that Kansas' electoral votes had gone to Weaver rather than Harrison, since Cleveland's cause was hopeless in the

[28] *Leavenworth Post*, October 26, 28, November 10, 1892; *Kansas Staats Anzeiger* (Wichita), November 17, 1892; *Kansas Telegraph* (Topeka), November 3, 1892; *Burrton Anzeiger*, October 31, 1892.

[29] *Der Waechter* (Kansas City), October 20, 27, November 3, 1892; *Hillsboro Anzeiger*, September 16–November 4, 1892.

[30] "The voice [vote] of the people [People's] is the voice [vote] of God!" *Kansas Staats Anzeiger* (Wichita), November 10, 1892. See also *Marysville Post*, November 25, 1892.

state. Though Populists claimed four years later that England was ecstatic over McKinley's victory, such "Anglophobia," if that is the word, was matched by the Republican statement in 1892 that "the English papers are all pleased over the result of the election" of Cleveland.[31] It had been a great day for Populism and fusion, and only the result in the House, where neither the Populists nor the Republicans had gained a clear majority, left a small cloud on an otherwise azure sky, and the Populists looked forward to enacting their whole program.

The small cloud in the House, however, quickly grew into a cyclone. The Republicans, whose preliminary canvass of the voters had been unusually complete and generally encouraging, could not believe that twenty thousand had switched to the Populists at the last minute, and beginning with charges that the Populists had voted thousands of "ghosts" from the Cherokee strip, they disputed returns for twelve seats. With the help of the Republican Supreme Court, which eventually decided the matter for lack of any other arbiter, they organized the House.[32]

During most of the session, however, a Populist House and a Republican House, each insisting it was the rightful one, fought the sensational "Legislative War of 1893." The war was long on words, intrigue, and pointed rifles but happily short on mayhem. Nevertheless, it did cut off effectively nearly all serious attempts to produce legislation for almost the entire session. Under the circumstances, the Populist passage of a law allowing redemption of foreclosed mortgages within eighteen months was a real achievement, but its effect was lost amidst Republican cries that the supposed party of reform had proved to be, as had been foretold, a party of anarchy.[33]

Two other matters hurt the Populists possibly even more than the lack of legislative achievement. One was the election of John Martin, a Democrat, to the United States Senate. Martin was known to be the most sympathetic and prominent Democratic fusionist, and Jerry Simpson, Governor Lewelling, and the presidential candidate, General Weaver of Iowa, saw

[31] *Scandia Journal*, November 18, 1892.

[32] J. K. Hudson, *Letters to Governor Lewelling* (Topeka: Topeka Capital Co., 1893), pp. 207-9.

[33] Karl A. Svenson, "The Effect of Popular Discontent on Political Parties in Kansas," (Ph.D. dissertation, State University of Iowa, 1948), p. 87.

Martin's election as a necessary move, particularly in the critical days of the "Legislative War." Weaver's attitude, especially, is worth noting because of his national prominence in both the Greenback and Populist parties; his acceptance of fusion even at a very auspicious time in the new party's history is evidence, as his biographer has said, that "throughout his career as an independent he was ready to cooperate if thereby the principles in which he believed would be advanced." Weaver's comment on Martin's election was that

the very best possible result was accomplished. . . . Judge Martin . . . has for years been openly in accord with the doctrines of the People's Party. . . . The judge is a free silver man, opposed to the National Banks, and in favor of an increase in the circulating medium. . . . I trust, however, that he is the last so-called Democrat to be elected by Populists' votes.[34]

A number of other Populists, however, notably Mrs. Lease, soured visibly at the spectacle of Populist votes electing a Democratic senator.

The second harmful result of the election was, paradoxically, victory. Without clear command of all branches of the state government, especially with such a disastrous legislative session, the Populists stood little chance of benefiting and a great chance of hurting themselves by the simple necessities of distributing patronage and enforcing prohibition. Governor Lewelling, gifted and humane but woefully inexperienced, had to distribute offices to Populists, to representatives of ethnic groups, and to office-starved Democrats, and in spite of his great efforts far too many incoming trainloads of grinning hopefuls too quickly departed, dour and disappointed. Attempts to distribute the patronage or explain away the dearth of it were sometimes crude and probably harmful, as when Fred J. Close, Lewelling's secretary, wrote one Jno. J. Jones of Topeka:

In reply to yours of the 5th inst. would say that the Governor himself is a Welchman [at least three generations earlier, he neglected to add] and of course has a kindly feeling for those of his native land [!], but other nationalities are also demanding

[34] Fred Emory Haynes, *James Baird Weaver* (Iowa City: State Historical Society of Iowa, 1919), p. 346.

recognition. . . . He has nothing that he can give to anyone at this time.[35]

The Populists had successfully avoided the prohibition question up to that point but could do so no longer. If the law was enforced, Democrats and others would cry foul; if enforcement was lax, many Populists and civic groups would scream corruption and thereby aid the Republicans. Letters piled high on the Governor's desk protesting that prohibition was not being enforced at Ellsworth, Hays, Valley Center, Atchison, and other points. One county attorney wrote implying that non-enforcement would be the wisest policy, while another demanded enforcement. Because of its power to appoint assistant attorneys-general and city police boards, the state administration was placed unwillingly in a no man's land between the warring wets and drys. If a safe middle road existed, Lewelling could not find it, and was shot full of holes in the crossfire.[36]

Populist belief in 1892 on such basic matters as sympathy for labor, welcome for immigrants, and praise for progressive foreign nations was no different from Populist belief in 1890. Switzerland was a better republic than the United States; Norwegian-Americans knew very well the evils of the national banking system; Swiss banking and mortgage laws should have American counterparts; the Leicester, England, borough-owned gas company was a boon to the consumer; Switzerland fifty years before had faced the problems the United States faced in the nineties, solved them, and "the little nation went upward and onward to its happy destiny"; Germany's public ownership of telephone and telegraph services was praiseworthy; nationalization of land, as Irishmen were demanding, would be good for the United States.[37] Foreign welfare ideas were simply grist for the Populist mill.

[35] Letter from Close to Jones, Topeka, March 13, 1894, in Lewelling MSS., in KSHS.

[36] Marko L. Haggard, "Prohibition, a Political Factor in Kansas" (Master's thesis, University of Kansas, 1947), pp. 276–77; letter from Chas. Stephens to Lewelling, Fort Scott, June 18, 1894, and letters from Ellsworth, Hays, Valley Center, Atchison, and other places, to Lewelling, in Lewelling MSS, in KSHS; W. L. Aaron to Attorney General John L. Little, Hays, February 14, 1893, and A. F. Edwards to Little, Parsons, June 17, 1893, in Attorney General MSS, in KSHS.

[37] *Advocate*, December 16, 1891; June 8, 29, September 14, 28, 1892; April 26, August 23, September 6, 27, November 29, 1893.

Such ideals, however, would soon face greatly changed political circumstances. In addition to the misfortunes which befell the Lewelling administration, the Populists would soon have to come to grips with women's suffrage, until then dormant, and a new organization known as the American Protective Association, the most intense expression of organized hatred of foreigners and Catholics the United States had known since the Know-Nothing movement.[38]

The year 1894 opened with the promise of brilliant political fireworks. Rumblings of discontent with Lewelling and certain ambitious individuals grew after four years of coexistence into an open gulf between the more idealistic and the more pragmatic members of the party, and before the year was out, it was anybody's guess who deserved which label. The 1892 elections had insured a future for Populism, but within two years many party members doubted that the future that had transpired had been worth fighting for.

[38] One suffrage bill, introduced by the Swiss-born Populist, M. Senn, passed the Populist Senate but got no further; Kansas, *Senate Journal* . . . *1893* (Topeka: Kansas Publishing House, 1893), pp. 731–32. J. C. Ruppenthal "Lucas Locals" column, *Russell Record*, April 3, 1893, in "Ruppenthal Scrapbooks," III: 323, 335, in KSHS.

CHAPTER SEVEN

POPULISM AGAINST ITSELF

1. Fusion and Faction

Tarnish marred the once shining armor of Kansas Populism as 1894 opened. Governor Lewelling had only one legislative session with which to make Populist dreams a reality, but that session could not have been scotched in a more effective way than by the "Legislative War." That inglorious fracas had led the reformers to the extremity of electing a Democrat to the United States Senate, and Lewelling's cautious handling of the episode only made him look like a man with a heart of gold and feet of clay. Many Populists who had never been happy with fusion and who had become administration appointees quit the government and by 1894 comprised a vocal if misanthropic cohort.

Beginning with the summer of 1893 and continuing through the campaign of 1894, the Republican press gleefully lent its columns to choleric ex-Lewellingites who were only too ready to shout "boodle" and "corruption." Far too much bias suffused the partisan press of those days to allow many judgments about the truth of the accusations, but only far more charity and benignity than lay within a Republican or ex-administration Populist breast could have excused certain deals. For example, Lewelling invited a British investment firm to join a group of state officials in the leasing of some mineral lands in Indian Territory; Fred Close, the Governor's private secretary, became the leading incorporator in an eighteen million dollar "Gulf and Inter State Railway." Accusations of personal corruption were served up as whipped cream on a rich, nutty pudding of tales about non-enforcement of prohibition, rake-offs on lotteries, policy rackets, and hideous mutilations of inmates at state institutions. Readers of all but the most faithful fusion Populist press got a steady diet of this, along with more bland ideological profundities, such as that which described Kansas as stumbling along under "an

149

administration created by Bellamyism, nursed by the principles of Doster and Herr Most, and made ridiculous by Simpson and Willits."[1] John J. Ingalls once uttered the remark that "The purification of American politics is an iridescent dream," and the outraged Populists threw him out of the Senate. By mid-point in Lewelling's term, the Populists not only had learned to respect the wisdom in Ingalls' remark but had begun to fear its sequel.

Bitterly ironical, too, were the hard times of 1893 and 1894. It seemed to the average voter that the very party that promised redemption from economic misery had only made it worse. As "ins" besieged by panic-pinched "outs," the Populists of 1893 had as little or less reason to look forward to the next election as the Republicans had had in 1889. Wheat farmers brought in fewer bushels in 1893 than in any year since the disastrous season of 1887, and 1894 was hardly an improvement. For every four bushels of corn harvested in 1892 there were only three in 1893, and 1894 was nearly as bad as the failure of 1890. The total dollar value of crops in 1893 and in 1894 was about one-half the amount in 1891 and 1892. This situation was not to improve materially until 1897. Forty-one banks closed in 1893 and 114 in 1894, with the result that three Kansas banks were doing business at the outset of 1895 for every four operating two years earlier.[2] The Panic of 1893 was a brutal reality, and in that nationwide disaster, Kansas was better off than other states only in that it had the dubious advantage of recent experience.

Economic conditions obviously needed a strong dose of reform at least as much as they had in 1889. But three ugly facts that had escaped people in the days of the Farmers' Alliance now became clear. In the first place, by 1893 Populism had a history, and a tell-tale gray one, while in 1889 it had

[1] Letter from Lewelling to Rowe Brothers & Co., Bristol, England, March 15, 1894, in Lewelling MSS, in KSHS; Kansas, Secretary of State, *Corporation Charters*, Book 39, pp. 511–14 (MS, volume in KSHS) ; *Topeka Capital*, May 31, 1894; J. K. Hudson, *Letters to Governor Lewelling* (Topeka: Topeka Capital Co., 1893), p. 14.

[2] Kansas, Board of Agriculture, *Seventh Biennial Report* (Topeka: State Printer, 1889), I, 279–80; *Ninth Biennial Report*, pp. 312–13; James C. Malin, *Winter Wheat in the Golden Belt of Kansas* (Lawrence: University of Kansas Press, 1944), pp. 143–51; Kirke Mechem (ed.), *The Annals of Kansas* (Topeka: Kansas State Historical Society, 1954), I, 160–61, 186.

been a pure white ideal. To many people who had been willing to try anything four years earlier, Populism had indeed been tried and found wanting. Second, the Panic of 1893 brought home afresh the fact that economic difficulties were national in scope and so reform would have to be national too. Even a clean sweep of state offices, a greater victory than the Populists had had in 1892, would help only slightly unless the direction of federal activity changed. The People's party had either to replace one of the old parties completely or to combine with one of them in a reform program, and the Democracy was the only choice. Third, the strategy of fusion was even more pressing in Kansas. There the People's party had actually become one of the two major parties in 1890, but only its alliance with the Democrats saved it in 1892. With worse worries expected in 1894, it looked as though fusion was the only hope.

Yet at the very time when fusion seemed the party's sole hope of success, faction rent it on this and other questions—another by-product of an administration in office but not in command—and its rosy future faded further still. Everyone agreed that reform of land, money, and transportation were still the basic Populist demands. Agreement ended there, however. Many Populists feared that unless the money question, which was thought to be the lowest common denominator in farmer and labor circles across the country, received the chief stress, other reforms would never get a trial. These people were fusionists. Many other Populists, however, saw no point in money reform unless land and transportation went with it and looked upon the Omaha platform of 1892 as the sempiternal bedrock of reform. This group thought fusion pointless, even poisonous. The first group accused the second of a lack of realism; the second accused the first of lack of principle.

Except for a few hard core leaders of each group, such as Governor Lewelling and Chairman Breidenthal among the fusionists and Mrs. Lease among the non-fusionists, or "middle-of-the-road Populists," as they called themselves, neither group had a stable, constant membership. Perhaps it would be better to call them fusion and non-fusion mentalities rather than groups, because neither of them included the same people at all times, or even held precisely the same set of attitudes and at the same time, yet both sides carried along their peculiar ideological baggage. A fusionist was a man willing to take half a loaf, willing to let many questions ride if the money-question reform would serve as a start toward other reforms, willing to accept electoral help wherever it could be found, willing to recognize that party machinery and organization were essential for success, anxious to avoid issues such as women's suffrage, which he might consider fine in the abstract but which would unquestionably alienate large masses of potential voters. A non-fusionist, on the other hand, wanted the whole Omaha platform or nothing at all. He distrusted Democrats as much as Republicans, was much more a moral idealist, much more, perhaps, an "authoritarian personality," and plumped for prohibition and women's suffrage as strongly as for any economic reform. Old third-party men led each group, and the Alliance and Populist credentials of the fusionists were at least as hoary as those of the non-fusionists. There was never any question of parvenu politicians pushing aside Populists of pride and principle for leadership of the party, because the politicians as well as the "men of principle" had been in the movement from its very beginning.

It would not do to say that Kansas Populism was ever clearly divided into the two groups, fusionist and non-fusionist. Not only did too many people share some of the attributes of both archetypes, but political campaigns blurred the already fuzzy lines even further. Nevertheless, the distinction between the two mentalities is useful for many reasons. The argument over fusion was, on the programmatic level, an argument over prohibition and women's suffrage, which more than any other issue raised the hackles of many ethnic groups, especially the Germans. The fusionists, in spite of personal sympathy for prohibition and women's suffrage in many cases (Breidenthal's, for instance), avoided them as political issues because they repelled the Democracy. That party was committed to following the wishes of the ethnic groups that largely made it up. Non-fusionists not only demanded that the People's party advocate prohibition and women's suffrage, which would obviously alienate the aliens, but they tended quite aside from those issues toward an abstractness, a rigidity of mind, which led them to approach the money question in terms of a "money power" and to proceed from there at times toward ethnocentrism.

The changing fortunes of fusion within the People's party answer the charge that the party shifted from devotion to principle to devotion to pelf. They show that Populism was always heterogeneous and that to ascribe the isolated remarks of extremists to the whole membership of the movement is an error. In many ways the presence of fusion meant the presence of ethnic support and the absence of ethnic antagonisms, and in the 1894 campaign, fusion was the central problem. That is why the convention and campaign of that year were so important.

Fusion with the Democrats had nearly been a fact in 1890, when the Populists rejected Charlie Robinson and nominated the unknown John Willits, and the Populist ticket missed narrowly in November. In 1892 Breidenthal was firmly in command, the party successfully dodged the prohibition and women's suffrage issues, and since Democratic presidential strategy called for the victory of electors who would not vote for Harrison, the Populists and Democrats reached an accommodation. Lewelling and Breidenthal planned to keep the fusion forces intact in 1894, but it was no simple job. Many of their closest advisers, such as Willits and G. C. Clemens, disliked fusion, and Democrats felt that their share of the patronage had been too slender.[3]

With prohibition and women's suffrage strongly in the wind in 1894, any dealings with ethnic groups would be touchy, but the situation became downright explosive with the addition of one more ingredient. This was organized nativism. In early 1887 a Clinton, Iowa, lawyer named Henry F. Bowers had founded a local anti-Catholic, anti-immigrant organization, which he called the American Protective Association. By 1894 this A.P.A. included hundreds of thousands of members concentrated in the older Middle West and on both coasts. Since it aimed mainly at minimizing Roman Catholic influence

---

[3] Dawn Daniels, "Lorenzo D. Lewelling—A Leader of the Kansas Populists" (Master's thesis, Northwestern University, 1931), pp. 23, 26–27, 63; Raymond C. Miller, "The Populist Party in Kansas" (Ph.D. dissertation, University of Chicago, 1928), pp. 163–64.

in politics and education and since it had strong support in many places from Orange Irish, Swedes, or other immigrants, its nativism was distinctly secondary to its anti-Catholicism, but many Irish and German Catholic immigrants believed it to be their special nemesis.[4]

The A.P.A. differed from the Know-Nothing movement of the 1850's not only in its acceptance of foreign-born support, but also in its plunge into politics almost from its beginning. In many states the A.P.A. slithered into Republican caucuses, primaries, and party machinery and tried to force that party to accept the A.P.A. program. Its votes were generally Republican votes, but although Republican politicians welcomed this support in many places, the group never controlled the national Republican party and was often of doubtful decisiveness on the state and local levels. The Republican party, however, was the sole political instrument of the A.P.A., except in a tiny minority of cases, and the Association is said to have been connected with the Republicans in Michigan, Minnesota, Washington, Nebraska, Wisconsin, and probably many other states. On the other hand, it had as an organization almost no connection whatever either with the Democratic party or with the People's party. There were a few instances, but they were extremely rare.[5]

Kansas was not among the strongest A.P.A. states, with fewer A.P.A. members in the total population than in Nebraska, Colorado, Missouri, Iowa, Wisconsin, and elsewhere, although at its peak it may have included as many as sixty-five thousand Kansans. There is no indication that it ever gained more than a foothold there in any party but the Republican. In 1894 the A.P.A. released its "Congressional Roll of Honor," which listed fifty-eight congressmen who had achieved this honor mainly by voting to cut federal appropriations for Indian schools run by religious denominations, most prominently the Catholics.

[4] Humphrey Desmond, *The A.P.A. Movement. A Sketch* (Washington, D.C.: New Century Press, 1912), pp. 7–11, 39–43, 45–49, 63–73; Donald Louis Kinzer, "The American Protective Association: A Study of Anti-Catholicism" (Ph.D. dissertation, University of Washington, 1954), pp. 78–88, 99–100, 102, 354.

[5] Kinzer, *op. cit.*, pp. 139–43, 146–47, 151–59, 231–32, 297–303, 315–21, 388; Desmond, *op. cit.*, pp. 29–34, 60, 73–77, 92; O. Fritiof Ander, "The Swedish-American Press and the Election of 1892," *Mississippi Valley Historical Review*, XXIII (March, 1937), 540.

One Democrat (from North Carolina), one Populist-Democrat (from Colorado), and one Populist (Hudson of Kansas) joined fifty-five Republicans, including such luminaries as Cannon of Illinois, Dolliver of Iowa, Nils Haugen of Wisconsin, Hepburn of Iowa, and Bellamy Storer of Ohio (whose wife later tried to pry a cardinal's hat out of the Vatican for their friend, Archbishop John Ireland of St. Paul). Besides Hudson, one other Kansan made the "Congressional Roll of Honor." He was Charles Curtis, a Republican, and President Hoover's running mate in 1928. The Great Plains, Bryan's stronghold in 1896, placed only three names on the "Roll of Honor," but the non-Populist Middle West was heavily represented, with Iowa, Illinois, and Wisconsin contributing twenty names alone. Although not every Populist, everywhere, all the time, was absolutely unconnected with the A.P.A., nevertheless neither Populist areas nor individual Populists gave the A.P.A. any appreciable support. During the Lewelling administration the A.P.A. asked the secretary of state of Kansas for a twenty-five-year charter, but it was turned down on the advice of the attorney-general on the ground that it promoted a religious test for public office. Both state officials were Populists. The principal fusion organ pointed out "the danger that Republicans will try to cultivate this religious war in order to keep office." The ancient voice of steadfast Populism, the Topeka *Advocate,* called the A.P.A.'s widely circulated and spurious "papal encyclical" proclaiming the duty of Catholics to exterminate all heretics on St. Ignatius Loyola day, 1893, "another fool fake" and "pure rot," and even the most extreme anti-Lewelling and antifusion Populist paper praised the secretary of state's action, called the A.P.A. a "bogus protective club," and said it was "bitterly fighting" the People's party. Not only was it true that the A.P.A. vocally opposed the Populists in Kansas, but the Populists were at least equally anti-A.P.A.[6]

Although Populists disagreed about fusion, all factions united in opposing the nativist A.P.A. But the non-fusionists,

[6] Kinzer, *op. cit.,* pp. 236–37, 255–56, 283, 477–78, 507–8; *Topeka Press,* May 9, 1894; Attorney General (John T. Little) MSS, in KSHS; *Advocate,* April 12, June 3, September 13, 1893; *New Era* (Topeka), September 23, 1893; "Ruppenthal Scrapbooks," III: 335, in KSHS.

although showing no active antagonism to Catholics and immigrants, were bound to damage the chances of fusion and repel the large foreign-born elements in the People's and Democratic parties by their insistence on having the People's party campaign for women's suffrage and prohibition. The extent to which they succeeded would be the extent to which the party, regardless of its intentions, would rid itself of the support of many ethnic groups.

As early as the summer of 1893, an anti-Lewelling, antifusion splinter group started to organize. It arose partly from its members' ideological devotion to prohibition and women's suffrage, partly from their disappointment over patronage perquisites, partly from disgust at having to deal with Democrats, partly from adroit deployment of Republican funds, partly from diffidence toward certain of Lewelling's deals. The core of Populism, its economic program, was not at issue. At any rate, in late March, 1893, a few weeks after the end of the "Legislative War," a nonfusion, strictly Omaha-platform, anti-Lewelling Populist paper called *The People* (soon changed to *The New Era*) began to appear in Topeka under the editorship of Cyrus Corning, an itinerant antifusion reform editor since 1890 or earlier. Corning was suspicious of politicians and was perhaps the only man ever to accuse the patriarchal Senator Peffer of political shenanigans in the form of an accusation of nepotism. John Brown, said Corning, was no fusionist—"he knew he was right and that was enough"—and any Populist who supported the "unholy thing" called fusion, and sang "John Brown's Body" again, was a hypocrite.[7]

By the fall of 1893 Corning's entourage included several prominent administration rejects. John Willits, the gubernatorial candidate in 1890, had been appointed to the State Board of Pardons and had been one of Lewelling's closest advisers, but in late 1893 he crossed into the Corning camp. He lost his patronage job the following spring. The practically defunct Citizens' Alliance, a mainstay of the 1890 campaign, was resuscitated and turned into an anti-Lewelling front by non-fusionists such as Noah Allen, another discharged officeholder, and W. F. Rightmire, a candidate for the Supreme

[7] *The People* (Topeka) [became *The New Era and the People*, June 10, 1893], March 25, June 10, September 9, 1893.

Court on the 1890 Populist ticket. W. H. Bennington, a Topeka lawyer who had been secretary of the Citizens' Alliance in 1890, and one-term Populist Congressman John Otis became ardent adjuncts of the Corning movement, and doubtless agreed with Corning that reform would never come to Kansas without "the complete turning under of bribers and bribe-takers-fusionists." Quite likely they joined him in his prayer,

May God in his mercy deliver the people of Kansas from any further inflection [sic] from the political harlots of Kansas who masquerade in the robes of righteousness while they riot in the offal of hell.[8]

By the spring of 1894 the *New Era* had established a rather extensive martyrology and demonology and was no less ferocious than the arch-Republican *Topeka Capital* in its ravings at the Lewelling government's alleged maladministration, turpitude, booze-running, and boodle. Its editorial policy, in case anyone might have missed it, appeared each issue in a masthead statement:

The New Era is right; Mrs. Lease is right; middle-of-the-road Populists are right; the administration frauds must be turned under or populism is forever doomed. True Populists will rally to the support of the New Era in its battle for reform as against republicans, democrats, and political prostitutes of the Lewelling stripe.

A "middle-of-the-road Populist," of course, was anything but moderate; supposed to indicate non-fusion, the term more closely represented the gutter than the middle of the road. Two additions to the Corning camp came in early 1894. One was the old she-bear, Mrs. Lease, and the other was the field marshal of the Kansas Republican party, Cyrus Leland. For many years Leland had guided his party according to the general strategy set by George R. Peck, general counsel of the Santa Fe Railroad, and Leland vacated his command temporarily in

---

[8] Hudson, *op. cit.*, pp. 5–6, 8, 39, 44, 193; Kansas, *House Journal . . . 1893* (Topeka: State Printer, 1893), p. 229; Raymond C. Miller, *op. cit.*, p. 264; *Russell Record*, February 13, 1893; *Kansas F.A. and I.U.* (Topeka), September, 1892–March, 1893; *Topeka Press*, June 1, 1894; *Ottawa Journal and Triumph*, June 7, 1894; *New Era* (Topeka), October 7, 1893, June 9, 1894; *Alliance Tribune* (Topeka), October 23, 1890; *The People* (Topeka), May 6, 1893.

1892 when Peck left the state. In 1894, however, Leland resumed his post and adroitly turned the "middle-of-the-road Populists" and the women's suffrage issue to the uses of the Republican party by destroying fusion and thereby wounding the Populists, perhaps fatally.[9]

Mrs. Lease apparently never got along with Breidenthal, although he sent her to Omaha in 1892 to lead the Kansas delegation to the national convention and once, at least, had intervened to smooth over bad feelings between herself and Lewelling, with whom she seems to have been still less cordial. The Governor had appointed her to the State Board of Charities in 1893, but she discovered that the job was commensurate with neither her talents nor her laurels, and by the fall of 1893 she was moving definitely toward the "middle-of-the-road" group. Before the year was out she was making public statements that the administration was riddled with corruption, and Lewelling fired her in late December. Shortly after that and after a meeting with Santa Fe lawyers, she was announced as one of the heirs of a five-thousand-dollar estate in Ireland, and from that time through 1894, she was unmatched as a champion of righteous antifusion reform. Mrs. Lease, and for that matter Corning and the rest of his group, may not have been consciously in cahoots with the Republican leadership, but there is evidence enough to indict if not to convict.[10]

2. Women's Suffrage, Prohibition, and the A.P.A.

The Populists plodded thus bruised and crippled to their 1894 state convention at Topeka on June 12. Lewelling and Breidenthal were determined to keep fusion alive, which meant a quick convention, a platform that dodged women's suffrage and prohibition, a stress on economic reform, and a ticket much like the successful one of 1892. Corning, Mrs. Lease, and as it turned out, Cyrus Leland, were equally determined to destroy fusion and fight for "principle," and in both cases a women's suffrage platform plank would turn the trick. The "middle-of-the-roaders" agreed with the administration forces

[9] *The Autobiography of William Allen White* (New York: Macmillan Co., 1946), pp. 232–33; Raymond C. Miller, *op. cit.*, pp. 42, 44, 275.

[10] *New Era* (Topeka), October 7, 1893, January 6, 1894; *Advocate*, March 14, 1894; Betty Lou Taylor, "Mary Elizabeth Lease: Kansas Populist" (Master's Thesis, Municipal University of Wichita, 1951), pp. 36–46.

only in favoring reform of land, money, and transportation and in condemning the A.P.A., and a bystander observed that

the Populist leaders—Governor Lewelling, Chairman Breidenthal *et al.*—are in a great stew today. They have a cut and dried programme, ignoring prohibition and woman suffrage, and like the old lady with the cow and the pail of milk, they are afraid the convention will kick it over.[11]

A carefully laid administration plan to avoid the women's suffrage issue never got past the first few minutes of the convention. The administration choice for temporary chairman could only fume while the delegates handed the gavel to one Ben S. Henderson, of Cowley county, a convert from Republicanism and an ardent suffragist. Henderson began the festivities with a rousing suffrage speech, welcomed to the speaker's stand a parade of suffragettes including Susan B. Anthony, Carrie Chapman-Catt, Rev. Anna Shaw, and Annie Diggs— "the heroin [!] of the movement," according to one paper— and made sure that a suffrage plank would get to the convention floor in spite of what the resolutions committee recommended.[12]

Although a valorous resolutions committee recommended a platform utterly silent on the suffrage question, in spite of the suffragettes who laid heavy siege to their meeting room, a minority report signed by eight members of the committee reached the floor at the convention's second session. This minority report amounted simply to the majority report plus a plank that declared the party in favor of the women's suffrage constitutional amendment on the ballot that fall. The delegates argued for hours over the minority report, and several of them showed that they had well in mind the effect of it on fusion and ethnic group support. Annie Diggs believed that the Republicans, who had ignored women's suffrage in their convention in Topeka a week earlier, "will have bid in vain for the German League and liquor vote" if only the Populists would endorse suffrage, and the widely respected Frank Doster, of Marion county, took a similar stand when he said that as far as he was

[11] *Topeka Democrat*, June 13, 1894.
[12] *Topeka Press*, June 12, 13, 1894; *Topeka Democrat*, June 12, 1894; *Topeka State Journal*, June 12, 13, 1894; *Winfield Daily Courier*, October 9, 1888; *Girard World*, June 14, 1894.

concerned the German vote, Irish vote, votes of all possible nationalities, and the Democratic vote were nothing to him as compared with principles. The defeated administration choice for temporary chairman, William Brown, a Kingman editor, scored Doster's indifference to the foreign voters and said: "I want to defend the foreign population against insinuations made in this convention." But ex-Congressman John Otis, a "middle-of-the-road" leader, retorted:

This question has simmered down to this. Shall the people control the People's party or shall the politicians control it? On one side stands the scheming politicians [sic] who say we must bid for the Democratic vote, the ignorant foreign vote. On the other side it is the educated thinking people of the party, the true reformers.

T. W. Barkley, a delegate from Ottawa county, was kinder to the immigrants but no less pro-suffrage: "The foreign voters are just as loyal to the party as any class of voters. It is not policy to put it in. It is not policy to do right. It is a duty." Several speakers later, Scotch-born Andrew Shearer, of Marshall county, "desired to be recognized on the grounds of his foreign birth" and announced that he "did not believe in catering to the foreign vote. We have come to the parting of the ways." In spite of a protest by R. H. Kane, of Dickinson county, that "he had been a People's party man since the days of Peter Cooper and . . . there was no cowardice in taking a stand that was for the interests of the party," Mrs. Diggs, the final speaker, seemed to express many delegates' feelings when she said that "the objections made to this amendment on the ground that it would lose the foreign vote" were pointless, since "it would be lost anyway and so there was no risk in adopting the plank." She probably meant that the Populist Senate and half-Populist House of 1893 would be blamed for putting the suffrage amendment on the ballot in the first place.

The vote was close—a margin of sixty votes out of over six hundred—but the minority report, in favor of women's suffrage, won. The convention added a clause saying that the women's suffrage plank should not be regarded as "a test of party fealty," but it was buried in the confusion of the campaign. A change in thirty votes, or less than 5 per cent, would have made the difference for the convention, for the Democrats who thereupon recoiled from fusion, and perhaps for the election result in November. A handful of delegates, unquestionably swayed by the appeals of the suffragettes and the turmoil attendant upon two dozen short but tumultous speeches, changed the course of Populism in 1894 and perhaps permanently. Breidenthal and the fusionists lost control of the convention on no issue but this, but it was enough to prevent fusion and repel many foreign-born Populists. It clearly demonstrated, though more for the benefit of historians than for the Populists themselves, that the Populists were certainly conscious of ethnic group voting, that many of them were favorable to these groups and anxious to have their help, and that even those who chose to disregard their votes did so, except for one or two, because their devotion to "principle" was stronger than their devotion to the immigrant. Their attitude to immigrants was in any case not an antagonistic one.[13]

As for the suffragettes, they originally had come to Topeka the week before to wring a suffrage resolution from the Republican convention but had failed and had then inflicted themselves and their issue on the Populists. There they left the Populists holding the bag. In their ardor they gave the impression that they would campaign for any party that came down on the side of women's suffrage, but it took them less than a day to turn in their newly donned Populist silks. The Populists got nothing but prayers, and even these they had to provide for themselves: just after the voting on the suffrage resolution a naughtily suspicious delegate called on the Rev. Anna Shaw for the "Populist whoop" she had promised the day before. The lady replied, "I know of no better whoop than that grand old hymn, 'Praise God from Whom all blessings flow,' " The delegates sang lustily, the suffragettes made their getaway, and of forthcoming blessings the Populists got not a trickle.[14]

The suffrage furore was not the last matter in that convention that had a close connection with fusion and foreign group votes. There was still prohibition. One of the most annoying

[13] *Topeka State Journal*, June 11, 13, 1894; *Topeka Press*, June 13, 1894; *Topeka Capital*, June 14, 1894; *Leavenworth Post*, June 14, 1894.

[14] *Ottawa Journal and Triumph*, June 21, 1894; *Topeka Press*, June 15, 1894; *Dickinson County News* (Abilene), June 21, 1894; *Lincoln County Sentinel*, June 28, 1894.

facts about women's suffrage, in the fusionists' minds, was that it seemed inevitably to mean that prohibition would never be gotten rid of, because the only way to do so was to resubmit the constitutional amendment effecting prohibition to the voters; and women voters, everyone thought, would never be persuaded to help end the drought. Yet many delegates hoped that this unfortunate situation could be eliminated, or at least eased, if the convention put itself on the line for more liberal liquor laws. In fact, a Democratic paper had prognosticated that if a suffrage plank went through "there will also be a big demand by conservative delegates to adopt a resolution demanding the resubmission of the prohibitory amendment to a vote of the people." And Andrew Shearer, apparently a bit remorseful about his pro-suffrage stand a few hours earlier, proposed to the convention a resolution that would give the state the control of the liquor traffic, with the profit element eliminated. But this particular convention, like many others, had its own self-appointed red-tape cutter. A Negro delegate from Pottawatomie county named Beck, the state coal oil inspector, who had fought the suffrage amendment partly on the ground that people were trying to make the People's party the stalking horse for all the "discarded issues" in the state, moved to lay Shearer's amendment on the table. The prohibition issue obviously had nothing more to do with Populist fundamentals than women's suffrage did, but the accepting of one made the accepting of the other the politic thing to do. Yet the convention decided to pass the tabling motion by a large margin, and the People's party had now, for all intents and purposes, put itself on record for prohibition as well as for women's suffrage. Fusion was well-nigh hopeless.[15]

There was only one other issue about which the more recent immigrant groups had any specal feeling. The convention had twice already swung and missed on the prohibition and women's suffrage issues, and it was on the verge of striking out. But at that point a Scotch-born Catholic lawyer from Fort Scott, a Lewelling appointee to the State Board of Pardons,

[15] Topeka Democrat, June 12, 14, 1894; Topeka State Journal, June 13, 1894; Topeka Press, June 13, 1894; Girard World, June 14, 1894; Olathe Tribune, June 22, 1894; Newton Journal, June 15, 1894.

J. F. McDonald, put before the convention a resolution condemning the A.P.A. This was the text:

The People's party of Kansas, having learned with deep regret that a new element has risen in our country, and we believe for the purpose of creating discord in the ranks of our party, and for the purpose of disrupting all labor organizations, its purpose being to array one class of citizens against another on account of religious faith.

Resolved, That the People's party, as its name implies, is the party of the people, and hence the enemy of oppression and tyranny in every form, and we do most emphatically condemn such conduct as un-Christian, un-American, and as totally opposed to the spirit of the Constitution of our country and we pledge our best efforts to defeat such organizations and to protect as far as we are able every individual of every nationality, religious creed and political belief in his sacred right to worship God according to the dictates of his own conscience.

The A.P.A. was not named explicitly, but nearly every newspaper, Republican, Democratic, or Populist, headlined it as the "anti-A.P.A." resolution, and the convention seemed clearly to recognize it as such. Uproar followed McDonald's entering of the resolution, and some delegate (perhaps Mr. Beck?) moved to table it. A voice vote on tabling was indecisive, but on a show of hands the motion to table was defeated, 218–298, and the convention voted immediately and nearly unanimously to adopt McDonald's resolution.[16] If the Populists could endorse women's suffrage and dodge resubmission, two ideas on which the Germans and most other ethnic groups had the strongest feelings, they could just as easily pass a condemnation of organized nativism and anti-Catholicism.

Where did the support for the anti-A.P.A. resolution come from? There was no roll call vote, but the editors who commented on the point agreed that both the suffrage plank and

16 *Topeka State Journal,* June 14, 1894; *Topeka Press,* June 13, 1894; *Census of 1895,* Vol. XXVII, Fort Scott ward 4, p. 10, in KSHS; Hudson, *op. cit.,* p. 193; *Topeka Democrat,* June 15, 1894; *Topeka Capital,* June 14, 1894; *Wichita Eagle,* June 14, 1894; *Wichita Herold,* June 14, 1894; *Leavenworth Post,* June 14, 1894; *Farmers' Voice* (Clyde), June 21, 1894; *Fort Scott Weekly Tribune,* June 21, 1894.

the anti-A.P.A. resolution came from the "same element," from "the anti-masculine delegates," the "middle-of-the-road populists . . . in control of the convention," and not from "the conservative, careful men in the convention."[17] If this is true, then the antiforeign Populists must have been few indeed, since even these more radical reformers, favorable to prohibition and to women's suffrage, found that no prejudices, no ethnocentrism, barred them from condemning the most widespread antiforeign and anti-Catholic organization in forty years. These "middle-of-the-roaders," moreover, were the steadfast non-fusionists, the very people least amenable to political compromise or rhetorical caution. Since there can be no question that the fusionists were friendly to ethnic groups and foreign ideas, and since the non-fusionists condemned the A.P.A. with equal strength in spite of their indifference to foreign-born voters, the putative nativists in the Populist party must have been scarce to the point of invisibility.

These three issues were a far cry from land, money, and transportation, the core of Populism, its chief reasons for existence, its main means of support. The actions of the 1894 convention, however, indicate that even when the Populists strayed from economic issues into other areas, they strayed in a direction that was neither neurotic, negative, nor nativistic. Each of the three issues—women's suffrage, the liquor question, the A.P.A.—related clearly to ethnic groups both personally and ideologically, and demonstrated clearly the Populists' attitudes toward ethnic groups and foreign matters. All this seems to lead to two conclusions.

First, a great many Populists were not antagonistic because they saw no point in being so. They simply did not pay much attention. It is hardly possible to psychoanalyze them, and surviving evidence—what they consciously did or unconsciously revealed—shows, if anything, that they were neither ethnocentric nor anti-ethnocentric.

Secondly, when on rare occasions the party consensus seemed to swing too far away from the ethnic groups, as it did in the 1894 convention on the women's suffrage and liquor questions, the balance was redressed by a pro-foreign act like

[17] *Downs Times*, June 21, 1894; *Newton Journal*, June 15, 1894; *Fort Scott Weekly Tribune*, June 21, 1894.

the anti-A.P.A. resolution.[18] These actions simply underscore the fundamental fact that the Populists were not a group of economists, or of political scientists, or of status-conscious intellectuals. They were not a wholesale lot of neurotics. They were a group of local politicians and farmers from a farming state that happened to be in a depression.

Prior to the passage of the women's suffrage plank there had been some doubt about Lewelling's renomination, because many delegates worried about the adverse effect that several administration scandals might have on the voters. After their show of independence on the suffrage question, however, the delegates renominated the entire Lewelling slate. One Republican paper judged that "the anti-administration Populists cut about as little figure in the convention as a conscientious man in the United States Senate."[19]

3. A Three-Ticket Race

The Democrats met about a month later, came out flatly against women's suffrage, adopted an innocuous plank opposing any religious test as a qualification for office (which might or might not have been taken as a slap at the A.P.A.), nominated a separate slate headed by David Overmyer, a Topekan who suddenly became a "German-American" in many precincts, and of course, completely fumigated themselves of any fusion tendencies. As in 1892, all three parties ostensibly agreed on major economic planks, since the Republicans were

18 From the *Topeka Capital*, a prominent Republican daily, June 14, 1894: "In going out of their way to denounce the A.P.A. the members of the populist convention dragged into the campaign a foreign issue which has nothing whatever to do with the opposing parties and principles. The American Protective Association is a secret society, non-partisan in its principles and in no way connected with the politics of Kansas. The convention might as well denounce the Masons or any other secret society. . . . The adoption of a resolution condemning the A.P.A. was a sop thrown to catch the Catholic vote. Just why such a resolution was offered can scarcely be understood unless it was meant as an offset for the suffrage plank, hoping thus to hold the foreign vote that does not believe in woman's suffrage. As to whether it was political sense the A.P.A.'s will be in position to answer in November."

19 *Topeka State Journal*, June 14, 1894. See also *ibid.*, June 11, 12, 1894; *Topeka Press*, May 27, June 14, 17, 1894; *Topeka Democrat*, June 4, 1894; *Topeka Capital*, June 15, 1894; *Salina Union*, June 15, 1894; *Girard World*, June 14, 1894.

bimetallists in Kansas. On other matters, however, the Republicans dodged women's suffrage as well as the A.P.A.; the Populists endorsed suffrage and damned the A.P.A.; and the Democrats damned suffrage but only slapped the wrist of the A.P.A. Fusion never had a chance. A few Populist editors put the best face on it and said wanly that the suffrage plank was politically wise, but others simply reminded the voters that the convention had said that suffrage was "not a test of party fealty."[20]

Antifusion Democrats and middle-of-the-road Populists, on the other hand, took every opportunity to say that the Populists had committed themselves to women's suffrage, and in the German editors' minds the Populists were pariahs. To everyone, women's suffrage meant prohibition without end. The Prohibition party platform differed from the Populist primarily in that one called explicitly for prohibition and the other called for it under the guise of women's suffrage; on economic issues, the two were very close. Ex-Governor St. John, the Moses of Kansas prohibition, was rumored to be on his way into the People's party after the Populists nailed down their suffrage plank, and a Republican paper called the Prohibition party the "Populist Aid Society." The administration was, as always, ground between the two stones of strict or lax enforcement of prohibition, advocated by various English-speaking members of the Populist party itself; and in spite of administration self-assurance, the German vote was evidently in full flight from fusion. "Middle-of-the-road Populists," straight Democrats, and an organization called the German-American League of Kansas all took the endorsement of women's suffrage to mean an endorsement of prohibition, and many Swedes and Irishmen were no happier than the Germans. One delegate to the Populist convention asked:

In due candor, what does the Populist party think they are going to do when they lose the support of all the best thinking and working Democrats? How do they expect to get the German vote,

[20] *Topeka Press*, June 7, September, 1894, *passim*; *Kansas Farmer* (Topeka), July 11, 1894; *Lincoln County Sentinel*, June 14, 1894; *Salina Union*, June 22, 1894; *Minneapolis Messenger*, June 28, 1894; *McPherson Opinion*, June 21, 1894; *Concordia Alliant*, June 14, 1894; *Westmoreland Alliance News*, June 22, 1894.

for they all well know that women suffrage means prohibition pure and simple?

And a Populist lawyer wrote gloomily to Governor Lewelling after the convention:

After the woman suffrage plank, and after the uncalled for resolution condemning the A.P.A.s—all my hopes were dispelled. In my judgment a party was never guilty of such egregious folly as ours at that convention. I was in hopes we would be left free to go before the people on the vital issues of the day, but [Frank] Doster and [Ben S.] Henderson were in the saddle and rode our party to the Devil in that Convention. The Germans will not touch us, the Democrats will not look at us, and the A.P.A.'s will bat us on every side, and there are thousands of them in our party in this State.[21]

Although the last statement was never borne out in the press or anywhere else, weeping, wailing, and gnashing of teeth were very appropriate. The fusionists retained the party leadership and the responsibility for the campaign, but the convention had burned the best bridges the party had for attracting Democratic and foreign-born support. The road to victory now seemed impassable.

In spite of its commitment to women's suffrage, the People's party in Kansas in 1894 kept a large part of its foreign-born support, never stopped trying to broaden it, and never took a hostile approach to immigrants or foreign matters. The Populists continued to compare favorably with their contemporaries as regards foreign references in their rhetoric. They kept up the press and partisan appeals that they had always made, and

---

[21] *Topeka Democrat*, May 15, June 6, 7, 14, 15, 1894; *McPherson Democrat*, October 26, 1894; *Girard World*, May 10, 1894; *New Era* (Topeka), July 29, 1893, June 16, 1894; *Ellinwood Advocate*, June 21, 1894; *Topeka State Journal*, June 11, 15, 1894; *Le Roy Reporter*, June 15, 1894; *Minneapolis Messenger*, June 21, 1894; *Topeka Press*, June 3, 6, 14, 15, 17 (first quotation), 1894; letters from Joel Miller [treasurer of Stafford county] to Lewelling, St. John, Kan., August 10, 1894, and from Rufus Cone to Lewelling, Wichita, June 21, 1894, in Lewelling MSS, in KSHS; letter from M. B. Nicholson to Lewelling, Council Grove, June 15, 1894, in Lewelling MSS, in KSHS (second quotation). See also, *St. Marys Journal*, quoted in *Junction City Sentinel*, June 30, 1894; *Scandia Journal*, June 15, 1894, November 9, 1894; *Seneca Courier-Democrat*, August 10, 1894; statement of Democratic congressional candidate Tully Scott in *Topeka Capital*, June 15, 1894.

again many immigrants worked for the party and ran for office. Andrew Shearer, who had been prominent at the state convention, had been president of the Marshall county Alliance in 1889. He was to nominate Breidenthal for Governor in 1900 and was thus a Populist throughout the life of the party. Shearer had been born in Glasgow, Scotland, in 1850, came to Kansas twenty years later and was successively a Liberal Republican, a Greenbacker, a Granger, an Allianceman, and a Populist, and finally ran for Congress from the Fifth District in 1902.[22]

In Barton county, Joseph F. Strothman, "one of our prominent farmers . . . and a good German scholar," ran again for state representative, and in Independent township, three farmers, German or German-wed, D. Frymiller, G. Schoepple, and William Grosshardt, were on the Populist slate. In nearby Rice county, C. D. Hansen, a Swede farming 240 acres, was secretary of the county Alliance, and in Lincoln county, the Germans reportedly "voted almost to a man" for W. H. Rahmeier, Populist for clerk of the district court. In Saline county, a young Swedish farmer, August Swedenberg, for several years a township trustee, ran for clerk of the court.[23]

The McPherson county Populist committee included several Swedes, some already mentioned, and others, including O. Swedlund, 52, a confectioner in McPherson city; J. F. Mullikan, the county assessor, married to a Scot; I. B. Klopfenstein, 29, a photoengraver at Inman who lived with his Swiss parents; and C. O. Aspergren, 28, a Swede who farmed 160 acres with his parents near Sharps Creek. German-Russian Joe Goering of Moundridge had been active since 1892 and remained prominent through 1902.[24]

A Prussian, William Ziegelasch, 44, who had come to Kan-

[22] Advocate, July 30, 1890; Topeka State Journal, July 25, 1900; Chicago American, October 22 [?], 1902, in "Populist Party Clippings," II: 170–71, in KSHS.

[23] Great Bend Beacon, October 11, 25, 1894; C. D. Hansen to Attorney-General Little, Raymond, Kansas, January 22, 1894, in Attorney General MSS, in KSHS; Lincoln County Sentinel (Lincoln), November 8, 1894; Salina Union, August 17, 1894; Census of 1895, Vol. XIX, Independent twp., pp. 5, 6, 8; ibid., Vol. CCCXIX, Raymond twp., p. 1.

[24] McPherson Opinion, June 14, 1894; Census of 1895, Vol. CCXIV, McPherson city, p. 24, and Inman city, p. 26; ibid., Vol. CCXVI, Harper twp., p. 11; ibid., Vol. CCXVIII, Meridian twp., p. 1.

sas in the mid-sixties and had become a grocer, made his first of three candidacies for probate judge of Geary county in 1894 and in 1898 was Populist county chairman.[25]

In Ellis county three tickets were in the field, and the Populists ran Anton Kuhn, 21, a Russian-born school teacher, for clerk of the district court; Miles Mulroy, 28, born in Wisconsin of Irish parents, for county attorney; and Dan McCarthy, Irishborn, for county commissioner. The county committee included Henry Tholan, 42, born in Germany and a farmer; Paul Dinges, 43, a prosperous Russian-born farmer; and Fred Solomon, 59, a German-born farmer, as well as Mulroy.[26]

The Rush county Populist convention, held in August, abounded in foreign-born delegates. Big Timber township sent David Zink, 58, a German married to an Englishwoman and a farmer of 240 acres; Joseph Herrman, 33, a Russian farmer; John E. Herrman, 46, also a Russian, who farmed 800 acres; and John Bollig, 40, another Russian farmer. Antoine Smrcka, who lived with his 63-year-old Bohemian mother on a 480-acre farm, represented Banner township, as did Joseph Schrater, 70, a Bohemian farmer, and Frank Richter, a farmer married to a Bohemian. Albert Albers, 56, a German farmer of a quarter section, with a wife and nine children, and Edward Connolly, 59, an Irishman, attended from Brookdale township, and Alois Bieber, 60, a Swiss with 320 acres, arrived from Lone Star township.[27]

Cloud county had an equally polyglot convention, including some new foreigners as well as many already prominent. George Kaad, 40, a Danish farmer with eight children, and T. A. Lynch, probably born of Irish parents, appeared for Grant township; P. H. Mahon, like Lynch born in New York but with Irish relatives living close by, and P. Hansen, 60, Danish-born, came from North Lawrence township. Lyon township sent John Eberhart, 59, a German farmer, and Anton Olson,

[25] *Junction City Tribune*, October 4, 1894.

[26] *Hays Free Press*, May 26, August 25, 1894; *Census of 1895*, Vol. CXVIII, Big Creek twp., p. 5, and Hays City, p. 11; *ibid.*, Vol. CXIX, Lookout twp., p. 7; *ibid.*, Vol. CXX, Victoria twp., p. 13, Walker twp., p. 4, and Wheatland twp., p. 14.

[27] *LaCrosse Chieftain*, August 10, 1894; *Census of 1895*, Vol. CCCXXVIII, Banner twp., pp. 1, 3, 4; *ibid.*, Vol. CCCXXIX, Big Timber twp., pp. 4, 6, 8, 11, and Brookdale twp., p. 4; *ibid.*, Vol. CCCXXX, Lone Star twp., p. 9.

29, a Norwegian who lived with his parents on two hundred acres. South Shirley township's delegation was entirely French, including A. M. Lafond, 57, Louis Savoie, 60, and A. Beaufort, 52, all French Canadian farmers, as well as D. Lagesse, 43, married to a French Canadian, and G. Perret, 44, the township assessor, born in France and farming eighty acres. Will Neitzel, 32, from East Sibley township, was born in Nebraska but lived near older Neitzels born in Prussia; and in the Solomon township delegation were two Butlers, an Irish name in the township, A. B. Halderson, 45, a Norwegian, and F. R. Hoyer, 49, a Danish farmer.[28]

In Mitchell county the incumbent Populist clerk of the district court had been called "the little dutchman" as a political trademark, but through some falling out with the county leaders, became by 1894 "the little office-seeking dutchman," and he was replaced by Adolph Busche, 46, of Tipton, a German-born merchant.[29]

In Lyon county two Swedes, Pete Fager, 32, and S. P. Sundholm, 54, farmers, were on the Waterloo township ticket, John Madden was nominated that year by the Populists for county attorney. Madden, 38, had been a Republican presidential elector in 1888, although not long before he had had Democratic ties, and switched to the Populists in 1892. He was born in Indiana but often acted as an Irish-American spokesman.[30]

The Republicans elected a much higher proportion of the foreign-born legislators in 1894 than they had in 1890, but the Populist representation was still considerable. Some of their 1890 House members had graduated to the Senate and were joined there by other foreign Populist senators. Hugh Reid, 48, of Crawford county, had been a Republican until 1876. Born in Ireland, he was married with seven children and had been in Kansas for twenty-four years. William Rogers, elected to the

[28] *Concordia Alliant*, May 31, 1894; *Census of 1895*, Vol. LXVI, Grant twp., pp. 5, 14, and Lawrence twp., p. 7; *ibid.*, Vol. LXVII, Lyon twp., pp. 2, 18, and Shirley twp., pp. 1, 26, 29, 32; *ibid.*, Vol. LXVIII, Sibley twp., p. 23 and Solomon twp., pp. 16, 17, 23.

[29] *Peoples Sentinel* (Glen Elder), October 13, 1894; *Census of 1895*, Vol. CCXLII, Pitts twp., p. 6.

[30] *Topeka Capital*, May 9, 1888; "Ruppenthal Scrapbooks," III: 17, in KSHS; *Emporia Tidings*, October 26, 1894; *Census of 1895*, Vol. CCIX, Emporia city, p. 1; *ibid.*, Vol. CCXIII, Waterloo twp., pp. 15, 19; *Emporia Tidings*, October 5, 1894.

Senate from Washington county, was born in Plymouth, England, in 1844, came to the United States at the age of three, fought in the Illinois 74th Infantry, and came to Kansas in 1869. A Republican until 1890, Rogers was a Methodist, had six children, was a farmer and stockman, contractor, builder, and money-loaner, and was a regent of the state university. Another Populist senator, John H. Reilly, of Labette county, born of Irish parents at Albany, New York, was a railroad engineer on the Missouri-Kansas-Texas. James Shearer, senator from Marshall county, was a farmer born in Shotts parish, Lanark, Scotland. He had come to Kansas in 1870 by way of Canada and had been active in reform parties since 1874. An original Populist, he had been secretary of his county committee in 1890 and 1891 and was perhaps the first installed president of a local Alliance.[31]

Five new foreign-born Populists entered the House of Representatives. Hugh Bone, 44, of Crawford county, was a miner born in Ayrshire, Scotland, had eight children, was a Protestant, had always been a third-party man, and was secretary-treasurer of the United Mine Workers of America. He had been elected to his first term in the House in 1892. J. A. Bucklin, of Thomas county, was a thirty-nine-year-old Swedish farmer. James Duffy, another miner, represented Cherokee county and had been a delegate to the state convention in June. He was 54 and had been born in Ireland. John J. Lambert, of Lincoln county, had been born in County Wexford, Ireland, forty-four years before, and had pre-empted his present farm. A former Republican, Greenbacker, Democrat, and Union Laborite, he was an original Populist. William Lewis, of Rawlins county, was a thirty-eight-year-old Englishman who had come to the United States at ten, had been in the mines and oil fields of Pennsylvania, and since 1886 had been a Kansas farmer. He was also an original Populist. In the Senate of 1894 the Populists had four foreign-born, the Republicans one, and in the House the Populists had five foreign-born and a probable Pennsylvania Dutchman, the Republicans eleven.[32]

[31] *Hand Book of the Kansas Legislature, 1895* (Topeka: Geo. W. Crane, 1894), pp. 59–60, 61, 62. These senators had been elected in 1892 for a four-year term.

[32] *Ibid.*, pp. 73, 75, 85–86, 98–99.

Not only did immigrants participate actively, but a great many were very concerned about women's suffrage, prohibition, the A.P.A., and other issues, if the English and German language newspapers accurately reflected the situation. Some Populist editors tried the "and you're another" tactic by dredging up an 1882 statement by the Democratic gubernatorial candidate, David Overmyer, in which he was supposed to have said that prohibition had not driven any decent German-Americans from Kansas or ended desirable immigration and that "only the very lowest class of Germans, such as are a dishonor to any country, are opposing the enforcement of the prohibition laws." The Populist *Topeka Press* tried a scare tactic: if the Republican ticket won, the rank prohibitionist nominated for lieutenant-governor would be only a heartbeat away from the governorship and "a reign of fanaticism worse than any that ever cursed the state." The paper took the silence of the German-American League of Kansas, which did not endorse the Democrats or anyone else, to mean tácit support of the Populists.[33]

But a German paper countered with a purported letter from Lewelling to Breidenthal written in 1892 in which Lewelling said that brewers were a class of people from whom he wanted no support, and German editors generally showed less sympathy than in the past for Populism, primarily because of women's suffrage and prohibition. Of eight German newspapers, four were Democratic, two leaned listlessly toward the Democrats, and two were Republican. Except for the last two, they had nothing against fusion on the Congressional or local level and presumably would have favored state-level fusion as they had in 1890 and 1892 except for those two repulsive issues. In addition, although a few grumbled that fusion had not brought the "Deutschtum" more offices, they probably would have gone along in 1894 since it was their only chance for any offices at all. Neither because of disappointing office hunts nor because of the gold-tinged financial theories that some of them held did the Germans object strongly enough to Populism to have made a *detente* on those grounds alone. Suffrage caused the break.

Some German editors accused the Populists of being cranks and calamity howlers but never, not even in the two Republican

[33] *Peoples Advocate* (Marysville), October 19, 1894; *Topeka Press*, September 5, 8, October 9, 18, 1894.

papers, did they accuse them of nativism in spite of their great sensitivity to it. Instead, it was the Populists' opponents who were "nativist, fanatic, canting, Anglo-Protestant Bourbons, which paradoxically [were called] the Republican party of Kansas." "Water heroes," "blue stockings," and "fanatics" the Populists may have been, but nativists, never.[34]

Republican Germans disliked the Populists because they were not dry enough, and the *Hillsboro Anzeiger* thought the "free-thinking" Populists would do poorly in the pious Mennonite region. The state W.C.T.U. set aside November 1, a week before the election, as a day of prayer for the success of the women's suffrage amendment, and reported some success among the Mennonites and a few Swedes in a campaign to influence the foreign-born to vote for women's suffrage. For the most part, however, the German papers of Kansas—urban, swimming wet, antisuffrage, highly sensitive to nativism—were most often Democratic in 1894. They welcomed Populist fusion, except when the new party fell in with women and water fanatics, but the Republicans except in special cases were untouchables.[35]

Kansas Swedes lacked a press to match the Germans', but English language Populist papers tried to make up for this by publishing reports that ten of eleven Minnesota Scandinavian papers had turned to the Populists since Republican gubernatorial candidate Knute Nelson had been found to be a tool of the railroad corporations, and by publicizing Swedish Populist speakers and other evidences of Swedish support whenever they could. It was an uphill fight. Many Swedes probably took a similarly anomalous position to that of Rev. Dr. Carl Swensson, of Lindsborg, who had been elected to the Kansas House of Representatives as a Republican in 1890 while advocating antimonopoly, mortgage relief, and public regulation of railways

[34] *Leavenworth Post*, October 12, June 15, 1894; *Kansas Telegraph* (Topeka), November 22, 1894; *Marysville Post*, September 14, 1894; *Der Waechter* (Kansas City), October 11, 1894; *Germania* (Lawrence), November 8, 1894.

[35] *Hillsboro Anzeiger*, September 21, 1894; *Our Messenger* (Topeka), October, 1894; for editorial opinion from September through November, 1894, see *Kansas Telegraph* (Topeka), *Marysville Post*, *Wichita Herold*, *Kansas Staats Anzeiger* (Wichita), *Leavenworth Post*, *Germania* (Lawrence), *Der Waechter* (Kansas City), *Hillsboro Anzeiger*. The last two papers were Republican and the others more or less Democratic.

and telephones, who had asked Governor Lewelling for a job in 1893, and yet who wrote an open letter to Lewelling in 1894, saying:

The plague of grasshoppers and droughts cannot be compared to the disasters which have been heaped upon our young and noble state by the doctrines and proclamations and public and private utterances of yourselves and other leaders of your party.

Populists had their Swedish speakers, Swedish testimonials, and Swedish literature, and remained forever hopeful of Swedish votes.[36]

A multitude of friendly appeals in the Populist English language press sought to lure Germans, German-Russians, Mennonites, Welshmen, Irishmen, Swedes, and Norwegians. Lewelling hired and fired the police board of Leavenworth, a city with a large foreign-born population, with fretful regularity in an attempt to salvage the Irish, German, labor, mining, and Catholic votes there as well as to placate every element on prohibition enforcement.[37]

Meanwhile, the other parties were active too. The Democrats harped on the Populist women's suffrage plank and the prohibitionism that went with it. The Republicans put their main stress on the troubles of the Lewelling administration and Populist "anarchism," especially as shown in the "Legislative War," although it had been a future Republican governor, Ed Hoch, who had battered down the doors of the Kansas House with a log ram. They also kept their own German and Swedish speakers and publications running full blast. Probably the Re-

[36] *Kansas Commoner* (Wichita), October 18, 1894; *McPherson Opinion*, October 18, 1894; *Larned Tiller and Toiler*, October 12, 1894; Emory K. Lindquist, "The Scandinavian Element in Kansas," in *Kansas: The First Century*, ed. John D. Bright (New York; Lewis Historical Publishing Co., 1956), I, 323; letters from Swensson to Lewelling, Lindsborg, March 28, 1893, and from A. A. Engstrom to Lewelling, Lund, Kan., May 15, 1894, in Lewelling MSS, in KHS; *Salina Union*, August 17, 1894; D. C. Zercher, *Orubbliga Fakta I Sammändrag; Manifest fran State Central Commite af Folkspartiet* (Topeka: Advocate Publishing Co., 1894) ; *Advocate*, August 1, 1894.

[37] *Mankato Western Advocate*, June 15, 1894; *Ellinwood Advocate*, November 1, 1894; "Ruppenthal Scrapbooks," III: 153; *Marion Times*, October 18, 1894; *Emporia Tidings*, October 5, 1894; *Larned Tiller and Toiler*, October 12, 1894; *Kansas Commoner* (Wichita), October 18, 1894; *Mankato Western Advocate*, October 12, 1894; Lewelling MSS, in KSHS, esp. May–September, 1894; *Leavenworth Labor News*, October 19, 26, 1894.

publican effort was the most smoothly professional of the three parties, but since they had to work under the added handicap of the A.P.A. albatross and seldom troubled themselves to get rid of it, they needed whatever smoothness they could muster.[38]

The anti-A.P.A. resolution was no passing fancy of the delegates at the June convention, to judge from the Populist press. A few papers preferred to forget all about it, but the great majority spoke out clearly. Almost no paper of any party actually defended the anti-immigrant, anti-Catholic secret society, although at least two Republican papers criticized the Populist anti-A.P.A. resolution in such terms as to bring replies from Populists that the Republicans were seeking the A.P.A. vote.[39] Whatever the political affiliation of the A.P.A. membership—if there were indeed "thousands of them in our party," as a Lewelling correspondent had suggested—they were silent through the campaign, and the press was unequivocal: the Populists and Democrats linked the A.P.A. with the Republicans, and the Republicans simply looked the other way.

From the *Topeka Advocate*—the most venerated and widely read Populist paper in the state, and at that time a Lewelling-Breidenthal organ, which called the A.P.A. furore "un-American, unpatriotic, and unreasonable"—down to the poorest country weekly, Populist papers damned the A.P.A. and linked it with the Republican party. The *Advocate* said it naturally fell in with the Republicans since each sought to deprive a certain class of its rights: the A.P.A., the Catholics; the Republican party, the producers. The *Emporia Tidings* was disgusted with the A.P.A., which opposed religious freedom, a principle "among others that nerved the arms of the colonists as they hurled their defiance at King George," and the Clyde *Farmers' Voice* said:

The republicans are intending to work the A.P.A. racket for all it is worth during the coming campaign. Of course this can only be done amongst the most ignorant and brutal. This organization would if it had its way take us back to the dark ages. Its

---

[38] *Junction City Sentinel*, June 16, 30, September 1, 1894; *Lindsborg News*, June 29, October 19, 26, November 2, 1894; Republican Party MSS, September–October, 1894, in KSHS; *Scandia Journal*, June 15, September–November, 1894; Lindquist, *loc. cit.*, I, 323.

[39] *Topeka Capital*, June 13, 1894; *Topeka Press*, June 14, 1894; *Garnett Eagle*, June 22, 1894; *Westphalia Times*, June 28, October 11, 1894.

active members are not only traitors to their country, but they are traitors to humanity.[40]

A dozen other Populist papers and a half-dozen Democratic ones could be cited to the same effect. Suffice it to say that the Populist editors overwhelmingly backed the anti-A.P.A. resolution, condemned the A.P.A. as a vicious, dangerous, and un-American organization, and tied it to the G.O.P.[41]

The Lewelling administration received advice to publicize the Populist anti-A.P.A. resolution in order "to cement the entire 80,000 [Catholic] votes to our party," and the leading Populist daily reproduced an alleged Republican letter to campaign workers which urged that they use the Populist resolution to attract A.P.A. votes. When someone tried to tar the third district Populist candidate for Congress with the A.P.A. brush, he summed up his and his party's attitude in an open letter.[42]

NEODESHA, KAN.
Oct. 9, 1894

J. M. Kennedy, Fredonia, Kan.
MY DEAR SIR:
Your letter concerning my relation to the A.P.A. is just received. In reply will say that I have never been, am not now, and so far as present intentions go, do not expect to be a member of that society. . . . While in the business I may as well say, in advance of any reports that may be started, that I am not a sheep thief, gambler, drunkard, opium eater or corporation attorney, and that I have never been hung or sent to the penitentiary.

Very truly,
J. D. BOTKIN

[40] *Advocate*, October 17, 1894; *Emporia Tidings*, June 29, 1894; *Farmers' Voice* (Clyde), June 14, 1894.

[41] *Ellinwood Advocate*, November 22, 1894; *Hays Free Press*, August 11, 1894; *Hutchinson Alliance Gazette*, June 14, 1894; *Independence Star and Kansan*, June 15, 1894; *Kingman Journal*, June 22, 1894; *Marshall County Democrat* (Marysville), October 26, November 2, 1894; *Peoples Advocate* (Marysville), November 2, 1894; *Newton Journal*, November 13, 1894; *Parsons Daily Eclipse*, October 26, 1894; *Kansas Commoner* (Wichita), October 18, 1894; *The Farmers' Advocate* (Winfield), November 3, 1894; *Great Bend Beacon*, June 28, 1894; *LaCrosse Chieftain*, November 2, 1894; *Leavenworth Post*, November 3, 1894; *Westphalia Times*, July 5, October 11, 18, 1894.

[42] *Topeka Press*, October 11, 1894; letter from R. M. Ruggles to Lewelling, Emporia, June 29, 1894, in Lewelling MSS, in KSHS; *Independence Star and Kansan*, October 9, 1894.

The three new issues that affected immigrants—women's suffrage, prohibition, and the A.P.A.—hardly had the campaign to themselves, however. In addition to these three, a few old concerns of Populist foreign relations reappeared, notably its attitudes to immigrants in general, to Jews, to immigration restriction, alien land, and pauper labor immigration.

A few Populist writers denounced New York slums flooded with "foreign sewage," the "off-scourings of eastern Europe," demanded an end to alien suffrage, and worried whether alien women would have the vote if women's suffrage passed.[43] But a much larger number looked favorably on Baron Hirsch's Jewish Colonization society; lauded the charity and community spirit of Nathan Straus, "the Hebrew philanthropist of New York"; praised Bjornstjerne Bjornson because his views, those of a great Norwegian philosopher, were Populistic; complimented German immigrants; and hoped that immigration would never stop. One Populist editor said that while the Republicans, from the gubernatorial candidate on down, cried, "Down with the foreigner! . . . tax to total exclusion, if need be, every poor immigrant who sets his face toward our promised land," the Populist motto remained "Equal rights to all, special privileges to none." A fusionist printed a letter from Governor Lewelling to the Kansas Immigration Company, which said that the world should know that Kansas welcomed anyone who will become a citizen and aid in its development. The leading non-fusion paper, too, said that immigration restriction was no answer to bad labor conditions:

Give us free access to our natural resources and an equitable distribution of the product, and we can find room and profitable employment for all the millions of Europe. It is not a decrease of wealth producers that we need, but a decrease of the leeches and parasites which rob the producers of the wealth which they create.[44]

[43] *Topeka Press,* April 10, 1894; "Ruppenthal Scrapbooks," III: 65, 69, 323, in KSHS; *Ottawa County Index,* June 14, 1894; *Olathe Tribune,* October 19, 1894.

[44] *Parsons Daily Eclipse,* November 1, 1894; *Topeka Press,* April 20, May 23, 1894; *Advocate,* May, 1894, *passim; New Era* (Topeka), August 18, 1894; *The People* (Topeka), April 29, 1893; *Ottawa Journal and Triumph,* July 26, 1894.

Fusionists and non-fusions alike agreed in detestation of the A.P.A. and in their welcome for the honest immigrant as a fellow member of the producing class.

Democratic publicists, with their party's traditional antipathy to Know-Nothingism and friendship for ethnic groups generally, took the same humanitarian position. Even some Democrats, however, said that "it is about time that a restriction of immigration takes practical form, and that the gates of our country be closed to the ignorant, lawless, impoverished people that swarm to this country. . . . These hordes recruited from southern Europe, western Asia, and northern Africa do not belong to this civilization."[45]

Nonetheless it was the Republicans who most frequently expressed antiforeign sentiments. The 1894 Republican candidate for governor, Edmund Morrill, was a strong immigration restrictionist, and the Republican candidate for congressman-at-large allegedly called the foreign-born "scum of Europe." Republican editorial writers demanded immigration restriction by literacy test for the "degraded class" of immigrants. Often their comments had a racist tinge, as in a cry from the *Topeka Capital* on the day before the Populists passed their anti-A.P.A. resolution: "There are few if any more urgent issues than this in the Nation at large. The restriction of immigration means the purification of American blood and it can not begin too early or go too far."[46]

Populist restrictionism, meanwhile, focused almost entirely around the problems of labor competition in a depression, landlordism, and the London banking power. The foreign-born tenants of alien landlords such as William Scully, who would never, in the Populist view, be landowners and therefore good citizens, were a serious problem, but education would solve it:

Let those among whom the new settlers locate see that they are informed concerning local affairs, and have the facilities for a thorough economic education. There is no better school for . . . this work than the Farmers' Alliance. Let these immigrants be

---

[45] *Council Grove Guard*, June 15, 1894; *Junction City Sentinel*, same.

[46] *Topeka Capital*, June 12, September 1, 1894; *Olathe Tribune*, June 22, 1894; *Larned Tiller and Toiler*, October 19, 1894; *Coffeyville Journal*, September 1, 3, 1894; *Minneapolis Messenger*, June 28, 1894; *Russell Journal*, June 14, 1894; *Marion Times*, October 4, 1894.

enlightened and converted as fast as they arrive . . . and no fears need be entertained of permanent settlers, even though brought here by corporations and designed for corporation purposes.[47]

As for pauper labor immigration, the Kansas Populists seemed unexpectedly to take a more humanitarian view the deeper the depression became. Even the economically-based restrictionism of 1890 and 1891 had often given way to a belief that the real difficulty lay not in the immigration itself but in monopolies, high tariffs, and an economic system that could not provide honest jobs for honest laborers. A search of the sources revealed but one sole proposal for a head tax on immigrant labor, and it was accompanied by a statement that the tax would be inoperative whenever "American citizens who want work have an opportunity to find employment at fair wages." In 1894 a letter to the *Advocate* raised the question of pauper labor and said "imported criminals and paupers augment the armies of the unemployed; intensify the sufferings; increase the danger; hasten the crisis." But immigration restriction was no answer. For one thing, "our country is large enough and possesses sufficient resources to supply first-class homes and all the comforts of civilization to the inhabitants of the earth." The real answer?

Of course we can stop pauper immigration if we decide to do so. We can, however, just as easily enact laws that will give every man, woman, and child constant and profitable work if they wish it. . . . Be it remembered that paupers and criminals are the products of perfidious and criminal legislation.[48]

This may be the view of a nineteenth-century idealist, and he and his fellows no doubt placed far too much confidence in the beneficent effect of good laws and good education. But it is hardly the view of a nativist, or a chauvinist, or a conspiracy-minded neurotic, or a racist.

That Populist's approach was more liberal even than that of

---

[47] *Advocate*, March 21, 1894.

[48] *Kiowa County Times* (Greensburg), June 8, 1894; Percy Daniels, *A Crisis for the Husbandman* (Girard: Western Herald Print, 1889), p. 119 [contains a resolution entered by Congressman Ben Clover as one section of a forty-section bill for a "graduated property tax" H.R. 6595, 52d Cong., 1st sess.]; *Advocate*, April 25, June 6, 1894.

the German-American League of Kansas. The League had organized mainly to try to stop prohibition and women's suffrage, but it also urged immigration restriction—"that lawless, diseased and indigent persons, the ripe and bitter fruit of despotism, shall be excluded from these shores"—as one of its main demands. The majority of Populists agreed with the League that this kind of restriction would be good, but they agreed also with its further desire to "emphasize the welcome with which the people of this country receive worthy, industrious, honest and law-abiding immigrants from the old world."[49]

The money question by 1894 was moving swiftly toward its later place as the one great issue in Populist politics. Here again, as in 1890, the Populists printed the "Hazzard Circular" story and denounced Rothschild and English and Wall Street bankers. But as they also had done earlier, they argued on economic grounds; they avoided hysteria; they avoided anti-Semitism; and if they showed any Anglophobia, they appeared to distrust Wall Street just as much as, if not more than, anything English. Kansas Republicans, bimetallists that they were, used many of the same arguments.[50]

The Populists worried a good deal less about these things than future historians have done. They were fighting a hard campaign, and by October it was clear that the outlook was gloomy. Women's suffrage had wrecked fusion and brought the Democrats into the fray with a ticket of their own. In this three-way race the People's party no longer had the ardor and uproar of 1890 to rely upon. If this were not enough, a fourth ticket appeared in September, the creation of the "middle-of-the-road" Populist group, the Cyrus Corning, Mrs. Lease, *New Era* group, which had done much to bring fusion to a crashing end.

This Middle-of-the-Road Populist ticket ran on the ostensible grounds that women's suffrage and non-fusion needed further help. But since the June Populist convention had already accomplished both, the Middle-of-the-Road Populist aims were rather hollow. At any rate, when the ticket emerged, Corning was slated for governor and several other disgruntled ex-

---

[49] *Topeka Press*, June 6, 1894.

[50] *Topeka Press*, April 8–10, 1894; *Salina Union*, June 15, August 17, 1894; *Kiowa Review*, June 27, 1894; "Populist Party Clippings," I: 193–96, 239–40, in KSHS.

Lewellingites were named for other offices. Mrs. Lease could swallow this much. Yet she dissolved her partnership with the Corning-*New Era* group at the very time the Middle-of-the-Road Populist ticket was officially filed and tied herself, however tenuously, to the Lewelling organization for the remainder of the campaign. The probable reason for her switch was the discovery that the Corning group had made a deal with Cyrus Leland, the Republican leader, to set up the separate ticket in order to decoy Populist voters from the Lewelling ticket. In addition, it suddenly seemed clear that as far back as the Populist convention in June, Leland had used the *New Era*, and the suffragettes, for the very purpose of raising the suffrage issue to break up Populist-Democratic fusion.[51]

Two days after the Middle-of-the-Road Populist ticket entered the lists, Breidenthal, as state chairman of the People's party, filed for a hearing to have it removed from the ballot on grounds that it was illegal on several counts under Kansas' Australian ballot law. Ten days later the attorney-general, secretary of state, and state auditor, all Populists, held the hearing. Breidenthal appeared for the People's party, and the representative of the Middle-of-the-Road Populist ticket was none other than Ben S. Henderson, of Cowley county, the same who had beaten the administration choice for temporary chairman of the June convention and then opened the floodgates of women's suffrage. The Middle-of-the-Road Populist ticket was thrown off the ballot for lack of genuine petitions and other reasons. But the very fact itself that Henderson represented the Corning group at the hearing, together with Populist press notices of surreptitious meetings between Corning, Henderson, and the Republican state leadership, left little doubt that the Middle-of-the-Road ticket, and very likely the suffrage issue at the June convention, had been Republican plants.[52]

Cyrus Leland had engineered a brilliant political coup. The Populists had been divided among themselves. Through Henderson's maneuvers at the convention they had endorsed the one issue sure to split off the Democrats and their foreign group

[51] *Topeka Press*, September 3, 4, 6, 9, 12, 13, 26, October 6, 8, 15, 16, 1894; *New Era* (Topeka), September 15, October 13, 1894; *Ottawa County Index*, October 18, 1894; *Girard World*, November 1, 1894; October 19, 1894; *Council Grove Guard*, October 5, 1894; Taylor, *op. cit.*, pp. 47–49.

[52] *Topeka Press*, October 5, 15, 17, 1894; *Salina Union*, October 26, 1894.

support, and fusion had been destroyed. By October it hardly mattered whether the further jobbery of the Middle-of-the-Road Populist ticket succeeded in getting on the ballot or not.

4. Bleak Results

Had the whole thing been less ignoble, great irony would have laid in the fact that the very people who had co-operated with the Republicans in these maneuvers, the Corning-*New Era* group, had insisted that they were the only Populists who were still steadfast, true-blue, down-the-line Omaha-platform reformers and that the Lewelling-Breidenthal Populists were unprincipled boodlers willing to sacrifice everything on the altar of fusion. And it is worth remarking that the few Populist expressions that could conceivably have been called nativistic or chauvinistic were almost all the outpourings of people like Corning and others of this tiny band of "steadfast men of principle" who were so rabidly non-fusionist that they came full circle, apparently, and fused with the Republican party.

It was the saddest November in Populism's short history. The Republicans swept everything except one congressional seat with a clear majority of the total state-wide vote. The Populist percentage was slightly larger than it had been in the last three-ticket year, 1890, but since it is improbable that the great decrease in the Democratic vote (its percentage was smaller than that of the Union Labor party in 1888) came through defections to the Republicans, probably many former Democrats stayed with the Populists and many former Populists reverted to the Republicans. To judge by returns from precincts filled with particular ethnic groups, the Populists had much success with the Irish, many Bohemians, the Welsh, the Danes, and some Germans. But although the Populists made inroads elsewhere, the Democrats kept most of the German-Russian Catholics, many German Lutherans, the German Swiss, and the Austrians, while the Republicans scored heavily among the Mennonites and to a considerable extent among the Swedes. Each party had its strongholds among both the heavily immigrant and heavily native-born counties.[53]

Fusion on the county and township levels had kept many

[53] Kansas, Secretary of State, Election Returns, 1894 (microfilm), in KSHS.

Populists in office, but the state ticket was wholly defeated. The women's suffrage amendment lost in nearly all counties except some in the western part of the state, which is hardly evidence for the Turner "frontier thesis," the idea that the frontier was productive of democracy, since these sparsely and recently populated counties, most of them hard hit by the economic bust of the late eighties, needed a certain level of voting population to maintain their county organization and their places in the state legislature. It may have been, as the state W.C.T.U. said, that just over half the Populists, or four for every three Republicans or four for every one Democrat, voted in favor of women's suffrage, compared with 88 per cent of the Prohibitionists; but at any rate, the issue was out of politics for a while and was not to threaten fusion again.[54]

No single factor can explain the Republican majority. Populist newspapers and party workers laid their loss to a "stay at home vote," but few of them went a step further and asked why voters had stayed at home. Some suggested that many Populists had left the state since 1892 to take up homesteads in the Cherokee strip, but a German editor was probably closer to the real answers when he said that "women's suffrage was, along with boodle, the straw that broke the Populist camel's back." The lackluster record of the Lewelling administration hurt gravely, together with the many charges of corruption and incompetency leveled at it by Republicans and dissident Populists, but Chairman Breidenthal and other leaders had a point when they insisted that the major reason for the defeat was not the administration scandals but nation-wide bad times, which hurt the Democrats across the country and the Populists in Kansas. Lewelling ran far ahead of his ticket, Breidenthal noted, and the Republican landslide was national, not just a Kansas matter.[55]

[54] *Olathe Tribune*, November 23, 1894; *Our Messenger* (Topeka), December, 1894.

[55] Letter from J. D. Bradley to Fred J. Close, Attica, June 7, 1894, in Lewelling MSS; *Industrial Free Press* (Winfield), November 8, 1894; *Mankato Western Advocate*, November 16, 1894; *Kansas Agriculturist* (Winfield), October 23, 1892 (comments on homesteading in the Cherokee strip). See also *Kansas Staats Anzeiger* (Wichita), November 8, 1894; Ecroyd, *op. cit.*, p. 220; James C. Malin, "The Kinsley Boom of the Late Eighties," Kansas *Historical Quarterly*, IV (May, 1935), 177; Diggs, *op. cit.*, pp. 99–100; *Topeka State Journal*, November 8, 9, 1894.

The Lewelling administration of 1893–1894 and the campaign of 1894 reflected several critical characteristics of Kansas Populism. Fusion did not occur in 1894, which made that campaign different from every other except the first one, in 1890. The reason was not that the Democratic party, or the ethnic groups borne along with it, found anything to object to in the People's party, but the noxious, peripheral, divisive issues of women's suffrage and prohibition. A slim majority of the Populist state convention brought about endorsement of women's suffrage (and thereby, prohibition), which prevented fusion. Hostility to ethnic groups was not involved, even among the delegates supporting women's suffrage, since their apparent yea-votes on the anti-A.P.A. resolution and the indifferent (not hostile) character of their speeches indicate the contrary. Unruliness, electric convention conditions, proneness to sentimental appeals, and a horror of "political bosses" kept them from nominating a fusion ticket in 1890, and these things coupled with the Lewelling record kept them from it again in 1894.

The Populists' predilection for fusion is important because it indicates not only that they were willing to work with the Democratic party and its ethnic group affiliates, not only that they lacked a rigid mental outlook and could take reasonable political steps to achieve reform; it is important also because some writers have thought it shows a lack of principle, a hypocrisy, an inconstancy derived from the overarching irrationality of the whole movement. Because of this it seems worth remarking that two changes did take place in Kansas Populism between 1889 and 1894, but both of them underscore the fact that the tone and character of the movement remained remarkably consistent.

The first change was a decline in numbers after the 1890 campaign. This took place immediately after that campaign, which was the most enthusiastic one. After some thousands of voters, a small number in comparison to the whole, had left, the Populist vote stayed at nearly the same level for several years. If there was a fundamental change in Populism, it took place immediately after the partly successful but generally disappointing first campaign of 1890. The loss of these marginal voters meant simply a lowered enthusiasm, not a change in the fundamental texture of the party.

The second change was from office-seeking to office-holding, from protest to the administration of government. The Populists during the Lewelling administration learned a great deal about governing, although imbroglios beginning with the "Legislative War" kept them from learning fast enough to avoid a series of ghastly blunders. Many of them turned from a quest for reform to a search for patronage. But what is striking is that although their governing ability may have been poor, the great majority of the Populists, including their top leadership, retained their moral fervor, their devotion to purpose, which everyone agrees they had before 1893. It is probably as true of the mass of the party, as it is certainly true of Lewelling and Breidenthal, that their rapid education in political realities did not mean, at the same time, a decline in their dedication to the reform program. It is worthwhile to point out that factions, deals, and personalities were important in the movement at least as early as the Union Labor days; that politics as distinct from statesmanship was nothing new to the Populists; that a pragmatic spirit of compromise had existed in 1890 as well as in 1894, although in neither year was it as successful as it was in 1892 or 1896 and after.

The Middle-of-the-Road Populist affair might be cited to dispute this view, but aside from the fact that it took place almost certainly with the connivance of the Republican high command, it had almost no support from the hundreds of Populist editors in scores of country towns, was shunned by local Populist conventions and county committees, and was led by individuals who in many cases were feuding personally with the regular state leaders.

These people should figure in a discussion of nativism in Kansas Populism because a few of the Middle-of-the-Road Populists had produced most of the examples of references to England, or Jews, or immigration restriction, that could be considered antagonistic. Yet even their exemplifications of apparent hostility must be granted partial or complete absolution upon reasonable analysis, and in any case, they were balanced, as in the *New Era's* columns, by evidence of positive warmth for foreign ideas and foreign people.

Furthermore, if one still insists that there was a radical, Anglophobe wing in Kansas Populism—and the "middle-of-the-road" leaders must be these people—it is undeniable that "middle-of-the-roadism" was the last refuge of a non-fusion attitude, a simple factional feud, an outright sellout by a few of the so-called old line, real Populists who ostensibly upheld the Omaha platform against the depredations of the regulars led by Lewelling and Breidenthal.

The case for nativism in Kansas Populism in 1894 falls flat. The "middle-of-the-road" group, the most radical faction on all matters and guilty of nothing worse than ambiguity on foreign matters, degenerated into a Republican fifth column. The delegates at the state convention who voted for a women's suffrage plank and thereby destroyed fusion did so out of indifference, not hostility, to ethnic groups. The state convention and the overwhelming number of Populist newspapers unequivocally condemned the chief nativist organization of the day, the American Protective Association. Immigrants participated, in large measure as usual, as candidates, party officials, or voters in the Populist cause. Populist attitudes toward immigration restriction, toward Jews, toward the Old World, were if anything more friendly than those of its opponents. Populism continued to have the same strongly democratic ideology that it had always had; it still was a program of economic reform to meet depression conditions; it kept the same humanitarian hallmarks it had in the days of its youth—and all this remained clear in spite of devastating defeat at the polls and darkening, widening depression.

Unless defeat and depression were to wreck it irretrievably, the People's party had to travel in a new tactical direction. From election day in 1894 into the spring of 1896, more and more Populists saw that their road had to be the parallel tracks of fusion and finance. The next stop was to be a battleground, and on that ground they were to fight the "Battle of the Standards."

CHAPTER EIGHT

FREE SILVER AND "UNDESIRABLE CLASSES"

1. A Single-Issue Campaign

For Kansas farmers 1896 brought the fourth consecutive near-failure in wheat, and corn production was nearly as poor. Not only had economic conditions not particularly improved since the late eighties for thousands of Kansas residents, but by then the rest of the country was in the throes of depression.[1] The result was a roaring reform campaign.

Several such political holocausts had hit Kansas since 1888 but 1896 was the first presidential year in decades in which the two great national parties faced each other on clear-cut issues deeply reflective of opposing economic viewpoints. Although Kansas had done a great deal for several years past to produce this situation and the reform sentiment that went with it, much of the original enthusiasm in the state had evaporated by 1896, and national politics and issues provided much of the drama and considerable of the direction of the Kansas campaign that year.

Fusion on the state and lower levels was hardly a question, since the Populists had won with it in 1892 and lost without it in 1894, and by this time the rank and file agreed and followed almost unanimously a group of moderate, pragmatic party leaders. Many Populist leaders, including Breidenthal, the state chairman, had been third-party men, had seen how a broadly based reform movement could succeed, and had learned that principles did not necessarily diminish when practical means to achieve them were used.

Until the midnineties free silver had not been an issue that alone would outweigh all other reforms, but it had been a major part of the reform program since the demonetization of silver in 1873, even getting strong support at the height of the Greenback agitation. The money question had been one prong of the

[1] James C. Malin, *Winter Wheat in the Golden Belt of Kansas* (Lawrence: University of Kansas Press, 1944), pp. 147–50.

Populist trident of reform issues—land, money, and transportation—since the beginning of the party, and Populist theoreticians had more and more come to stress that issue, not only because it had been part of the original program, and part of the Omaha platform in 1892, but because it had seemed justified by the Panic of 1893.

The reluctance of some Populists to base a campaign almost solely on free silver was greatly dissipated by 1894 or 1895, and by 1896 a fusion campaign run on free silver lines, even though its presidential candidate was a Democrat, held no terrors for most Kansas Populists. The Kansas leaders could reason from their personal experience and the party's history that it was absurd to send the People's party down to the dismal oblivion of the Greenback and Union Labor parties by insisting on every syllable of the program adopted at Omaha or earlier when one of their most fundamental, most radical planks stood a very good chance of becoming national policy by the election of a "Popocrat" President. Some historians have understood the Populists' relative silence in 1896 on issues other than the money question to mean a great shift from their original positions, and that money reform was a Democratic, not a Populist, issue. But the Democrat Cleveland, whom they had come to detest, was no silverite, and General Weaver, the Populist presidential candidate in 1892, was no goldbug. Admittedly, some important Populist voices, such as the Topeka *Advocate*, resisted the move to a single money plank as late as January, 1896, but the switch to silver was quick and complete. It was a sign of shrewdness and dedication to an old Populist issue that now seemed to have a real chance of success. Furthermore, many Populists had been running exclusively on the silver issue for some years, and thoroughgoing Populists like Governor Lewelling and Jerry Simpson approved of a silver campaign well before the 1896 conventions. How Populists felt about the single-issue campaign was summed up aptly in an open letter from a McPherson county fusion Populist to a leader of the 1896 "middle-of-the-roaders":

I consider the perservation [*sic*] of the life of our nation of greater importance than the preservation of any party. The conflict now on is between the trusts, combines and corporations and their agents, backed by the British monetary influences and their **patriotical** descendents [*sic*] of the Toryism of Revolutionary days advocating the single gold standard on the one side, and the American patriots enlisted in the cause of humanity on the other.[2]

After Bryan's selection by the Democrats at Chicago, General James B. Weaver of Iowa, the Presidential candidate of the Greenbackers in 1880 and of the Populists in 1892, placed him in nomination for the Populists. Seconding speeches came from General J. G. Field, of Virginia, the Populist vice-presidential candidate in 1892; Jerry Simpson, of Kansas; and Ignatius Donnelly, of Minnesota, lately returned to the fusion camp after a bout of "middle-of-the-roadism," apparently taking to heart his 1891 statement that "we believe that the party that, in such a crisis as this, shortens its platform, lengthens its muster roll."[3]

Like the national leadership, the party wheel horses in Kansas had the great courage to risk the very existence of the party that had brought them into office and fame on the chance of achieving one of their most deeply held principles. Jerry Simpson and former Governor Lewelling clearly felt this way, and the mass of the party was so immersed in the silver question that candidates for county attorney or county superintendent of schools had nothing to report about the local situation but "only talked feenance."[4]

The Populists and Democrats had no trouble reaching an ac-

[2] Kansas City Journal, October 30, 1911; Raymond C. Miller, "The Populist Party in Kansas" (Ph.D. dissertation, University of Chicago, 1928), pp. 164, 271; Donald H. Ecroyd, "An Analysis and Evaluation of Populist Political Campaign Speech Making in Kansas, 1890–1894" (Ph.D. dissertation, State University of Iowa, 1949), pp. 27, 190; James C. Malin, "The Kinsley Boom of the Late Eighties," Kansas Historical Quarterly, IV (May, 1935), 177; John D. Hicks, "The Political Career of Ignatius Donnelly," Mississippi Valley Historical Review, VIII (June, 1921), 126; Advocate, November 22, 1893, January 8, 1896; Kansas City Sun, November 3, 1893; Great Quadrangular Debate (Salina, Kan.: Press of Republican Job Rooms, 1894), pp. 9, 63; Dawn Daniels, "Lorenzo D. Lewelling—A Leader of the Kansas Populists" (Master's thesis, Northwestern University, 1931), p. 63; Topeka Press, April 2, 1894; New Era (Topeka), October 28, 1894; Annie L. Diggs, The Story of Jerry Simpson (Wichita: Hobson Printing Co., 1908), p. 120; printed letter, B. Evans to J. F. Willits, Eureka, September 15, 1896, in "Populist Party Pamphlets," VII, in KSHS.

[3] Lee A. Dew, "Populist Fusion Movements as an Instrument of Political Reform, 1890–1900" (Master's thesis, Kansas State Teachers' College [Pittsburg], 1957), p. 81; Hicks, op. cit., p. 120.

[4] Diggs, op. cit., p. 58; Daniels, op. cit., p. 63, letter of Lewelling of April 17, 1893, and Russell newspaper of August 15, 1896, in "Ruppenthal Scrapbooks," V: 243, in KSHS.

commodation, and at their state conventions, one day and one hundred miles apart, each accepted a Democratic-named slate of presidential electors and a Populist-named slate of state officers. The same electors appeared on the ballot under the Democratic and the Populist headings, and both were committed to Bryan. The vice-presidency posed a problem, because Arthur Sewall, the Democrat, was a national banker and thus unacceptable to many Populists, while Tom Watson, the fire-eating Georgia Populist, was no favorite of the Democrats. But the Kansas fusionists agreed that their electors would simply vote for the one that received the larger vote in the rest of the country. This obviously worked in Sewall's favor, and as the campaign progressed, Watson got short shrift in Kansas to the dismay of some party members.

Harmony might have resounded at the Populist convention at Abilene on August 5 more loudly than it did, since State Senator John W. Leedy upset the Breidenthal-supported candidate, ex-Congressman W. A. Harris, for the gubernatorial nomination. Other nominees included Frank Doster, who had been so indifferent to foreign-born support at the 1894 convention, for chief justice; Jerry Botkin, the 1888 Prohibitionist candidate for governor, for congressman-at-large, and L. C. Boyle for attorney-general. Some of this may not have been wholly to Chairman Breidenthal's liking, but he had always got along well with these people, and in contrast to the 1894 convention, the changes in plan did not seem to stem from Republican-inspired maneuvers. By far the most eloquent Republican comment came in William Allen White's most famous editorial, the one that catapulted him into national prominence for the rest of his life as "the sage of the grass roots":

What's the matter with Kansas?
We all know; yet here we are at it again. We have an old moss-back Jacksonian who snorts and howls because there is a bath-tub in the State house; we are running that old jay for governor. We have another shabby, wild-eyed, rattle-brained fanatic who has said openly in a dozen speeches that "the rights of the user are paramount to the rights of the owner"; we are running him for chief justice, so that capital will come tumbling over itself to get into the state. We have raked the ash heap of failure in the state and found an old hoop skirt of a man who has failed

as a business man, who has failed as an editor, who has failed as a preacher, and we are going to run him for congressman-at-large. He will help the looks of the Kansas delegation in Washington. Then we have discovered a kid without a law practice, and have decided to vote for him as attorney-general. Then for fear some hint that the state had become respectable might percolate through the civilized portions of the nation, we, have decided to send three or four harpies out lecturing, telling the people that Kansas is raising hell and letting the corn go to weeds.

. . . .

Whoop it up for the ragged trousers; put the lazy, greasy fizzle, who can't pay his debts on an altar and bow down and worship him. Let the State ideal be high. What we need is not the respect of our fellow men, but a chance to get something for nothing.[5]

The Middle-of-the-Road Populists did not sabotage this convention as they had the one of 1894, but they waged an active campaign and this time succeeded in getting their ticket before the voters. Possibly they were subsidized by the Republicans, and although they had to do without the help of Mrs. Lease, by then back in Pennsylvania, they shouted at the voters that they were the real Populist party, the real votaries of the Omaha platform, the unreconstructed, unsubverted, unfused rank-and-file reformers. Yet these simon-pure bearers of the truth supported the Democrat, Bryan, for President. Since they did this with a separate slate of electors, one must be pardoned for suspecting that this was not done to help Bryan but to split his Kansas vote.[6]

Some of the Middle-of-the-Road Populists' voter appeals smelled no better than their methods. John F. Willits, W. H. Bennington, Cyrus Corning, W. F. Rightmire, and Abe Steinberger led the movement as in 1894 and were joined by a reputed former G.A.R. commander named Paul Vandervoort, of

[5] Topeka Cooperator and Press, August 4, 6, 1896; Kermit E. Opperman, "The Political Career of Senator William Alexander Harris" (Master's thesis, University of Kansas, 1938), p. 22; Raymond C. Miller, op. cit., p. 292; Edith Connelley Ross, "The Administration of John W. Leedy," in A Standard History of Kansas and Kansans, ed. William E. Connelley (Chicago: Lewis Publishing Co., 1918), II, 728–29; interview with W. J. Breidenthal, Topeka, September 11, 1960; Advocate, August 12, 1896; Emporia Gazette, August 20, 1896.

[6] Topeka Cooperator and Press, October 5, 7, 9, 11, 13, November 2, 1896; Raymond C. Miller, op. cit., p. 304.

Omaha, who presents a clear-cut case of a Populist anti-Semite and nativist. A reform lecturer, at least since 1891, Vandervoort not only took a very extreme position on the money question but extended his slams at Jews and other immigrants to many totally unrelated areas and often made statements like "all the Jews and Shylocks of Lombard Street, France and Germany are shipping the scum, dregs and filth of the dirtiest haunts of vice in the crowded cities of the old world to our shores." The Topeka organ of the Middle-of-the-Roaders was the only "Populist" newspaper that consistently expressed antiforeign, Anglophobic sentiments, but even there, references that could be construed as anti-Semitic were infrequent and were always tied closely to bankers.[7]

To regular Populist editors, the "middle-of-the-road" group were leeches. One called Vandervoort and Willits, when they stumped the state in November, "Two Hoary Frauds," and another repudiated them as soreheads. A third said:

Van de Vort [sic] the Judas of Populism, the slimy traitor of Nebraska, the A.P.A. leader of Omaha and Bennington and Willits the willing tools of Cy Leland are stumping Kansas in the interests of McKinley. They are a trio of which the republicans are ashamed. . . .[8]

Some of the regular Populists, together with silver Republicans and Bryan Democrats, talked about the money question in terms of a "money power," much as they had in 1890, but in almost no instances did any of them come close to the bigotry of Vandervoort and some other Middle-of-the-Roaders. The money question was the main issue in Populist speech making, as it had been in former years, and some naturally gave it the "money power" treatment, but they had nothing against anyone other than Jewish, English, or Wall Street bankers. Their refer-

[7] Vandervoort to editor, *Advocate*, February 22, 1893; *Advocate*, April 5, 1893; *Stockton Alliance Signal*, October 27, 1892; "Acceptance Address by Hon. Paul Vandervoort, delivered at Indianapolis, December 28th, 1892," in paperback book [cover and title page missing] (Indianapolis: Vincent Publishing Co., [1893?]), in "People's Party Pamphlets," VII, in KSHS; Middle-of-the-Road Populist material in "People's Party Pamphlets," VI, VII; *Winfield Free Press*, October 8, 1896; *Kansas City Sun*, August 7, 1896; *Topeka Cooperator and Press*, July 2, 15, 18, 25, September 19, 1896.

[8] *Farmers Voice* (Clyde), October 8, 1896; *El Dorado Industrial Advocate*, October 23, 1896; *Kiowa Review*, October 21, 1896; *Olathe Tribune*, October 16, 30, 1896.

ences to England were often connected directly with the "spirit of '76," but the references to Jewish bankers were not extended to Jews in general.[9]

They applauded silverite foreign countries and carefully exonerated the people of Europe from the blame heaped upon their goldbug governments. Sneers at Rothschild, at the Belmonts, and at Englishmen who benefited from American gold monometallism had a realistic basis in the great power these people actually held,[10] and Englishmen and Americans, Jews and Gentiles, were reviled without distinction as "a foreign and domestic money power." One Populist believed that all absentee landlords, whether English or American or any other nationality, all "rob the people just as much," and when Populists hoped to rid the country of the ilk of "Mr. Ickleheimer," of the Wall Street gold brokerage firm of Heidelbach, Ickleheimer & Co., they very demonstrably wrapped up McKinley, J. P. Morgan, Cleveland, "Herr Most, our leading anarchist," H. C. Frick, Mark Hanna, and George Pullman in the same package. Anticapitalist they may have been, but not anti-Semitic. And probably it is worth saying just once more that a considerable number made no references of any kind to the English, to Jews, to Wall Street, or to malevolent bankers. The 1896 standard bearer, William Jennings Bryan, stated clearly what the Populist attitude had been all along:

Our opponents have sometimes tried to make it appear that we were attacking a race when we denounced the financial policy

[9] Ecroyd, op. cit., p. 186; Parsons Daily Eclipse, October 8, 1896; The Money of the Constitution (Washington, D.C., 1896), p. 31; songs nos. 4 and 5 of Bryan and Leedy Free Silver Flambeau Club, detached pages in "People's Party Pamphlets," VII, in KSHS; Independence Star and Kansan, October 23, 1896; Lyndon Peoples Herald, October 15, 1896. The only exceptions are Farmers Voice (Clyde), November 12, 1896; Ottawa Journal and Triumph, October 20, 1896; Girard World, October 15, 29, 1896.

[10] Parsons Daily Eclipse, October 22, 24, 1896; W. H. Farrell, The Crisis (Revised), Or, The Way to Settle the Gold and Silver Question ([Leavenworth]: Press of Ketcheson & Reeves, 1896), pp. 59–60; S. S. King, Seed Time and Harvest (Kansas City: The Author, 1894), p. 123; S. S. King, A Few Financial Facts (Kansas City: E. R. Calender Printing Co., 1895), pp. 120–24; An English View. Our Financial System from a British Standpoint (Pueblo, Colo.: Single and Bradfield, Printers [1896?]); Address to the Silver Republicans of Kas (Topeka: Republican Silver League, 1896); Advocate, February 20, 1895; Council Grove Courier, October 30, 1896; "Ruppenthal Scrapbooks," V: 239, in KSHS.

advocated by the Rothchilds [*sic*]. But we are not; we are as much opposed to the financial policy of J. Pierpont Morgan as we are to the financial policy of the Rothchilds. We are not attacking a race; we are attacking greed and avarice, which know neither race nor religion. I do not know of any class of our people who, by reason of their history, can better sympathize with the struggling masses in this campaign than can the Hebrew race.[11]

If in spite of this one still insists that a trace of nativism or anti-Semitism did exist among the Populists, it was more than matched by Democratic statements, by Republican complaints that the Democratic tariff position was an English policy, or by such remarks as that of then-Old-Guard William Allen White that gold was "American, democratic, Saxon" and silver was "European, socialistic, Latin."[12] Populists continued to praise foreign institutions and foreigners as individuals and lashed out anew at the A.P.A. If there was an A.P.A. candidate, it was not Bryan.[13]

2. The Literacy Test for Immigrants

On another issue which bears on nativism, the Populists occupied a middle ground between the Republicans and the Democrats, as they nearly always did on non-economic questions. This was the proposal to restrict immigration by using a literacy test. A variety of restriction schemes had been tossed into the congressional hopper for several sessions, but in the Republican-dominated Fifty-fourth Congress, elected in 1894, Senator Henry Cabot Lodge and Representatives Sam McCall, of

[11] "Bryan and Sewall Silver Club. Constitution and By-laws," in "Populist Party Pamphlets, 1890–1896," in KSHS; *Parsons Daily Eclipse*, November 2, 1896; *Advocate*, August 21, 1895; *Farmers Voice* (Clyde), October 29, 1896; *Emporia Times*, November 6, 1896; *Olathe Tribune*, November 6, 1896; William J. Bryan, *The First Battle, A Story of the Campaign of 1896* (Chicago: W. B. Conkey Co., 1896), p. 581.

[12] W. P. Harrington, "The Populist Party in Kansas" (Master's thesis, University of Kansas, 1924), p. 92; G. Webb Bertram, *Merchant of Venice (Modernized)* (n.p., 1896?), in "People's Party Pamphlets," VI, in KSHS; *Downs Times*, October 22, 1896; Dew, *op. cit.*, p. 92, quoting White.

[13] *Advocate*, August 28, September 4, November 6, 1895, August 18, 1897; *People's Party Campaign Handbook* (Hiawatha, Kan.: Press of the Harrington Printing Co., 1898), *passim*; Donald L. Kinzer, "The American Protective Association" (Ph.D. dissertation, University of Washington, 1954), p. 433.

Massachusetts, together with other members inspired by the New England-based Immigration Restriction League, spearheaded a serious drive to restrict immigration by requiring an immigrant to demonstrate his ability to write in some language. All political parties in Kansas at one time or another had urged some form of immigration restriction, usually on the grounds that contract or pauper labor put American workers at an unfair competitive disadvantage. Populist Senator Peffer entered a restriction bill that aimed mainly (if it resembled other statements he made) at consular inspection of immigrants before they left Europe. The consular inspection method obviated the return to Europe of certain undesirables prohibited under previous laws after they had already arrived at an American immigrant depot.[14]

Senator Lodge, however, considered consular inspection "impracticable," and by the mid-nineties such straightforward labor-based restrictionism had given way to a new idea, the literacy test, which would have cut off immigration from southern and eastern Europe while permitting apparently more assimilable groups to keep coming. The literacy test was clearly based on the assumption that there was a distinction between good and bad races of immigrants, whereas labor restrictionism was rooted in economic competition. But when the literacy test began to draw widespread and diverse support, including endorsement from such groups as the Boston Merchants Association, the Boston Chamber of Commerce, the Seattle Chamber of Commerce, the Chicago Board of Trade, the Commercial Travellers of the United States, and many influential eastern professional and academic people, it seemed to be the one form of restriction that had any chance of passing the Congress, and labor restrictionists jumped on the bandwagon.

In May, 1896, the House debated the question, and over the protests of German-born Republican Congressman Richard Bartholdt, of St. Louis, the floor leader for the literacy test bill, Democrats and Republicans offered and spoke for amendments clearly in the labor interest.[15] Bartholdt insisted that he was not

---

[14] *Congressional Record*, 54th Cong., 1st sess., January 22, 1896, XXVII, 855.

[15] John Higham, *Strangers in the Land* (New Brunswick, N.J.: Rutgers University Press, 1955), pp. 70, 72; Barbara M. Solomon, *Ancestors and*

a nativist, but admitted that in his mind the only valid reason for immigration restriction was the "deterioration . . . in the character of our immigration." The literacy test would cut down the volume of immigration but continue to permit the influx from the more desirable nations. Amendments of the labor restriction type were tacked on, however, and the bill passed, 195–26, without a roll call. The Senate took up the bill in its lame duck session and quickly passed a weaker version that went to a Senate-House conference.

Each house then debated the conference report. At that point came the only remarks by a Kansas congressman in the whole debate. Republican Charles Curtis, one of the two Kansas representatives on the "A.P.A. Congressional Roll of Honor," declared: "I am in favor of more stringent immigration laws. I believe that all criminal, pauper, contract-labor, and ignorant classes and anarchists should be denied admission to our shores." On the final vote, the Kansas delegation split, with four Republicans and two Populists voting for the bill and two Republicans voting against. Whether they were voting for and

---

Immigrants (Cambridge, Mass.: Harvard University Press, 1956), chaps. V–VII, *passim; Congressional Record*, 54th Cong., 1st sess., XXVIII, 3531, 5418–21, 5470–72, 5478–81, 5484–85. Lodge's position is in: U.S. Congress, Senate, *Senate Report 13, Foreign Immigration*, to accompany S. 112 (55th Cong., 1st sess. [n.p.]), p. 23: "The results of all the tables given above may be summarized as follows: They show that the illiteracy test will affect almost entirely those races whose immigration to the United States has begun in very recent times, and which are most alien in language and origin to the people who founded the thirteen colonies and have built up the United States; that it would tell most heavily against those classes of immigrants which now furnish the paupers, diseased, and criminals, excluded by existing law, and is therefore a continuance of the present policy of the United States which has met with general acceptance; that the immigrants who would be excluded by the illiteracy test do not go out into the Western and Southern states, where immigration is needed, and become an agricultural population, but remain almost entirely in the Atlantic States, and in the great centers of population where the labor market is already overcrowded; that the illiterate immigrants who would be excluded by the bill proposed by the committee are largely congested in great cities and furnish a large proportion of the slum population; that the illiteracy test would shut out those classes of immigrants which statistics show contribute most heavily to pauperism, crime, and juvenile delinquents, and that with two exceptions none of the excluded races, as is shown by the letters of the governors of the different States, are desired in twenty-six States of the Union from which reports have been received. In one word it may be said that this measure will exclude a larger number of undesirable immigrants and a smaller number of desirable immigrants, so far as statistics can be relied upon, than any restriction which could be devised."

against the literacy test, or for and against the labor restriction portions, is impossible to say.[16] Similarly ambiguous were the favorable votes of both Kansas senators, Populist Peffer and Republican Lucien Baker. In the Senate twenty-seven Republicans voted for and six against (all but one from the northern plains or mountain states); twenty-five Democrats voted against and four for (David B. Hill, of New York, and one senator each from Texas, Virginia, and West Virginia); two Populists voted for; and three Populists joined ten Republicans and ten Democrats in not voting at all. Populists leaned mildly toward the bill, Democrats opposed it, and Republicans supported it.

President Cleveland handed down a ringing veto just before he left office, partly on the grounds that illiteracy was merely a pretext for keeping out certain immigrants who might very well prove to be useful citizens and that the provisions intended to help labor were unwise since labor's difficulties stemmed from depression, not immigration. The House overrode the veto but the Senate never reconsidered the matter.[17]

In Kansas during the mid-nineties immigration restriction had much the same direction and support it had had earlier. Almost exclusively it aimed at reducing labor competition. Literacy testing appeared in a few Republican editorials, but except for these, editors of all three parties alike mentioned immigration restriction but seldom, and when they did they argued its necessity almost always on labor grounds.[18] The race-based literacy test idea, like active personal discrimination against Jews and other groups, came from the East and was not a major issue in the Kansas campaign in 1896.

3. After Seven Lean Years

The German press in this campaign was a study in contrasts. Those that had been traditionally Democratic were strongly sil-

[16] *Congressional Record*, 54th Cong., 1st sess., XXVIII, 5421, 5484–85, 5517, 6446; *ibid.*, 54th Cong., 2d sess., XXIX, 235–41, 1228, 1235, 1677; U.S. Congress, House of Representatives, *Report 1079, Amending the Immigration Laws*, to accompany H.R. 7864 (54th Cong., 1st sess. [n.p.]), pp. 1–2.

[17] *Congressional Record*, 54th Cong., 2d sess., XXIX, 1937–38, 2667–68, 2946–47.

[18] *Advocate*, December 4, 1895, June 30, 1897; notice of Republican rally at Fort Scott, October 31, 1896, in Angle MSS, University of Kansas; *Coffeyville Daily Journal*, March 9, 1896.

verite even though Cleveland had been their idol in former years, and Republican papers kept a stiff upper lip and kept supporting gold. Both camps claimed that their policy was the only possible one for German Americans. But Germanic immigrants did not embrace silver simply because fusion demanded it, since there was a conspicuous absence of German, Austrian, or Swiss names at the Gold Democrats' state convention on August 25. The Democratic papers published in large type an old letter of Prince Bismarck's in favor of silver, pointed out that bimetallism was the policy of the German Central party (the German Catholic Center), and ran serially a treatise supporting bimetallism by Dr. Otto Arendt, a German economist. J. D. Botkin, Populist candidate for congressman-at-large, presented no difficulty for the Democratic *Marysville Post*, in spite of the fact that he had been the Prohibitionist candidate for governor in 1888, though the Republican Kansas City *Kansas Staats Zeitung* was distressed at this dry background. The *Staats Zeitung* played up Archbishop Ireland's Republicanism as heavily as the Democrats played up Bismarck, and the *Leavenworth Post* accomplished a neat tour de force in backing Bryan and the rest of the Democratic ticket except Leedy, because Morrill, the incumbent Republican governor, had been "all right" on prohibition enforcement and the *Post* preferred him to Leedy, an unknown quantity. The *Hillsboro Anzeiger* praised the Republican-supported prohibitory law as a Christian policy, but the *Post* still regarded the Republican party as the party of " 'honest money' and dishonest profits, the party of rings and monopoly" whereas Bryan represented "the producing classes, the workers, the farmers." Perhaps the policies of a German newspaper at that time depended mainly upon which political party was supporting it financially.[19]

English language Republican and Populist papers and speakers talked on both sides of the silver question, quoting or refut-

[19] *Marysville Post*, September 4, 11, 18, 25, October 9, 1896; *Germania* (Lawrence), October 29, November 5, 1896; *Kansas Telegraph* (Topeka), September 17, 24, October 29, November 12, 1896; *Kansas Staats Zeitung* (Kansas City), October 1, 8, 15, 22, 29, 1896; *Wichita Herold*, October 22, 1896; *Leavenworth Post*, October 2, 17, 19, 30, November 4, 6, 1896; *Hillsboro Anzeiger*, September 4, 18, 25, October 2, 9, 23, 30, 1896; Kirke Mechem (ed.), *The Annals of Kansas* (Topeka: Kansas State Historical Society, 1954), I, 62; *Advocate*, September 2, 1896.

ing Dr. Arendt and Bismarck, and in the absence of a local Swedish paper, the Populists imported speakers and out-of-state sheets in an attempt to offset the great prestige of Dr. Carl Swensson of Lindsborg and other members of the Swedish gold cohort, though the Populist effort seems to have been too little, too late. It was not until the following February that Swedish silverites set up a state-wide organization, and they did so somewhat ruefully since they felt that Swedish voters had supported the gold standard.[20]

By endorsing local candidates the Populists in Ellis county had no trouble fusing with the Democrats, who were controlled that year by the German-Russian Catholics, but the silver party had no luck at all with the Mennonites farther to the South, among whom the Republicans fruitfully sowed the ideas that the Democrats had caused the Panic of '93 and that Bryan was a visionary whose election would bring about a return of pre-Civil War slavery. Foreign-language treatises on the money question, from both sides, were more common than ever, with the Republicans utilizing Italian and Norwegian perhaps for the first time and Populists publishing "Coin's Financial School" in English, German, Swedish, and Bohemian and other tracts in these languages and Norwegian.[21]

The Populists sought the Irish vote by publicizing the Irish birth or connections of candidates or by once more hanging the A.P.A. label on the Republicans—"The A.P.A. objects to the government painting warships green"; "President Hubbard of

[20] *Hutchinson Gazette*, October 15, 1896; *Coffeyville Daily Journal*, September 2, 1896; *Marysville People's Advocate*, October 2, 1896; *Ottawa County Index* (Minneapolis), October 22, 29, 1896; *Russell Journal*, October 8, 1896; *Industrial Free Press* (Winfield), October 1, 1896; *Ottawa Journal and Triumph*, October 20, 1896; *Industrial Advocate* (El Dorado), October 2, 1896; *McPherson Opinion*, October 22, 1896; *Lindsborg News*, October 2, 9, 1896; *Advocate*, February 3, 1897; J. C. Ruppenthal interview, Russell, September 16, 1960.

[21] *Hays Free Press*, October 3, 1896; *Marion Times*, October 29, November 12, 1896; Cornelius C. Janzen, "Americanization of the Russian Mennonites in Central Kansas" (Master's thesis, University of Kansas, 1914), p. 114; "The money plank of the Democrats was not understood at all by the great majority" of the Mennonites; People's Party State Central Committee, *Agitate, Educate, Organize* (Topeka: The Committee [1894 or 1896]), in "People's Party Pamphlets," VI, in KSHS; "Republican Campaign Literature, 1896," in KSHS; circulars from the Republican State Central Committee, 1896, in Angle MSS, University of Kansas, indicating interest in the nationality background of voters.

the state A.P.A. says that 90 per cent of the members are Republicans"—and while the Republicans printed widely the pro-gold proliferations of John Ireland and other bishops, the Populists snickered that Ireland's political bedfellows that year were the atheist, Robert Ingersoll, and the anarchist, Johann Most.[22]

Whatever the result, both parties were certainly conscious of the foreign-born vote, and rightly or not in all cases, considered it subject to bloc appeals. It is worth noting that these were almost always translations of tracts on silver or gold aimed at informing the non-English-speaking voters about the main issue of the campaign. The Catholic issue cut across ethnic lines, and the bulk of the bloc appeals consisted of slight variations, either in language or endorsements, on the money theme.

The Republicans probably had the greater success, what with at least six imported German speakers crisscrossing the state. The Populists had fewer speakers, but one of them, a former Democratic candidate for lieutenant-governor, gave over eighty speeches for Bryan, silver, and the Populists. He was Friedrich W. Frasius, a north German who had come to the United States in his youth and to Kansas in 1867, when he settled at Clyde in Cloud county. After 1892 he kicked over the Democratic traces through disgust with Cleveland's policies and became a redoubtable Populist in spite of a little disgruntlement in 1897 with Governor Leedy's patronage methods.[23]

Frasius was not the only foreign-born worker in the Populist campaign, and in addition to many who had appeared previously, others from many ethnic groups were candidates or party

[22] *Downs Times,* October 15, 22, 1896; *Osborne County News* (Osborne), October 22, 1896; *Kiowa Review,* October 14, 1896; for A.P.A. quotes, see *Advocate,* April 8, May 13, 1896 [for additional quotes, see *Advocate,* September 11, 1895, January 15, March 25, 1896]; *Newton Journal,* October 13, 23, 1896; *Westphalia Times,* October 29, 1896; *Kansas City Sun,* May 1, 22, 1896; *Coffeyville Daily Journal,* October 15, 1896; *Stockton Alliance Signal,* October 29, 1896; *LaCrosse Chieftain,* October 23, 1896.

[23] *Kansas Staats Anzeiger* (Wichita), October 24, 1888; *Kansas City Sun,* July 20, 1894; letters from Geo. Wagner [secretary of Shawnee county Populist committee] to "To Whom It May Concern," Topeka, March 1, 1897, and Frasius to John W. Leedy, Topeka, March 10, 1897, in Leedy MSS, in KSHS; *McPherson Opinion,* October 8, 1896; *LaCrosse Chieftain,* October 26, 1900; *Great Bend Beacon,* October 19, 1900; *Westmoreland Signal,* October 5, 1900.

officers. In Wyandotte county H. M. Herr, a 45-year-old German who came to the United States in 1869 and to Kansas in 1881, ran for probate judge, and at the other end of the state Alfred Lawson, 47, a Swedish farmer and rancher, became the state representative from Trego county. An Englishman, William Blincow, 61, was probate judge in Thomas county, and a Bohemian, Joseph Kuchera, the Populist county treasurer, was joined by another "naturalized Bohemian citizen" running, a Populist paper said, against "a lot of rotten American commissioners" in Republic county. William Moore, 53, an Englishman, also ran in that county for state representative.[24]

The Irish Catholic colony at Blaine, in Pottawatomie county, was overrun with Populists, and the whole township ticket was either Irish-born or second generation. An example was Eugene F. Cronan, who lived with his Irish-born parents and was in the loan, insurance, and real estate business, was on the county committee, and ran for justice of the peace. Elsewhere in the same county J. W. Fitzgerald, 59, an Irishman, ran for state representative, and Frank Bothe, who was "young . . . capable, honest . . . [and] belongs to the sturdy German nationality," sought the clerkship of the district court.[25]

Several nationalities appeared on township tickets in Osage county. John Graham, an Englishman, ran for justice in Superior township; Arvonia had its Welshmen, and Olivet and Grant townships included D. W. Carlson, 36, who farmed 160 acres; August Anderson, 36, with 140 acres; C. J. Rapp, 64, with 1,100 acres; and John Gunnason, 39, all Swedish-born farmers, as well as Forvald Swenson, 62, a Norwegian. During this campaign another Swede, Ole Ostrom, who had come to Russell county in the early eighties to become a mail carrier, electioneered so devotedly for Bryan that he broke down and had to be

[24] Kansas City Sun, September 13, 1896; W. W. Reno and R. J. Hopkins (eds.), The Kansas Blue Book: Containing the Portraits and Biographical Sketches of the Members of the Legislature of 1897 (Topeka: Crane & Co., Printers, 1897), p. 62; Advocate, September 22, 1897; Republic County Freeman (Belleville), September 10, October 22, 1896; Census of 1895, Vol. CCXV, Rose Creek twp., p. 15, in KSHS; ibid., Vol. CCCLXXXII, Morgan twp., p. 8.

[25] Westmoreland Signal, August 28, October 2, 9, 1896, October 5, 1900; Census of 1895, Vol. CCXCII, St. Marys twp., p. 33; ibid., Vol. CCXCIII, Clear Creek twp., pp. 1, 7, 9, 10, 11, 12, 15, 21.

consigned to the state asylum for three months after Bryan lost the election.[26]

Even in the overwhelmingly Republican Swedish township of Diamond Valley in Morris county, the Populists mustered a ticket, which included Emil Forsberg, 29, and Gust Haglund, 53, Swedish-born farmers; David Blomberg, 44, born in Illinois but married to a Swede; and Charles Owens, 52, an English-born farmer with 800 acres. In McPherson county many of the usual Swedish Populist contingent reappeared with their German and German-Russian confreres, and in Labette county the candidate for state representative was Bengt Johnson, a Swede who came to Kansas in 1869 to farm and raise livestock. Johnson had been in the mercantile and milling business in Sweden and had been a founding Populist and Allianceman, having served as president of his local Alliance for three years.[27]

Two other legislative candidates, both Canadian-born and both successful in the election, were Parker F. Carr, of Stafford county, a farmer and bridge-builder who had been a Populist since 1889, and C. W. Fairchild, of Kingman county, a veteran of two terms as county attorney and a former Greenbacker. In Cowley county Henry Buss, 52, a German-born and well-to-do farmer ran for county commissioner, and in Geary county J. J. Muenzenmayer, a native of Untertürkheim, Württemberg, ran for state representative. Muenzenmayer, a Civil War veteran with a large family, was a Methodist and former Democrat, and had been a farmer, stonemason, and an implement and hardware dealer.[28]

For these men and for scores of thousands of others, the Bryan crusade proceeded apace. It was unquestionably one of the most vibrant, crucial, moving presidential campaigns in American history, and if not everyone suffered temporary derangement as a result, like Ole Ostrom, the Swede in Russell

[26] *Lyndon Peoples Herald*, October 22, 1896; *Census of 1895*, Vol. CCLXXV, Grant twp., pp. 4, 7, 17, 20, 22; *ibid.*, Vol. CCLXXVI, Olivet twp., p. 20; interview with J. C. Ruppenthal, Russell, September 16, 1960.

[27] *Council Grove Courier*, October 16, 1896; *Census of 1895*, Vol. CCL, Diamond Valley twp., pp. 8, 15, 16, 19; *McPherson Opinion*, August 13, 1896; Reno and Hopkins, *op. cit.*, p. 58.

[28] Reno and Hopkins, *op. cit.*, pp. 38, 44, 70; *Industrial Free Press* (Winfield), October 29, 1896.

county, Kansas, the current of emotion ran swift and deep. As it happened, of course, the Jordan was not crossed. It was figured that a switch of thirty-five thousand votes in four states would have given Bryan an electoral victory, but McKinley and "honest money" carried the day across the nation.[29]

In Kansas the "Popocrats" had better luck. They swept the presidential contest, the entire state ticket, six of the eight congressmen, and decisive majorities of both houses of the legislature. Of the foreign-born in the new legislature, there was one German-Russian Democrat; one German Democrat elected with Populist support; two Canadians, a Scot, an Irishman, and a German among the Republicans; and two Canadian, two Swedish, one English, and one German Populist. Of a number of the most heavily immigrant voting districts, two moved from their 1894 position toward the Bryan ticket for every one that moved toward McKinley.

The Middle-of-the-Road Populists? They had the support of none of the party officials, two or three editors out of hundreds, and exactly 1,240 voters in the state from a total major-party vote of 332,378, of which 168,041 were Populist-Democratic. It would be overgenerous to say that one Populist in a hundred was a Middle-of-the-Roader.[30]

For the first time, after trying for seven years, the Populists had full control of the government of Kansas. This achievement took place simultaneously with the liquidation of the People's party as a national force after the defeat of its fused national ticket of 1896. In Kansas the Populists were from their earliest days the second major party, and the Democrats came to them begging, but nationally this was not so. Absorption of the Populists into the Democracy in 1896 suddenly ended them as a significant party. In view of their previous happy concubinage, the Kansas branches of the two parties needed only a prod from this shotgun of national fusion to send them prancing to the altar to contract a permanent union.

Many Bryanite observers felt that much of McKinley's margin came from foreign-born workers who either through igno-

[29] Harrington, op. cit., p. 96.
[30] Reno and Hopkins, op. cit., passim; Kansas, Secretary of State, official voting returns for 1896 for 71 selected voting units of high ethnic concentration (microfilm), in KSHS.

rance or coercion voted against the interests of workingmen. Although this was not a problem in Kansas, since "new" immigrants were scarce and Bryan won the electors, it could have been a marvelous opportunity for Populists to express the nativism they have been accused of. Instead, the *Advocate* thought that a German, for example, who voted for gold did so because it was the currency of the fatherland, and as soon as he found out that not only many Germans but the mass of Americans "except the money-changers" were bimetallists, he would become one too.

The foreigner is, as a rule, sure to find out in time where his interests lie, and vote that way. From a lack of familiarity with the language he may be backward in taking up a new issue, but the intelligent foreigner is sure to go with the native American if you give him time enough to investigate and fully understand the bearings of this currency question.[31]

To the rabid excitement of the campaign of 1896, the Leedy administration was a decided anticlimax. Leedy was a better politician than Lewelling, his letters show an overpowering interest in patronage, but he was less of a reformer. The legislature concerned itself at its opening with a pointless bipartisan foray into the resubmission question and with such oddments as a bill "to give statutory force to the ten commandments." The main issue of the session was the regulation of railroad freight rates, which had been a long-time Populist hope, but when the bill finally emerged from a House-Senate conference it was so battered that Leedy felt he had to veto it and call a special session for another.[32]

The lackluster Senator Peffer was involuntarily retired and went on to run for governor on the Prohibition ticket in 1898 and then to canvass Kansas for the Republicans in 1900. The ex-Confederate officer and ex-Democrat whom Breidenthal had

[31] *Advocate*, December 30, 1896.

[32] Leedy MSS, in KSHS, include dozens of letters asking for and receiving patronage appointments. A few were requested on ethnic grounds, though most letters simply stressed the eminent moral fitness of the candidate. The file on cities and towns is largely taken up with prohibition enforcement. *House Journal . . . 1897* (Topeka: State Printer, 1897), p. 898; Raymond C. Miller, *op. cit.*, pp. 308–9; Karl A. Svenson, "The Effect of Popular Discontent on Political Parties in Kansas" (Ph.D. dissertation, State University of Iowa, 1948), pp .72–78.

backed for the governorship, William A. Harris, went to the United States Senate to fight for nationalization of the Pacific railways and other reforms.[33] Meanwhile, the Leedy administration and the Populist legislature were creating a record that could most charitably be called "undistinguished."

When the heavily Populist Kansas delegation to the new Fifty-fifth Congress arrived in Washington, it confronted further efforts to pass a literacy test bill much like the Lodge-McCall bill of the previous Congress. Populist Senators Allen of Nebraska and Turner of Washington opposed it very vocally, but again the Senate passed the measure, again the Populist senators split, again both Kansas senators (Populist Harris and Republican Baker) voted in favor, and again the party line-up showed the Republicans almost unanimously for the bill, the Populists split, and the Democrats against. In both the second and third sessions of the Fifty-fifth Congress, however, the House refused to consider the bill. When the final attempt to get it on the floor lost, 101–104, with 150 representatives not declaring themselves, the whole Kansas delegation with its six Populists and two Republicans either joined the opposition or did not vote.[34]

By then it was 1898. The onrush of war turned men's thoughts away from the inglorious idea of literacy testing and restriction on racist grounds, salubrious prosperity had dissolved many of labor's suspicions, and literacy testing went into a slumber from which it did not awake until years after Populism had expired. Throughout the heyday of the literacy test scheme in the nineties, Kansas Populists never supported the test or the racist notions that underlay it. Kansas restrictionism, such of it as there was and so far as its rationale was explained, rested almost wholly on grounds of labor sympathy. This kind of restriction they did support, even when it was attached to the literacy test. Republicans more noticeably supported the work of the Immigration Restriction League, the notion of a great and insuperable difference between older, assimilable immigration and newer, non-assimilable immigra-

[33] *Topeka Cooperator and Press*, November 9, 1896; "Ruppenthal Scrapbooks," IX: 155, in KSHS; *Downs Times*, October 13, 1898; *McPherson Republican*, October 12, 1900; Opperman, *op. cit.*, pp. 30–32.

[34] *Congressional Record*, 55th Cong., 2d sess., XXXI, 116, 312, 427–30, 689, 4806; *ibid.*, 55th Cong., 3d sess., XXXII, 196–97.

tion, and the literacy test, although in Kansas even that support was only infrequently expressed.[35]

The main issue of the 1896 campaign had not been a state matter at all but a question soluble only by federal action. This made it extremely difficult for the Leedy administration, even without its internal problems, to satisfy the voters. Reform was ebbing fast. The new battle cry of the nation would be *Cuba libre*, and it was a poor prophet who believed that Populism's seven lean years would be followed by seven years of plenty.

[35] *Topeka State Journal,* February 18, 1898; *Advocate,* June 22, 1898; *Hutchinson News,* February 7, 1898.

CHAPTER NINE

DENOUEMENT

1. Jingoes and Humanitarians

After 1896 the Populist story became, in Gray's phrase, "the short and simple annals of the poor." Few of them realized it on the morning after Bryan's defeat, but Populism was mortally stricken. Fusion on the national level had ended its independent existence, and it was only a matter of time before the People's party in Kansas, without hope of presidential victory, the affecting of broad reforms on questions of principle, or federal patronage, would almost have to follow suit. Furthermore, the seven or eight years of agricultural depression and the dismal aftermath of the Panic of 1893 were giving way to what would become two decades of prosperity, and Populism, the off-spring of deep depression, withered into obsolescence. Soon a new reform movement, to be called "progressivism," would take shape across a more prosperous country.

If these factors caused a gradual attrition, another suddenly exploded with massive force to shatter the already weakened party. Foreign war and foreign expansion, the prime concerns of the McKinley administration, had never been part of the hard core Populist program. But they related so closely to the psychological baggage of many Populists that they left the party for good, although they had never faltered before fusion, free silver, or the foreign-born.

In the middle and late nineties many Americans became jingoes—people marked by an emotional, perhaps hysterical, desire to enter a foreign war—in their attitudes toward the Spanish colony of Cuba. Jingoism probably had a very close connection with nativism. Both attitudes are nationalistic, one an antipathy to foreign people, the other an assertion of aggressive national pride. John Higham, the leading historian of post-Civil War nativism, suggests that this was the case: although the nativists and the Jingoes were not identical groups, they shared a nationalistic psychology that in the first case was defensive and was manifested in a drive toward immigration restriction and that in the second case was aggressive and led to a compulsive desire for overseas adventures.[1] Apparently with a similar connection in mind, a leading critic of the Populists has accused them not only of nativism but of jingoism as well, particularly in connection with the fomenting of the Spanish-American War. This critic admitted that jingo sentiment was strong among goldbug Democrats and Republicans of both monetary persuasions but maintained that it was stronger still in those parts of the country where Bryan and the "yellow press" were allegedly supported in twain. The congressional resolution of May 20, 1897, to recognize Cuban belligerency got its main support among Democrats and Populists together with trans-Mississippi Republicans. But although the Bryan area was strongest for war, the critic continued, it was hostile to annexation of territory conquered by American forces, while, on the other hand, eastern business elements were cool to war but were ardent annexationists. The Populists' initial fervor on the Cuban question resulted from frustration over the defeat of Bryan, and after they had been balked in the 1896 campaign, the Bryan supporters channeled their subsurface anxieties and frustrations into a bellicose demand for foreign war.[2] (All this assumes, of course, that support of Cuban belligerency or war was tantamount to jingoism.)

Nobody can argue that the Populists were not nationalists, nor that foreign concerns do not depend greatly upon domestic events. But what shape did Populist nationalism take? Was it so neurotic?

In Kansas, at any rate, the Populists' nationalism rested not on any urgent need to demonstrate American industrial and political might—if anything, they were overconfident about the rightness and self-sufficiency of American democracy—nor on notions of *Realpolitik* that the United States needed to prove her newly acquired status as a world power. It rested rather on the older nationalism of the early nineteenth century, the same

[1] John Higham, *Strangers in the Land* (New Brunswick, N.J.: Rutgers University Press, 1955), pp. 75–76.

[2] Richard Hofstadter, "Manifest Destiny and the Philippines," in *America in Crisis* ed. Daniel Aaron (New York: Alfred A. Knopf, 1952), pp. 177–83; Hofstadter, *The Age of Reform* (New York: Alfred A. Knopf, 1955), pp. 87–91.

inbred spirit of '76 with its suspicion of Great Britain, the same Jeffersonian-Jacksonian suspicion of despotisms whether political, financial, religious, or of a privileged class, the same spirit that compared Europe invidiously in political freedom, economic opportunity, material abundance, and humanitarian benevolence to that experiment in democracy, the uncorrupt and innocent United States.

Traditionally, there had been a certain defensiveness about it, perhaps, but more significantly, this nationalism contained a warmth, sympathy, and generosity that invited the stranger to partake of superior American virtue at the same time he was proudly informed of it. In the light of this, it is easier to understand how the Populists at first apparently supported what they understood to be the Cuban people's struggle to liberate themselves from Spanish despotism, and perhaps offered American assistance, and then found abhorrent the pressure for American acquisition of Cuba and the Philippines. Not frustration over the loss in 1896 but their humanitarian nationalism led many Populists to take a closer look at the bloody Cuban struggle when they were relieved momentarily after the election from the press of domestic concerns. To them the United States was the mother of republics, the guardian (since President Monroe's famous doctrine) of Latin American liberty, which bound the country to assist these suffering people. But when the Spanish-American War soon became a war of conquest and acquisition, they quickly backed away.

The Populist press, like everyone else, had printed news stories about the New Orleans Mafia murders in 1891 and the Venezuelan boundary dispute in 1895, but at that time, they were upstaged by economic questions. During the 1896 campaign some of them sang, to the tune of "My Old Kentucky Home,"

> We'll weep no more over Venezuela's woe,
> Till we rescue our homes from decay;
> We'll preach no more on the doctrine of Monroe,
> Till the Populists carry the day.[3]

Some Populists, moreover, feared that active intervention in the Cuban insurrection might bring about an Anglo-American

[3] Chas. A. Sheffield, *Echoes from '76* (Minneapolis: C. St. John Cose, Publisher, 1896), p. 9.

alliance, and others wanted some assurance that "plutocratic magnates" would not capitalize on Cuban intervention to make it a bond-issuing spree like the Civil War. Some Populists wanted to spread the American eagle over Canada, "from the arid wastes of Mexico to the eternal snows of Greenland," as a prelude to "the parliament of man, the federation of the world," or shared the general middle western sentiment for some aid or recognition of the Cubans. A young Kansas Republican took an even more expansive view than that—and a more decidedly jingoistic one—when he said, "The people of this great, liberty-loving nation will not stand aloof and see the moth-eaten, effete monarchies of Europe, bulldoze, badger, and steal the territory of our sister republics on this side of the Atlantic." Yet some Populists thought differently. After Jerry Simpson returned to the Congress in 1897, he fought appropriations for battleships because a standing navy seemed to him a threat to liberty, fought army appropriations, fought the sending of relief money to Cuba because "charity should at least begin at home," opposed the annexation of Cuba because "a large number of very undesirable citizens" would make matters even worse for many Americans already on strike or out of work, spoke against recognizing Cuban belligerency in 1897, and voted against the war in 1898. Populist Senator Harris, like Republican Senator Baker, voted that a state of war existed in Cuba (which meant recognition of Cuban belligerency and private assistance to the insurgents) but that strict American neutrality be maintained, and the Senate agreed with them in May, 1897, 41–14.[4] The text of the resolution, which never got beyond the Foreign Affairs Committee in the House, read:

Resolved by the Senate and House of Representatives, etc., That a condition of public war exists between the Government of Spain and the government proclaimed and for some time maintained by

[4] G. C. Angle to editor, Fulton Independent, January 3, 1896, in Angle MSS, University of Kansas; "Ruppenthal Scrapbooks," III: 81, in KSHS; Kansas Commoner (Wichita), July 14, 1898; Topeka Press, December 24, 1896; Congressional Record, 54th Cong., 1st sess., XXVIII, 3592 (remarks of Rep. Baker); ibid., 55th Cong., 1st sess., XXX, 1201–2, 2240–44, 2460–61; ibid., 55th Cong., 2d sess., XXXI, 707, 803, 1186, 3820–21, 4388 ff., 4400 ff.; George W. Auxier, "Middle Western Newspapers and the Spanish-American War," Mississippi Valley Historical Review, XXVI (March, 1940), 526–30; Ray A. Billington, "The Origins of Middle Western Isolationism," Political Science Quarterly, LX (March, 1945), 45–47.

force of arms by the people of Cuba, and that the United States of America shall maintain a strict neutrality between the contending powers, according to each all the rights of belligerents in the ports and territory of the United States.

As the country moved closer and closer to war in the early months of 1898, Kansas Populist editors steered clear of rabid chauvinism and took their customary middle ground between the Republicans and the Democrats on questions not directly economic. Perhaps one can say that the Republican press tended to be the most cautious of the three parties on the question of active intervention in Cuba, the Democratic the most activist, and the Populists in between, but there are important exceptions and qualifications. As to the *degree* of their pro- or anti-war feeling, not much distinguished the presses of the three parties, but the *reasons* behind their attitudes differed markedly. Undoubtedly the Populist papers were nationalistic, but in early 1898 their clearer motivation was the wish that something be done about the "brutal and inhuman treatment" of the Cubans by Spain. To them the Cuban insurrection was another case of liberty struggling against an oppressive European despotism. They saw an obvious parallel between Cuba in 1898 and the United States in 1776, considered Spain a pushover, and hoped that help would come quickly for the Cubans. But what kind of help was called for? They were by no means unanimous in demanding an official American expeditionary force and in some cases clearly restricted their appeals to food and financial aid. The De Lome letter of February 9, 1898, and the sinking of the *Maine* a week later seemed to some of them calculated Spanish insults to American honor, but neither one was a *casus belli,* and would be properly atoned for by a thorough apology to the United States and a recognition of Cuban independence. Especially as war grew imminent, the Populist papers discovered other reasons for taking a moderate view.

One was that war would be at best only a temporary relief from hard times and would hardly bring about the real remedy, a more equitable distribution of wealth. Another was that a war would only benefit bondholders, as not only would the United States issue bonds to finance the war, as it had done during the Civil War, but the United States would become the underwriter of Spanish bonds on Cuba, bonds that otherwise would never be paid. Jingoism was nothing but a trick to raise newspaper circulation. The *Advocate* ran a cartoon depicting a paunchy senator saying to a clerk who was standing by a ticker tape, "Now, when I yell 'War! War! War!' three times, you watch the stock ticker," and commented:

The Maine disaster has given the cowardly jingoes who occupy public positions or run small dailies an opportunity to add to their assininity [*sic*]. The war scarer is in it to line his pocket, and his policy sells more papers than that of honesty and pure patriotism.

War certainly seemed inevitable to the *Advocate* by March, 1898, but although the paper recognized that the American people sympathized deeply with the Cuban insurgents "who are making a heroic fight for their freedom and independence," the question of active intervention was something else: "Would it be best to sacrifice the lives of many thousands more of sailors and soldiers in a war with Spain if it can possibly be avoided?" Senator Harris, ex-Senator Peffer, and the *Advocate*'s editors all believed that "no sane man" wanted war. Although one Populist paper could declare that, while "most men would rather fish than fight," we might as well "hurry up and get Spain thoroughly licked before the fishing season opens," another one could paraphrase the Democratic *Wichita Beacon* thus: "If Wall Street and Lombard Street can make more money out of war than in times of peace, there will be war. If peace is more profitable, there will be peace. Gold is the chief influence on earth." Not all Populist papers were as cautious as the *Advocate*, but hell-or-high-water interventionism was not the common pattern.[5] The Populist press, moreover, devoted much more space to the usual economic issues, such as railway rate legislation and the money question, than to the Cuban question in the early months of 1898.

Kansas Republican papers did not let the Cuban issue overwhelm them, either, but their generally cautious approach was highly seasoned with a consistent anti-Spanish bias. While the Populists were often caught between a humanitarian desire to intervene on behalf of the Cubans and a fear that a war would

[5] Quotes from *Advocate*, March 2, April 6, 1898, and *Kinsley Graphic*, March 25, 1898; see also, *Advocate*, *Peoples Voice* (Wellington), *Kansas Commoner* (Wichita), *Kansas City Sun*, *Kinsley Graphic*, February–April, 1898.

only benefit the plutocrats, the Republicans faced a dilemma of their own. As Republicans they felt bound to stay in step with what they took to be the dignified saraband of the Mc-Kinley administration, but as their blood rose at the chance to outstomp the black and treacherous Spaniard, they sometimes tapped out the more frenetic rhythms of jingoism. With important exceptions, the Republicans usually took pains to deny that they were jingoes and praised McKinley's policy as one of "reasonable conservatism," but along with this position they evidenced a very persistent undertone of bellicosity and anti-foreigner feeling. Only very rarely did Republican editors support intervention on the basis of humanitarian relief of the Cubans, although they interpreted the De Lome letter and the *Maine* disaster, if not as grounds for war, as very serious insults to the United States that necessitated abject apologies and an indemnity from Spain.[6]

Both incidents gave Republican editors, whether they were interventionists or not, further proof that the Spaniards were a treacherous breed. The *Topeka Capital* believed United States intervention was needed to restore law and order in Cuba, to return "the starving people to their farms and homes before they are exterminated by the cruelties of Weylerism," and to deal with a problem growing out of "the very character of Spain, its stubbornness, the popular illiteracy, . . . the senseless national pride." If the *Capital* shared its bellicosity with only a few extremists in the Populist and Democratic camps, its strong suspicion of hereditary defects among the Spaniards was shared almost exclusively with its fellow Republicans. Moderate Republicans who admired the McKinley policy of caution and deplored the prospect of great loss of American life in Cuba also considered the Spaniard "by nature cruel, treacherous, wholly untrustworthy," and believed both sides, the Spanish and Cuban, equally guilty of tendentious propagandizing.[7]

Meanwhile the columns of the two most famous Kansas

[6] *Wichita Eagle*, February 16, 1898; *Topeka Capital*, February 18, 1898; *Topeka State Journal*, February 10, 17, 19, 21, 1898; *Salina Republican*, February 23, 1898; *Hutchinson News*, February 12, 15, 16, 1898.

[7] Quotes from *Topeka Capital*, February 11, April 2, 1898, and from *Salina Republican*, February 21, 1898; see also *Topeka State Journal*, February 23, April 7, 1898; *Wichita Eagle*, April 11, 1898; *Hutchinson News*, February 16, 1898.

editors of the time, E. W. Howe and William Allen White, both Republicans, showed deep opposition to American intervention in Cuba, and viewed both sides, the Spanish and Cuban, with distrust. Howe, or one of his writers, scoffed, "Jim Orr says he would hate to to [sic] be killed while fighting to free a lot of halfbreed Spanish and Africans, because it would be too much like falling dead at a dog fight," and an Emporia Gazette editorial, quite possibly by White, declared that

as between Cuba and Spain there is little choice. Both crowds are yellow-legged, garlic-eating, dagger-sticking, treacherous crowds—a mixture of Guinea, Indian and Dago. One crowd is as bad as the other. It is folly to spill good Saxon blood for that kind of vermin. . . . Cuba is like a woman who lets her husband beat her the second time—she should have no sympathy.

In sum, when Republican papers were interventionist they showed the same kind of sympathetic approach to the Cuban populace that many Populists showed but added the ingredient of racial bias and a stress on inbred Spanish treachery. More often, however, the Kansas Republican press was caught between loyalty to McKinley and love of a fight and, in a few cases, coupled excoriation of the foreigner with coolness toward war.[8] Perhaps the *Emporia Gazette* of White and the *Atchison Globe* of Ed Howe were as far out of the mainstream of Republicanism as Mary E. Lease and Paul Vandervoort were from the mainstream of Populism in 1894 and 1896; but if these strong ethnocentrists cancel out each other, it is still true that anti-Spanish and anti-Cuban stereotypes were more common in the Republican than in the Populist papers of the period.

Democratic editors no more agreed among themselves on the Cuban intervention issue than their Republican or Populist opposite numbers. One was ready to accommodate Spain "any morning before sunrise," but expected that financiers and bondholders would stay McKinley's hand against Spain. Another, however, saw no cause for war if Spain would only pay the damages for the *Maine* and expected that a war would only serve bondholders and give the national banks "a new lease on

[8] Quotes from *Atchison Globe*, April 7, 1898, and *Emporia Gazette*, February 23, 1898; see also, *Globe*, February 6, 7, April 5, 1898; *Gazette*, February 15, April 8, 1898.

life." But while they contradicted themselves they gave few signs of ethnocentrism.[9]

When the question of Cuban intervention became a practical question in the United States Congress, all Kansas representatives except Jerry Simpson supported it, but, as in the press, for varying reasons. Two weeks before the House voted to intervene in Cuba, Populist Congressman Ridgely and Republican Congressman Broderick each entered a joint resolution recognizing Cuba's independence and calling for United States "intervention," but only the Populist added that funds should be appropriated for the "starving Cubans." When the intervention resolution passed, Congressman Botkin, the only Kansas representative who spoke that day, made it clear that he was voting to end inhuman barbarism and to mete out retributive justice to Spain. The 2 Republicans joined 5 of the Populists and 318 other congressmen on April 13 to authorize the President to take armed measures in Cuba. Jerry Simpson was one of 19 House members who voted against the resolution. He did not explain his vote, but a newspaper in his district claimed, perhaps speciously, that his opposition came from a desire to leave less discretion in the hands of McKinley and Hanna than the April 13 resolution provided. If this is true, it was coupled with the consistent antimilitarist, anti-expansionist, anti-war attitude that Simpson held throughout the 1897–99 Congress. Furthermore, again paralleling the Populist press, two of Simpson's colleagues quickly entered strong protests, not against the war, but against the financing of it by bond issues.[10]

Before the Spanish-American War began and during the first few weeks of it, Kansas people seldom gave much thought to the great question that rapidly emerged and soon dominated national politics: What should be done with conquered Spanish colonies? The separate problem of annexing Hawaii to the United States had met with much opposition in the early and middle nineties, and on April 20, 1898, the Senate agreed that

[9] *Ottawa Journal*, March 31, 1898, and March–April, 1898, *passim; Paola Western Spirit*, March–May, 1898, *passim; Junction City Sentinel*, March–April, 1898, *passim.*

[10] *Congressional Record*, 55th Cong., 2d sess., XXXI, 3341, 3401, 3745–48, 3820–21, 4388 ff., 4400 ff.; *Peoples Voice* (Wellington), April 18, 1898; *Hutchinson News,* April 14, 1898.

Cuba would not become an American colony. But when Commodore Dewey destroyed the Spanish fleet in Manila Bay in early May, many Americans took it for granted that the whole Philippine archipelago was also ours, and stateside expansionism steadily mounted. Nearly everyone expected the annexation of Hawaii and Puerto Rico; a long occupation of Cuba seemed very probable; and voices crying for Philippine annexation grew louder as the summer passed.

Annexation soon became the McKinley administration's policy and, therefore, the official policy of the Republican party. To encourage the annexation of the Philippines (and a fortiori Puerto Rico, Cuba, and Hawaii), the Republican press around the country brought up military, strategic, and commercial arguments in favor of it, adding in many cases that destiny had sent Dewey into Manila Bay or that the United States was duty bound to carry the torch of civilization into that backward area.[11]

Kansas Republican papers generally echoed these opinions. Papers that had leaned most decidedly toward Cuban intervention in the spring were very anxious to see not only Hawaii, Cuba, and the Philippines annexed for reasons of trade, manifest destiny, and national glory, but looked forward to taking Nicaragua, then being talked of as the site of an isthmian canal, as well. Others that had followed McKinley cautiously in the spring on the Cuban intervention issue now followed him more confidently on annexation. One paper that had warned against Cuban annexation in April demanded that voters support McKinley and Philippine expansion in November, and after McKinley's re-election in 1900, exulted, "The sun is not to set upon American soil and the work that Dewey did in Manila bay is not to be in vain." Another looked forward to the annexation of Cuba, Puerto Rico, and the Philippines, and possibly Canada if the French Canadians—a "never assimilating race . . . please excuse us from calling them 'fellow citizens' "—were excluded. The Republican chorus of approval was interrupted rarely, but again the papers of E. W. Howe and W. A. White, the principal opponents of intervention among

[11] Fred H. Harrington, "The Anti-Imperialist Movement in the United States, 1898–1900," *Mississippi Valley Historical Review*, XXII (September, 1935), 214.

the Republicans in the spring, took a nonconforming (if self-consistent) line of opposing annexation. Howe's *Globe* said, "The only redeeming feature in assuming the responsibility of providing for the Filipinos is that they don't wear much, and their dry goods bills would not be considerable"; and White's *Gazette* asked, "Are we going to allow ignorant black wild men in our new territories to vote?" Such sour notes, however, were hardly heard amid the hymnody of awe at the rising star of empire.[12]

An even greater unanimity marked the Populist and Democratic presses, but their unanimity was in the opposite direction. Whether they had been cool or warm toward Cuban intervention in the spring of 1898, these papers almost all opposed Philippine annexation on the grounds that it would lead to a large standing army and navy, that American soldiers were being "forced into fighting the oppressed instead of oppressors," that American labor would have to meet Filipino competition, that the cost of governing the new colony would be huge, that "after all our war for humanity turned out to be one of conquest as all Europe prophesied." One important Populist paper wavered on the question, but made a clear distinction between imperialism for humanitarian purposes and imperialism for commercial advantage. With such views, Populist editors had erected another bridge of fusion between Populism and the Democracy in Kansas. Together they joined Gold Democrats and Bryan Democrats across the country in an anti-imperialism that contrasted deeply with Republican expansionism. But as the campaigns of 1898 and 1900 demonstrated, theirs was the less popular side.[13]

Any generalizations on the party press of the period on the

[12] *Topeka Capital*, May 8, 1898; *Topeka State Journal*, February 11, May 10, November 2, 1898; *Hutchinson News*, April 11, November 1, 2, 3, 4, 5, 1898, November 8, 1900; *Salina Republican*, April 14, December 12, 13, 1898; *Atchison Globe*, December 14, 1898 (see also October 27, November 4, 1898); *Emporia Gazette*, May 2, November 3, 4, 1898; *Russell Record*, October 22, 1898; *Wichita Eagle*, May 6, 7, October 28, 1898.

[13] *Jerry Simpson's Bayonet* (Wichita), May 8, 1899; *Peoples Voice* (Wellington), October 27, December 2, 1898; *Kinsley Graphic*, December 2, 24, 1898; *Kansas Commoner* (Wichita), December 1, 22, 1898; *Junction City Sentinel*, November 25, December 23, 1898; *Ottawa Journal*, October 6, November 17, December 22, 1898; *Paola Western Spirit*, December 2, 1898; *Advocate*, May 11, July 20, November 2, December 14, 1898; Harrington, *op. cit.*, pp. 214, 218–19.

Cuban intervention and territorial annexation questions must be qualified—there are exceptions on every point—but this much can be said. There was a definite tendency among the Republicans to behave coolly toward intervention but warmly toward annexation. The Populists, on the other hand, waveringly opposed intervention and later joined the Democrats in steadfastly opposing annexation.

The contradictions of both, however, are more apparent than real. The Republican press was consistent not only with the McKinley administration's policies but with superficial national gain. When war seemed of doubtful value they were cautious, but the prospect of national advantage through colonial acquisition intrigued them. On both points they evidenced anti-Spanish and other stereotypes. In the Populist press, on the other hand, humanitarian sympathy for the oppressed Cubans slightly outran certain fears that a war would create a bondholder's paradise, and humanitarian opposition to American conquest capped an older opposition to standing armies and navies, to labor competition, and to government expenditure to benefit the capitalists who would be the greatest beneficiaries of war. Populist anti-imperialism was therefore by no means purely idealistic but almost never did it include any of the anti-foreigner feeling, the ethnocentrism, that marked several prominent Republican papers in their discussions of both the intervention and annexation issues. To judge by their newspapers and congressional activities, it seems hardly likely, after all, that the Populists concealed a "profoundly nationalistic and bellicose" mentality under "a patina of pacifist rhetoric."[14]

Unfortunately for the People's party, the rank and file were by no means as anti-imperialist as its press. For several reasons many people found 1898 a good opportunity to break their long engagement with Populism. Bryan and free silver had been downed, the business cycle was rising seductively, and "popocratic" fusion by then approached the status of a complete and final merger. But when the leaders of the party capped all these things with a marked disdain for imperialist annexation, many Populists, the majority perhaps ex-Republicans, returned to their old party or were freshly con-

[14] Hofstadter, *Age of Reform*, p. 85.

verted. They were a minority of the Populists, but a large one, and when the Republicans waved the flag for war and empire, the Populist deserters were many. In spite of fusion, free silver, and a seven-year barrage of Republican pleas and insults, in spite of on-again, off-again flirtations with prohibition and women's suffrage, in spite, perhaps, of the presence of certain ethnic groups, these people had stuck with Populism. But with the removal of economic distress and the union of Populism and the Democracy, they had had enough and made their exit through the popular and patriotic route of war and empire.

2. The 1898 Campaign

The Populists' rapid descent lowered their strength nearly to that of the Democrats in 1898. With the defection of a great many people to the Republican policies of war and empire and with the reform impulse generally ebbing, there were fewer and fewer party members left who had much objection to being identified with the Democrats, and the Kansas campaign of 1898 flowed smoothly out of fusion headquarters and down the drain. It was an astute man who prophesied in April that "should there be war with Spain the Pops would stand no more show in the election this fall than an armless man at a hugging match."[15]

Only one minor and inconsequential factional split bothered the Populists in 1898, and in the campaign the foreign-born vote was more earnestly sought after than ever. The incumbent state ticket was renominated at the state convention at Topeka on June 15, and the resolutions committee, which included the Scot, Andrew Shearer, and the Swiss, Christian B. Hoffman, sent to the floor a platform that contained no references to immigration, aliens, or the foreign-born and a resolution opposing an alliance with Great Britain for the conduct of the Spanish-American War.[16] The main attack of the campaign was silver once more, McKinley appearing as the tool of Hanna, Wall Street, and the "money power."

There was little difference in ideology between the Democrats and the Populists. While the Republicans attempted to underscore the opposition of some leading Populists to resub-

[15] *Ottawa Journal*, April 14, 1898.
[16] *Advocate*, June 22, 1898.

mission of the prohibitory amendment, a perennial German plea, and the paucity of German patronage rewards in the Leedy administration, the Populists set out to capture the German vote with a new stratagem that they probably felt should have been tried years earlier. This was a German newspaper financed and operated by the party itself. F. W. Frasius, the former Democrat who had helped the Populists in 1896, circularized the Populist State Central Committee in April, 1898, offering to edit a German language Populist weekly if the state leaders could guarantee a thousand subscribers at a dollar apiece. Frasius pointed out that too many Kansas Germans were dependent on Republican papers from within and outside the state. The Central Committee immediately accepted the offer, got in touch with the county chairmen, and before long the new paper, the *Topeka Volksblatt*, was merrily chirping the Populist line *auf deutsch*.[17] The *Volksblatt* contemptuously called the Republican gubernatorial candidate, Stanley, a hypocrite and a pharisee on the liquor question and a man who threw sand in the people's eyes with regard to prohibition and corporations. It listed fifteen legislative accomplishments of the Leedy administration, including a banking law, a stockyards law, a textbook law that foiled "the book trust" in its attempt to bilk the public school student, labor laws, and anti-Pinkerton law, and others. It opposed further involvement in Cuba and elsewhere as harmful to American soldiers and workingmen and scored the Republicans as monopolistic enemies of labor. Charles Curtis, the Republican congressman from the fourth district, was a corporation carpetbagger, the Republican party was the party of the prohibition craze, and German-Americans all over the state were tumbling over themselves in a rush to get on the Populist bandwagon—other German papers to the contrary notwithstanding. If this were not enough, the

---

[17] *McPherson Republican*, November 4, 1898; printed letter, F. W. Frasius to State Central Committee, Topeka, April 20, 1898, and letters from W. T. Tipton [state secretary] to J. C. Ruppenthal [Russell county chairman], Lansing, April 25, 1898, Tipton to Ruppenthal, April 20, 1898, Taylor Riddle [state chairman] to Ruppenthal, Topeka, September 12, 1898, Riddle to Ruppenthal, September 30, 1898, Tipton to Ruppenthal, Topeka, October 27, 1898, and Riddle to Ruppenthal, Topeka, October 29, 1898, in "People's Party MSS," in KSHS.

editor, A. Lemkau, toured the state to address the faithful in German.[18]

The Swedes, the second largest foreign language group, were not favored with a newspaper in their own tongue, but Nels Anderson, of Topeka, made Swedish stump speeches in several areas. To Carl Swensson and others, however, the Republican ticket was "the Swede ticket," and Republican papers pointed out to German readers that had not some of the Populists in the legislature defected to prohibition, resubmission would have passed (as it also would have if the Republicans had voted for it). Germans read that Leedy appointed only one German to office—as chairman of the Livestock Sanitary Commission— and they were told that their American patriotism could best be proved by a Republican vote, to endorse McKinley's conduct of the war. Other Populists lauded England for its many co-operatives, whooped it up for German-American Populist candidates, and accused the Republicans of desperation so great that they had to drag in the A.P.A. issue for one last time.[19]

In view of the election results, however, it is not likely that the Republicans were the desperate ones. The Republicans seemed to do everything right, even when they claimed that "an English paper has made a canvass and reports that ninety per cent of the Catholics and all the Jews are against the United States," when their gubernatorial candidate turned out to be a temperance man, and when their national leaders, paralleled by the Kansas Prohibition party, labored for a literacy test to restrict immigration.[20]

For one thing, the Republicans had the help of most of the German language press, which up to that time had usually been very Democratic and satisfactorily fusionist. The Populists,

[18] *Topeka Volksblatt*, September 6, 13, 20, 27, October 4, 11, 18, 25, November 1, 8, 1898; letters from W. T. Tipton to J. C. Ruppenthal, Topeka, October 19, 31, November 5, 1898, in "People's Party MSS," in KSHS.

[19] *Advocate*, September 14, 1898; *Lindsborg Record*, November 4, 1898; *McPherson Republican*, November 4, 1898; *Independence Star and Kansan*, October 28, 1898; *The Better Way* (Minneapolis), November 3, 1898; *McPherson Opinion*, October 27, 1898; *Parsons Daily Eclipse*, October 25, 1898; *Emporia Times*, October 7, 1898.

[20] *Russell Record*, May 7, 1898; *Our Messenger* (Nickerson), March, 1898.

said the German editors, were overrun with cranks, prohibitionists, suffragists, and enough female campaigners to make a witches' sabbath. Populist Governor Leedy had done nothing about resubmission and very little about anything else except railway rates and had not given much patronage to the Germans. The Republican, Stanley, gave them hope of better days. Nearly all of the German papers, and papers in Swedish areas as well, were outspokenly opposed to further militarism or annexation, however, and this together with the Germans' knowledge of Stanley's prohibitionism (officially, at least) makes it somewhat puzzling that they supported the Republicans both nationally and on the state level.[21] The simplest answer is that Republicans had bought control of these papers, and Popocratic writers sometimes hinted at this. Perhaps they felt patriotically constrained to support McKinley, although not his expansionism, since he was a wartime President. Prohibition and resubmission were still important, but these issues worked in different directions than formerly, since the Democrats had dropped their resubmission plank and Republican candidate Stanley notified the Germans that he was a resubmissionist. Many of them had been lukewarm toward bimetallism in the first place and devoted less space to campaign matters in 1896 than in earlier years. Finally, prosperity was returning to German farmers as to everyone else, and reform voting was not as economically attractive as it had been.

Nevertheless, many foreign-born Kansans participated on the Populist side as they had in previous years. In Pottawatomie county, A. Urbansky, 60, Prussian-born and perhaps a Jew, ran for the Kansas House of Representatives on the fusion ticket. Peter Thielen, an Iron Cross winner in the Franco-Prussian War, was a Populist wheel horse at Dorrance in Russell county, and German delegates Henry Rosey and Louis Ascher, of Jefferson township, noised it about the Geary county convention that Stanley was anti-German. In Republic county

---

[21] *Kansas Staats Zeitung* (Kansas City), October 20, November 3, 10, 25, 1898; *Kansas Telegraph* (Topeka), August 18, 25, September 1, October 6, 20, 27, November 3, 10, 1898; *Germania* (Lawrence), November 10, 1898; *Leavenworth Post*, October 26, 30, November 2, 1898; *Wichita Herold*, October 13, 20, 27, November 17, 1898; *Marysville Post*, October 21, November 4, 1898; *Lindsborg News*, October–November, 1898; *Kansas Volksblatt* (Newton), October 20, 1898.

John Brown, 52, who had come to the United States twenty years before from Aberdeenshire, Scotland, ran for county attorney, and on the same ticket the court clerkship was sought by J. J. Shimek, a Bohemian-born general-store operator. Second generation Swedish and Swiss Populists John Hanson and I. B. Klopfenstein graced the McPherson county ticket, and Samuel C. Martin, 40, a native of the island of Guernsey, an ex-Republican farmer and stockman, became the second consecutive English-born Populist to go to the legislature from Rawlins county.[22]

A Dane, Olof Larson, made a race for clerk of the district court in Osage county, and in Ellsworth county C. A. Ingermanson, 35, a Swede, and Joseph Sekavic, 54, a Bohemian, represented Langley and Palacky townships on the Populist county committee.[23]

From Rooks county a 45-year-old Canadian-born farmer, E. E. Smith, went to the legislature as a Populist, and in Rush county the Populists named Conrad W. DeWald, a German-Russian, for clerk of the district court because of his knowledge of German. Many foreigners were delegates to the county convention, most of them Germans or German-Russians. Big Timber township sent Mike Legliter, 43, a Russian farmer of 840 acres; Joseph Schemberger, Sr., and Joseph Schemberger, Jr., Russian farmers; John C. Schaffer, 22, a Russian with a German wife, a farmer of 360 acres, and the township assessor; John Legliter, 68, a Russian farmer of 210 acres; and Caspar Bieker, 27, a Russian farmer of 145 acres. John Serpan, a Bohemian farmer of a quarter section, and Hugh Moran, who farmed with his Irish parents, represented Banner and Brookdale townships, and Ed Heraghty, 59, an Irishman, joined Fred Oelkers, 45, a German, as farmer delegates from Fairview

[22] *Westmoreland Signal*, September 2, 1898; conversation with Prof. John Noonan, Manhattan, October 16, 1961; "Ruppenthal Scrapbooks," V: 601, in KSHS; *Junction City Tribune*, September 2, 1898; *Republic County Freeman* (Belleville), October 27, 1898; *McPherson Democrat*, October 28, 1898; *Census of 1895*, Vol. CCXIV, Inman city, p. 26, in KSHS; *ibid.*, Vol. CCXVIII, Marquette twp., p. 11; *ibid.*, Vol. CCXCII, St. Marys twp., p. 5; R. M. Ruggles *et al.*, *The Kansas Blue Book* (Topeka: Crane & Co., Printers, 1899), p. 209.

[23] *Lyndon Peoples Herald*, August 18, 1898; *Census of 1895*, Vol. CCLXXVI, Melvern twp., p. 20; *Ellsworth Populist*, October 5, 1898; *Census of 1895*, Vol. CXXII, Langley twp., p. 1, and Palacky twp., p. 13.

township. Two Germans, J. B. Kleihege, 53, a storekeeper and farmer, and C. Rodeman, 52, a farmer, came from Hampton and LaCrosse townships. Heavily German-Russian Pioneer township sent J. W. Schlegel, 39, and John Rothe, 44, both Russian-born farmers, and from the ethnically mixed Lone Star township came G. A. Krueger, 36, a German, Louis Schloemer, 58, married to a German, and Alois Bieber, 64, a Swiss farmer.[24]

Yet despite foreign-born participation and the Populists' appeals to ethnic groups, too many obstacles faced the fusion forces in 1898. It was hard to fight the kind of logic that William Allen White's *Emporia Gazette* was offering in behalf of the Republicans—"If you endorse Leedy you endorse De Lome—each said McKinley was a weak man"—and the Populist opposition to overseas expansion was evidently so unpopular that Republican papers were able to quote Populist anti-annexation articles verbatim to let them fall of their own weight before the voters. It was probably an issue that the Republicans did not need to embroider in order to persuade many Populists to switch their votes.[25]

The Populists were crushed. The Republicans swept every state-wide office and most of the congressional seats. They took a majority in the Kansas House, where the eight foreign-born representatives were split evenly between the two parties (two Canadians, an Irishman, and an Englishman to the Republicans; two Canadians, an Englishman, and a Swede to the Populists). Many Populist newspapers accurately attributed the result not to an increase in the Republican vote but to ten or twenty thousand "Popocrats" who stayed at home on election day. Few of these editors bothered to inquire further why so many silverites had not voted, and those who did came up with unconvincing answers: the failure of the legislature to pass a railroad freight rate act; over-confidence; loss of voters to the Cherokee strip (although it had been open for several years

[24] Ruggles, *op. cit.*, p. 191; *LaCrosse Chieftain*, September 2, October 21, 1898; *Census of 1895*, Vol. CCCXXVIII, Banner twp., p. 4; *ibid.*, Vol. CCCXXIX, Big Timber twp., pp. 3, 4, 5, 7, Brookdale twp., p. 2, Fairview twp., pp. 5, 7, and Hampton twp., p. 3; *ibid.*, Vol. CCCXXX, LaCrosse twp., p. 6, Lone Star twp., pp. 9, 17, and Pioneer twp., pp. 3, 14.

[25] *Emporia Gazette*, front-page box, October–November, 1898; *Hutchinson News*, November 2, 1898.

by then); disgruntlement with the Leedy administration, which was involved too deeply with patronage and with boodlers (in spite of the fact that dissatisfaction with Leedy was noticeably slighter than with Lewelling in 1894); and inclement weather, which they offered to explain the fact that the Populist decline was mainly in rural areas, while the cities had held more steadily to their previous levels.[26]

Although the father of Kansas prohibition, John P. St. John, droned sepulchrally that the Populists had lost because they had appealed to the "slum vote in the cities by . . . declaring for resubmission," and had lost more among the better classes than they had gained among the depraved, it was more likely not the Leedy administration's reputed corruption but its lack of luster that accelerated the withering of reform. Taylor Riddle, the Populist state chairman in 1898, figured that the Republican vote slightly increased in forty counties (about one-third of the total number), probably from new voters, but elsewhere the Republicans had not gained. The Populists actually gained more from the Republicans than the Republicans gained from them, he said, but fusion lost much more heavily from abstention. The Middle-of-the-Road vote, meanwhile, had gone "almost solidly" to the Socialist party.[27]

3. And Afterward

Despite its complete control of the state government from 1897 to 1899, Populism had accomplished almost nothing. Its reform banner was in shreds. Better commodity prices were blowing away the clouds of depression, and the Republicans had pre-empted the more popular side of the war and annexation issue. Obviously Populism was on its deathbed.

In the lame duck session of 1899 the last band of Populist congressmen showed a steadfast devotion to principles and thereby dug their own graves deeper still. Jerry Simpson fought an increase in the standing army, saying "I say to you here and now that I do not believe that this Republic can ever prove to

[26] Ruggles, op. cit., passim; Salina Union, November 11, 1898; McPherson Democrat, November 11, 1898; Parsons Daily Eclipse, November 10, 13, 1898; Newton Journal, November 11, 1898; Annie L. Diggs, The Story of Jerry Simpson (Wichita: Hobson Printing Co., 1908), p. 206.

[27] Unidentified newspaper (November, 1898) in "Stanley" volume, "Kuhn Scrapbooks," in KSHS; Kansas Commoner (Wichita), December 8, 1898.

be a great colonizing nation," spoke against further army appropriations, which were "beyond question . . . to carry on a war of conquest in the far-off Orient," and joined his Populist colleagues in voting against naval appropriations while Republican Charles Curtis supported them. When the new Republican Congress met the following winter, Simpson's successor supported a tariff to protect American interests against Puerto Rican and Philippine goods while one lone Kansas Populist congressman, Ed Ridgely, demanded free trade with the new colonies and their captive markets.[28]

Two years later, with Bryan heading the national ticket again and with John W. Breidenthal the gubernatorial nominee of both parties, the Populists and Democrats were well-nigh indistinguishable. Initial opposition because of Breidenthal's favorable views on prohibition evaporated, but the Popocrats swept to a resounding defeat on a platform that restated the old economic appeals in a year of prosperity and declared itself against "militarism, imperialism, and the desire for foreign conquest," as well as against political absolutism either by McKinley in the Philippines and Puerto Rico or by Queen Victoria in South Africa.[29]

In this 1900 campaign (the last Populist attempt of any significance) appeals to the foreign-born voters were more abundant than ever. Populist papers pointed with pride at the "flop" to Bryan taken by Dr. Samuel Sale, rabbi of Temple Shaare Emeth in St. Louis, who had been chaplain of the 1896 Republican national convention, after Dr. Sale announced "as one citizen to another" that he looked for Bryan to end American imperialism. Germans appeared on Populist slates and the state organization distributed some German language speeches by Carl Schurz and others supporting the Popocrat platform. Certain Populist editors warned workingmen to bear in mind the threat of "Mongolian and Malay cheap labor," which was a by-product of McKinley's imperialism. But the same papers balanced restrictionist labor appeals with boasts about Rabbi Sale's new-found Bryanism and the Bryan support coming from

[28] *Congressional Record*, 55th Cong., 3d sess., XXXII, 1001–6, 1958, 2329, 2918–19; 56th Cong., 1st sess., *ibid.*, XXXIII, 2051, 2056, 2297, 2416, 2428.
[29] *Topeka Capital*, July 26, 1900; *Emporia Times*, October 26, 1900; interview with W. J. Breidenthal, Kansas City, September 12, 1960.

the German (Jewish?) employees of B. Kuppenheimer & Co. and the J. V. Farwell Company in Chicago. Under McKinley, Cuba was an "American satrapy," and American rule in the Philippines an autocracy. "A prominent German farmer" argued in a Populist sheet that the United States, instead of becoming more and more like a monarchy, should emulate the non-imperialist, non-militarist government of Switzerland.[30]

The fusionists must have been encouraged by the general support they received from the German language press, which with one major exception supported their ticket. Imperialism had them especially worried, although labor and antimonopoly considerations reappeared after a relative absence of several years. Populist-colored arguments also cropped up, such as that John Hay took orders from Lord Pauncefote and that Bryan was defeated by the money power while McKinley won with the support of trusts and tariff barons; and Breidenthal's favorable attitude toward prohibition proved for some the only major stumbling block.[31]

Popocrat English language papers frequently proclaimed that Bryan was running away with the campaign in Illinois, South Dakota, and other places, and reprinted resolutions of various *Turnvereins* condemning Republican imperialism. The same general appeals were made to Swedish voters, and a final effort appeared to tie the A.P.A. to the G.O.P. Nevertheless, the Republicans kept up their foreign appeals, too, especially to the Swedes and Mennonites, and to judge by the election returns that year several ethnic groups that had dallied with reform in the nineties, such as the Danes and the Welsh, ap-

[30] *Great Bend Beacon,* October 26, 1900; *Marysville Advocate-Democrat,* October 19, 26, November 2, 1900; letters from J. H. Curran [state secretary] to county chairmen, Parsons, May 5, 1900, and Curran to J. C. Ruppenthal, Parsons, June 28, 1900, and Topeka, August 9, 1900, in "People's Party MSS," in KSHS; *Parsons Daily Eclipse,* October 19, 20, 31, 1900; *Westphalia Times,* October 25, 1900; *Ellis County News* (Hays), September 29, 1900; *Independence Star and Kansan,* October 12, 1900.

[31] *Kansas Telegraph* (Topeka), July 12, September 13, 20, October 4, 25, 1900; *Wichita Herold,* November 1, 8, 1900; *Kansas Staats Zeitung* (Kansas City), September 27, October 25, November 1, 8, 29, 1900; *Germania* (Lawrence), October 5, 12, 19, 1900; *Marysville Post,* September 7, 21, November 2; *Leavenworth Tribune,* October 17, 30, 1900; *Westphalia Times,* October 11, 1900, published a column entitled "W. J. Bryan über die Wahlfragen" ("Bryan on the campaign issues"), as did other English language papers in German areas.

parently shifted toward the Republicans in 1900 or shortly afterwards.[32]

Populist sympathy for victims of oppression and imperialism underlay the one new issue produced in this campaign. As it was expressed by the Sixth Congressional District convention, the Populists extended their sympathy to the South Africans "In their defense of home and country against British aggression." It was almost inevitable that the Boer War should become a Populist concern, what with their disgust with American imperialism during the preceding two years, their appreciation of underdogs, and their sensitivity to British machinations more than any other. The McKinley administration was roundly damned for its heartless failure to recognize the Boers, and the Populists expected thousands of German voters to react by voting Populist. The old Populist hackles rose at the thought of British oppression:

We should do away with the Fourth of July; its celebration offends our British brother, and we should not offend our sensitive brother with unpleasant memories. When kindly England captures Boer prisoners, they should strap them to a cannon and blow them to atoms, as they did Sepoys in 1857. Two African Republics are crushed out by that red coated bully of the world England, but this Hanna McKinley administration had not one word of sympathy. . . . 200,000 soldiers of a powerful nation crush 20,000 patriots, who made three removes to satisfy England, but gold lay under Johannesburg, and greedy England must have it.[33]

[32] *LaCrosse Chieftain*, October 26, 1900; *Salina Union*, October 19, November 2, 1900; *Olathe Tribune*, October 5, 1900; *Parsons Daily Eclipse*, October 31, 1900; *Marysville Advocate-Democrat*, November 2, 1900; *The Better Way* (Minneapolis), October 4, 1900; *Kansas Populist* (Independence), October 26, 1900; *Peoples Voice* (Wellington), November 1, 1900; *Hillsboro Post*, October 26, 1900; *Scandia Journal*, October 19, 1900; *Lindsborg Record*, October 5, 1900; official election returns, in KSHS.

[33] Quote from *LaCrosse Chieftain*, October 26, 1900. See also *Osborne County News* (Osborne), November 8, 1900; *Marysville Advocate-Democrat*, October 5, 12, 1900; *Peoples Sentinel* (Glen Elder), October 18, November 1, 1900; platform of Populists, Sixth Congressional District, Colby, in J. W. Morphy MSS, in KSHS. At least one advertiser in the Populist *Osborne County News* had not caught up with the idea that Populists were Anglophobic. In the issue of November 8, 1900, there appeared an advertisement for Chamberlain's Colic, Cholera, and Diarrhoea Remedy, endorsed in a letter dated November 4, 1897, from Vryburg, Bechuanaland, by Capt. C. G. Dennison of the British army, who found it most useful for the bowel complaints of his men when they were about to capture the "rebel" stronghold of Galishe, South Africa.

After ten tumultuous years the Populists of Kansas trudged through the 1900 campaign with a list of issues surprisingly like the Alliance platforms of 1889 and 1890. A few issues had changed: outworn demands for mortgage relief had given way to demands for structural changes in government, such as direct election of senators and federal judges and the initiative and referendum, leading to more direct rule, by the people; a maximum freight rate law had been passed, removing that issue; and opposition to Puerto Rican and Philippine colonialism had been added recently. But there still remained the old hatred of national banks, the demand for governmental currency issue only, bimetallism and the sixteen to one silver-gold parity ratio, antimonopoly, government ownership of utilities, a tax structure more equitable toward labor, including an income tax, and an anti-British feeling, this time occasioned by the Boer War. The last of the Populist congressmen heaped shrill scorn on alien landlords and "centralization of property" in any hands, individual or corporation, home or foreign.[34] The death rattle of Kansas Populism sounded remarkably like its birth squalls.

Belief in the strength of anti-imperialism led the Populists to think that the Germans, Irish, Dutch, and the Scandinavian voters would go overwhelmingly "Popocratic." If they did, however, they had the field to themselves. Bryan lost; the state ticket lost; congressmen lost; the legislature was lost; two consecutive elections were lost; and Populism was dead. The following year the Republican legislature passed a law prohibiting any candidate from accepting the nomination of more than one party, thus outlawing fusion,[35] and those who had not already returned to the Republicans because of war and empire either drifted into independency, perhaps to be caught up in the Republican insurgent progressivism of the next decade, or became firm Democrats.

If many old Populists became insurgent progressives, however, they must have cast querulous glances at such novel bedfellows as William Allen White, Joe Bristow, or Ed Hoch, who had been among the most skillful practitioners of the art of Old Guard thuggee upon Populist principles and partisans back in

[34] *Jerry Simpson's Bayonet* (Wichita), May 14, June 19, 1900; *Congressional Record*, 56th Cong., 1st sess., XXXIII, 836–38.
[35] *Parsons Daily Eclipse*, November 2, 1900; Harrington, *op. cit.*, p. 108.

the turbulent nineties. Those who seek to comprehend American culture by constructing trends in its history may find it peculiarly anomalous, but much insight lies in the remark of a Topeka judge in 1910 who saw "a vast difference between Populism and insurgency," regardless of whether one agrees with his further observation that any likening of the two was "a libel on the Populists."

A few stalwarts kept a shadow of the People's party on the ballot as late as 1906, but they could not even match the vote of the Socialists. Third-party voting in Kansas shortly after 1900 was slight, slighter than it had been in the eighties before Populism began.[36]

[36] Letter from H. W. Lutz to writer, Holton, October 16, 1960; letterheads bearing formerly prominent names in "People's Party and Democratic State Committees, Legislative Bureau, Manuscripts," in KSHS; Jas. H. Lathrop (ed.), *The Phonograph of Human Liberty. Organ of the Populist Party* (Topeka, October, 1902), p. 14, *passim*; *Topeka Capital*, April 13, 1904; December 28, 1906; March 13, 1908; *Kansas City Journal*, June 23, 1910.

CHAPTER TEN

CONCLUDING REMARKS

The foregoing chapters have narrated the story of the Populist movement in Kansas, with special reference to the relations between the Populists and non-American ideas, groups, and persons. Although a sizable body of literature appeared during the 1950's that asserted that the Populists were deeply hostile to things non-American, the Kansas story does not support those assertions. In fact, it supports something more like the opposite of each of the outstanding points of criticism.

The Populists have been accused of nativism, both of a personal kind and of an ideological kind; instead, they were friendlier and more receptive to foreign persons and foreign institutions than the average of their contemporary political opponents. They have been accused of "conspiracy-mindedness"; for them, however, tangible fact quite eclipsed neurotic fiction. They have been accused of anti-Semitism, both personal and ideological; instead they consistently got along well with their Jewish neighbors and consistently refrained from extending their dislike of certain financiers, who happened to be Jews, to Jews in general. They have been accused of chauvinism and jingoism, especially with reference to the Spanish-American War; instead, such lukewarm support as they gave collectively to Cuban intervention was based on quite different grounds, and as a group they strongly opposed the imperialism that the war engendered. Finally, they have been accused of selling out their vaunted reform principles by seeking political fusion with the Democratic party, especially in 1896, and thus of revealing a neurotic instability; but instead, fusion was for them a legitimate means to the accomplishment of real, if limited, reform. In the case of Kansas, the largest of the wheat-belt Populist states, the five principal criticisms of Populism voiced by recent writers not only do not square with the facts, but should be replaced with a viewpoint so much in contrast as to be practically the opposite. Briefly put, this viewpoint is as follows.

Populism in Kansas was a political response to economic distress. From the early days of the Farmers' Alliance, the progenitor of the People's party, to about 1892, relief of economic difficulty was virtually the sole reason for the party's existence; after 1892 this purpose was alloyed to some degree with the desire of the party to perpetuate itself as a political organism. In both periods, however, economic difficulties remained the party's chief reason for being, and relief of them its main objective. Populism called for the enactment of a set of legislative reforms by state and federal governments and accepted the extension of governmental power involved in such enactment. In its most complete and ideal form, the Populist program appeared in the national party platform of 1892, the "Omaha Platform," but this platform bore no more nor less relation to the practical operations of the party than platforms usually do. In Kansas the People's party placed its emphasis consistently on the three questions of land, money, and transportation, which were the issues causing greatest distress in that particular state. Since monetary reform seemed to have the broadest political appeal of all the reforms called for in the Populist program, it received more stress than the rest of the program at the time (1894–97) when the party seemed to have its best chance of succeeding.

As Populism followed the ways of practical party politics in the program that it offered and in the issues it chose to stress, it took a practical approach to its sources of support as well. Economic distress cut across lines of religion, of nationality origins, of race, of previous political affiliation, even of occupation and of wealth and status. To so great an extent was this the case that it is not even accurate to say that the Populists accepted or sought the support of third-party men, Republicans, Democrats, immigrants of many kinds, organized labor, city dwellers, and others, to broaden their agriculturalist base. For these groups were in and of Populism from the beginning. The job of the party leaders was therefore not so much to attract new groups but to be sure that the party program appealed to each of those groups already there and to spread the Populist message to further individual members of the existing coalition, of which the lowest common denominator was a desire for one or more specific economic reforms.

As a result, large numbers of every politically consequential foreign-born group then in Kansas, with the exception of the Mennonites, became active Populists. Party leaders received this support warmly and eagerly, except for one or two occasions: the 1894 state convention and probably the one of 1890. At those times, certain influential leaders supported the non-economic issues of women's suffrage and prohibition so vocally that they led the party to take positions unacceptable to many foreign-born groups. Even here, however, the attitude of these leaders to the foreign-born was one of indifference not of hostility. The fact of the matter seems to be, to judge by statements made by the delegates on the floor of the 1894 convention, that many Populists were simply unconcerned with ethnic groups or foreign matters; they were neither favorable nor hostile, except when they thought they might justifiably appeal to ethnic bloc votes or when they cited examples of enlightened foreign institutions to document their own reform program. To the great majority of Populists, in 1894 and at other times, foreignness and certainly Jewishness were simply not affective categories. For practical political reasons, among others, the Populists expressed themselves favorably toward foreign groups, either abroad or close at hand. This was certainly true of the fusionists; it was true of the non-fusionists except when women's suffrage and prohibition got in the way; it was even true, at times, of the Middle-of-the-Road group, which combined an antibanker (including English, Anglo-Jewish, and Wall Street banker) rhetoric with some benevolence toward immigrants as individuals.

Many leading Populists were in fact first or second generation immigrants. In the 1890's the Populists surpassed the Republicans in the proportion of their state legislators who were foreign-born. Foreign-born Populists abounded among county-level officeholders, county committeemen, precinct workers, and delegates to county, district, and state political conventions. Wherever an ethnic group existed, there existed as well its Populist voters and Populist leaders, with the exception of the Mennonites, who were undeviatingly Republican. The Populists, however, had immigrant blocs of their own, especially on the frequent occasions of county and state-level fusion with the Democrats. The party organization appealed to foreign-language groups with pamphlets, newspapers, and campaign speakers. They presented much the same arguments to their polyglot audience as the party was making to the English-speaking voters. The only difference was in window dressing, such as testimonials from Prince Bismarck and from German political economists in support of silver coinage. At their 1894 state convention, and prior and subsequently in their newspapers, the Populists forthrightly condemned the American Protective Association, the most influential and widespread nativist organization since the Know-Nothings.

On three contemporaneous issues relating directly to immigrants, the Populists took positions that might seem at first glance to have been nativistic, but in each case their attitude to the immigrant was neutral or favorable. When they attacked "alien" landholding, they were attacking landlordism, not the immigrant small landholder. When they called for an end to contract or "pauper labor" immigration, they clearly excepted "worthwhile" or "sturdy" immigrants and based their position on labor competition, not on racism. When their congressmen supported the Lodge-McCall literacy test to restrict immigration, they apparently did so as the only practical way to enact the bill's riders, which would have lessened labor competition, and almost never expressed approval of the philosophy of superior and inferior, desirable or undesirable, races put forward by Lodge and the Immigration Restriction League. In each of these three instances the Populists based their actions on reasonable economic grounds, if not especially perceptive or laudable ones. Their aim was to attract the political support of organized labor, of tenant farmers, and very likely of Irish-Americans.

The rhetoric of Populism was highly charged with nationalism, but it was a nineteenth-century kind of nationalism that did not include the nativistic or anti-Semitic characteristics of some twentieth-century right-wing nationalists. Only two foreign groups fell under the censure of any considerable number of Populists. This censure was a consequence of two issues firmly rooted in economic realities and in neither case did they grow out of or were they extended to racial or nativistic antagonism. The two groups were English or Anglo-Jewish financiers and English or Anglo-Irish landlords, respectively responsible in part for money stringency and for large land-holding. Many Populists feared that the trend toward tighter money and tighter land would continue unchecked unless these two groups, *and their American or Gentile associates,* were stopped. In both cases the antipathy of the Populists clearly extended to all malevolent financiers, monopolists, and land barons, whether English or American, whether Jew or Gentile, whether native or alien. For the Populists, or many of them, to have laid their troubles at the door of a mixed group of English, Anglo-Jewish, and American capitalists may have been naïve and simplistic, but the point is that the common denominator of their hostility was not nativism or anti-Semitism but distrust and dislike of a truly unsympathetic economic class. In some cases their anti-English attitude transcended this economic base, since the economic problem meshed so well with the rather widespread anti-English attitude shared by many nineteenth-century Americans as part of the American Revolutionary tradition. But the English people escaped the censure placed upon certain financially powerful Englishmen, and Jewish financiers escaped any blame whatever as Jews, although a few of them, as investment bankers, shared the criticisms heaped by the Populists, or rather, some of their more outspoken rhetoricians, upon the wickedness of powerful financial interests in general. This was certainly the case with the terms "Shylock" and "Rothschild," which appeared with some frequency in Populist literature but which were cachets not of Jewish conspiracy but of oppressive finance.

So far did Populist expressions of friendliness to Jews as individuals, in Kansas and elsewhere, to Jews as a group, to English immigrants, to English institutions such as co-operatives and public ownership of utilities, outweigh the expressions that might be construed with effort as Anglophobic or anti-Semitic, and so specious are the grounds upon which the Populists have been accused of Anglophobia, anti-Semitism, or nativism, that these accusations must simply fall without support. There is an exception that proves the rule. A handful of Populists sometimes let their antipathies include "racial characteristics" of these two groups, especially the English, and thereby they evidenced irrationality and prejudice. They were atypical. Many, in fact nearly all, of these Populists were attached to the Middle-of-the-Road Populist splinter group in 1894 and 1896. This group attempted to overthrow the recognized state leadership, whose reform credentials were at least as old and respectable as the dissidents'; it was in all probability subsidized by the Republican state organization; and it received the support of less than 1 per cent of the rank and file at the polls in 1896 and of the Populist press.

In what, then, did their nationalism consist? It is difficult to answer such a question, because to accuse such a pragmatic, anti-intellectual people as these agrarians of having possessed "concepts" or "ideas," much more a "system," is itself a distortion. They did, however, possess felt attitudes that were forced into words to form the rhetoric of their speeches and editorials. Needless to say, the scribes and leaders of Populism came closer than anyone else to expressing these views in logical form, subject, of course, to political exigencies. But it can be assumed that their rhetoric must have been congenial to the rank and file—otherwise they would have been unable to attract and to hold that rank and file. Nonetheless, the rhetoric is undoubtedly more radical, more logically organized, and much more explicit than the views of the mass of the party. In their rhetoric, Populist nationalism consisted of a feeling that the United States was a different *kind* of political society from any that had ever existed before and therefore more worth preserving than any previous one. America was not just another nation-state but an embodiment of certain ideals. It was the embodiment of democratic republicanism: a society where the people rule, where the governed consent to their governors, where the rights of life, liberty, and property are protected because this very protection is the object of their own self-government. It was the embodiment, too, of economic democracy: where resources wanted only honest labor to be translated into the reality of abundance, where opportunity was equal, where the distribution of the nation's wealth was equitable. It was the antithesis of Europe and Europe's corruption, decadence, parasitical upper classes, stagnation, and economic and political oppression. It was a place, in short, where the people rule for themselves and for the protection of their natural rights. Or, at least, so it should have been.

Yet who were the people? The answer is already implied.

The people were those who believed in the ideals of democratic republicanism, of economic democracy, and of freedom from European conditions of life. The people were those who actively sought the preservation of those ideals. They were those who labored by their own hands, who had equal opportunities to labor and to accumulate, who used the resources of the United States to produce their own and the nation's wealth. They were those who created wealth rather than those who manipulated wealth already produced. Very often this legitimate wealth-producing activity was defined by the Populists as agricultural and laboring activity; those who farmed or labored were by definition the real people. This corresponded conveniently both to what might roughly be called the Jeffersonian-Jacksonian tradition and to the actual political bases of the People's party's support. Translated into the rhetoric of a political campaign, it often meant emphasizing "the producing classes" or the common bonds of "the farming and laboring people."

The conscious derivation for all of this was the American Revolution, and secondarily, the War of 1812. These struggles successfully created a nation embodying this set of ideals.[1] Such conscious roots made it easy, of course, for some Populists to look upon the machinations of English financiers as a third and final attempt by England to subjugate America. It was primarily through the American Revolution that a nation of, by, and for the people was created and through it that all that was wrong with Europe and Britain was left behind.

Consequently, it was up to the people—often implying the farmers and laborers—to see to it that this nation, this unique society, did not perish from the earth. Who threatened its extinction? Certainly not the refugee from European misery, at least so long as he, too, believed in American republicanism and opportunity. In this unique kind of nation the doors were open to those who wished legitimately to share its benefits. The goods of this nation were not to be shut up inside for the exclusive use of those already there but rather to beckon as to a

[1] Except for frequent claims to have been at one time "Lincoln Republicans," few Populists looked back to the Civil War as a watershed for these ideals. Perhaps it was not yet sufficiently ancient and myth-ridden. Perhaps, too, this was another way of avoiding giving pause to the ex-Southerners attracted to the Populist ballot.

flourishing haven those who wished to escape the oppression of a decadent Europe. The nation was, in Lincoln's words, a last, best hope of earth. The immigrant was to show his good faith in these ideals by becoming a citizen and remaining permanently (as the Populists' alien land law provided) and by not attempting to destroy the opportunity of individuals already possessing it (as Populist demands for an end to "pauper labor" immigration showed). For an immigrant to take away the job of an American laborer was unnecessary anyway, since opportunity and America were virtually synonymous.

The "worthwhile" or "sturdy" immigrant was not, then, the enemy of American nationality. In fact, he seemed to justify the Populist approach to American nationality—certainly he did in the case of immigrant agricultural colonies in Kansas, which had been very successful—and he was therefore quite welcome. But who then *was* the enemy? To most Populists who thought about the matter beyond their immediate economic distress—and by no means all of them thought through their views of American nationalism with anything like the completeness that this sketch might imply—the enemy lay in certain recently emergent opportunities for malevolence. America was shifting from a predominantly rural and agricultural nation to one predominantly urban and industrial. This shift was in no way evil in itself. Populist spokesmen such as Senators Peffer and Harris had expressly denied any hope of turning back the clock, and if they were not absolutely delighted with a process that seemed to be toppling the farmers and their allies from political and economic predominance (if indeed they had ever possessed it), they were determined to live with such a trend. What is more, they were determined to see that these changes should benefit all the people and not just a few; that they should take place in such ways as to guarantee democratic republicanism and economic democracy. The majority of them therefore accepted industrialization but condemned monopoly, accepted banking and finance but condemned usury and financial sleight of hand, welcomed accumulation but condemned economic feudalism, welcomed enterprise but condemned speculation. It was not industry and urbanism that oppressed them, they thought, but their abuse.

For most Populists these considerations identified the enemy well enough. An appealing program, aimed conveniently at the relief of immediate distress as well as at the placing of new trends within the old ideals, could be constructed without further ado. A rhetoric quickly emerged that concerned itself with attacking landlordism, transportation monopoly, and money shortages, and this rhetoric remained the basic vehicle of Populist ideas from start to finish. In a minority of cases, however, it seemed convenient to personalize the enemy, and in doing so, some Populists passed the bounds of precise statement. At times, American financiers and monopolists such as the Belmonts, Morgans, and Vanderbilts, English financiers such as the Rothschilds, American and English land and mortgage loan companies, and prominent American statesmen such as Sherman, McKinley, and Cleveland, together seemed to form a common and inimical class dedicated to the people's overthrow. Ever since the Civil War this group seemed to have conspired to bring about the economic destruction of the farmers and their allies. This minority of Populists thereby dealt with the money question in terms of a "money power." Yet even they nearly all used the term "conspiracy" in a general sense to mean the common attitudes of an entrenched and powerful minority, and only a tiny proportion meant by the term an explicit conspiratorial agreement, as when they referred to Ernest Seyd and the "Hazzard Circular" of the sixties and seventies. But most Populists did not voice this line, a fact more remarkable if one grants that rhetoric tends to be more radical than the general feeling of its political following. This "conspiracy" was, in addition, a financial one and not a Jewish or English one. To look at a close-knit community of interest and to see in the mind's eye a conspiracy is not necessarily great irrationality but rather a lack of factual knowledge about the competitive methods of late nineteenth-century capitalism. If antibanker, antimonopoly, or anticapitalist statements formed fairly frequent themes in Populist rhetoric, Populists of every hue made it clear that it was usury, irresponsible economic power, and minority rule that they were opposing and not the industrial revolution, urbanism, or capitalism and banking as such. The abuse of new trends, not the trends themselves, had driven them, they felt, from their once uncontested eminence. Now they wanted to regain that eminence and accepted the fact that it could never again be theirs alone. If agrarian class predominance was over and done with, plutocratic class predominance should be scuttled before it progressed any further. Then economic democracy would be reborn.

The Populist view of American nationality, with its stress on democratic republicanism and economic democracy, was therefore intended to be at once majoritarian, individualistic, and humanitarian. That it was a nationalism naïvely humanitarian rather than aggressive appeared very clearly in the Populists' approach to the Cuban insurrection and the Spanish-American War. They sympathized deeply with the insurgent Cubans and viewed their uprising as a struggle for freedom and democracy much like the American uprising of the 1770's. In Kansas this sympathy expressed itself in a moral support for the insurrectionists that sprang from a confident view of their own moral righteousness. Nonetheless, the Populist press and Populist congressmen held back from armed intervention, took a cautious attitude to the blowing up of the *Maine,* restrained themselves from anything more vigorous than sympathetic gestures toward the Cubans in spite of the Spanish "despotism" and "Weylerism" they believed the Cubans to be suffering, and in unison with their Democratic neighbors hoped that war could be avoided. This was very close to the Republican position also. When war came, they supported it as everyone else did, but until then their humanitarian sympathy for the Cubans was checked by the fear that a war beginning with Cuban intervention could only benefit large financial interests. The Kansas Republicans' coolness toward Cuban intervention resulted mainly from the caution that McKinley maintained into April, 1898, and the desire of the Kansas Republicans to support their own administration. The Populists avoided the Republicans' scornful references to Cuban or Spanish racial inferiority and far more frequently than the Republicans took a humanitarian view of the matter. In Kansas the Populists were not violent jingoes. Furthermore, unlike the Republicans in their area, and other people elsewhere, the official Populist position on the question of American imperial expansion for commercial or military purposes, which arose after Dewey's victory in Manila Bay, was to join the Democrats in opposing expansion and in demanding that the United States leave the Philippines and other potential colonies alone. They were interested in the spread of American democratic ideals, in the overthrow of Spanish oppression of Cuba, if this could be done without the commitment of American armed forces, but not at all in American conquest or colonization. Populism in Kansas apparently lost many adherents because of this stand, but it remained the official party position nevertheless.

It is worth noting that Populist opposition to imperialism was much more firmly expressed than Populist sympathy to the Cuban insurrectionists, because the Democratic party was also much less firm on the latter question than on the former. As a matter of fact, official Populist rhetoric was tailored to fit the political exigencies involved in getting along with the Democrats not only on the war and imperialism issues but on most other questions as well. Political fusion with the Democrats on all levels marked Kansas Populism very strongly, and to some writers, fusion has meant that the Populists lacked any real dedication to the principles they so vigorously espoused. But the Populist movement chose political means to accomplish its program of economic reform; it was a political party, not a pressure group or an ideological front; for better or worse it therefore bound itself to use partisan methods. If one looks no further than the Omaha platform of 1892 to find out what Populism stood for and then observes that many planks in that platform were soft-pedaled in 1892 and later for the sake of fusion and political success, one might assume that Populist devotion to reform principles was a sham. But this is a superficial view. Fusion was the only apparent way to achieve any reforms, any accomplishment of any principles at all, and the degree to which the People's party was willing to fuse with the Democrats in Kansas was the degree to which it possessed political common sense. The identification of fusion with dedication to principle, rather than with a sellout, comes into even greater relief as soon as one recalls the shabby story of the Middle-of-the-Road Populists, those self-styled simon-pure reformers who almost certainly connived at the defeat of the reform party with the local Republican organization. The prevalence of fusion sentiment indicates as well the willingness of the Populists to seek out and accept the support of the foreign-born blocs that ordinarily made their political home in the

Democratic party. It also indicates their pragmatic approach to political action, their willingness to use an obvious means at hand to achieve legitimate political ends, and their flexibility, which stood in such contrast to the rigidity of the Middle-of-the-Road Populists.

The political horse sense that provided them with their receptivity to fusion was a natural outgrowth of the immediacy of the distress from which their movement sprang. It accounted, too, for the apparent anomaly of a radical program based on conservative ideals. For the Populists of Kansas were not a collection of rag-tag calamity howlers, ne'er-do-wells, and third-party malcontents, as William Allen White and others have suggested, but a large body of people of diverse occupational, wealth-holding, and status levels. As a group they were hardly distinguishable from their Republican neighbors, except for a probably higher mortgage indebtedness, and their greater degree of political and economic awareness. The great majority could be called "middle class," and they were interested in preserving what they considered to be their middle-class American ideals and substance. These were being threatened, they felt, not by the facts of industrialism and urbanism but by their existing *shape*. To change that shape, they settled upon the device of a political party.

Their view of the future was one in which many wrongs would have to be righted, many present trends would have to be redirected to conform to old ideals, for that future to become acceptable. Yet they were confident that this would happen. In several ways they were confused, ill-informed, and behind the times. They were unaware of urban problems, for example, and they never understood that money reform was basically a solution only to agricultural problems, if indeed to them, and not a solution for growing monopoly or for inequities of wealth distribution. Yet if this is true, it is true as well to acquit them of nativism, anti-Semitism, conspiracy-mindedness, jingoism, lack of principle, and of living in some neurotic agrarian dream world. They were bound together not by common neuroses but by common indebtedness, common price squeezes, common democratic and humanitarian ideals, and common wrath at the infringement of them. From this wrath rose the Farmers' Alliance, and from the Alliance their ultimate instrument of

protest, the People's party. The Populists were far too concerned with land, money, and transportation, and also, later
on, with the mechanics of winning and keeping public office,
to have much time to worry about whether their ideals were
mythical or their anxieties neurotic. Tight money and foreclosure sales were the products of nobody's imagination. Even
in their rhetoric they were too busy preaching positive reforms
in a depression to be concerned with racism or anti-Semitism
or agrarian Arcadias; and in their practical political activities,
they took all the help they could get.

The Populists were liberal nationalists bringing to radical
social changes a radical response. By such means they meant
to re-assert what they considered to be the fundamental ideals
upon which their society had previously depended—in their
view of history—and must continue to depend—in their view
of political philosophy. They undertook this task in the Kansas
of the 1890's, with its particular kind of social structure, its
particular distribution of wealth and income, its specific economic conditions, and its peculiar laws and traditions. These
particularities form the limits of historical analogy, and they
give no grounds for making the Populists the gawky ancestors
of Father Coughlin or of Senator Joseph R. McCarthy. They
make it very difficult to call the Populists the descendants of
the Jeffersonians and Jacksonians or the precursors of Progressivism or the New Deal, although with these movements the
Populists shared a considerable body of ideals. They make it
unrealistic even to equate the Kansas Populists with Populists
of other regions or other states.

This particular set of facts, however, allows the Populists of
Kansas to be judged on their own grounds. The verdict is very
simple. They were people who were seeking the solution of
concrete economic distress through the instrumentality of a
political party. By this means they would not only help themselves but they would redirect, not reverse, the unsatisfactory
trends of their time to correspond with the ideals of the past.
This involved profoundly the political co-operation of the
foreign-born, and it involved a deep respect and receptivity for
non-American institutions and ideas.

BIBLIOGRAPHICAL NOTE
AND ACKNOWLEDGMENTS

The principal types of contemporary sources used in this book are newspapers, manuscripts, interviews, books, articles, and pamphlet literature of the Populists and others, and a miscellany of almanacs, legislative handbooks, documents of private organizations such as churches, and federal and state documents. The bulk of this material is in the Kansas State Historical Society at Topeka.

Nearly everyone working in Kansas history discovers that newspapers provide him with the most abundant, continuously available, and generally useful kind of source. This was true in the present case, with less ephemeral examples of Populist publications, such as pamphlets, running close behind. This study drew on 173 Kansas newspapers for the period from 1886 through 1900, some for only one issue, some for as many election campaigns during that time as they were in existence, some for every issue for over a decade. These papers represent every locality in Kansas where there was Populist activity, or immigrant settlements, or both, as well as, to provide a check, some areas where there were neither. They include such widely circulated or otherwise influential papers as the *Topeka Capital, Topeka State Journal,* Topeka *Advocate,* Independence *Star and Kansan, Mc-Pherson Democrat,* Ottawa *Journal and Triumph,* and the Winfield *American Nonconformist and Kansas Industrial Liberator;* such papers as *Jerry Simpson's Bayonet,* the *Ravanna Record,* the Pawnee Rock *Alliance Globe,* the Cherryvale *People's Party Plaindealer,* and the *Blue Rapids Weekly Motor,* and dozens of others, which reflected the feeling of a locality or a faction or sometimes of a single person; and twenty-nine foreign-language papers, most of them German. Some papers were Democratic, some Populist, some Republican; some had minor party viewpoints, and a few were politically uncommitted. My intention was to sample newspapers representing every area, faction, ethnic group, or special viewpoint, if it existed in print, that related to the problem of Populism and nativism or immigrants in any significant way. To arrive at a balanced selection from the extensive newspaper holdings of the Kansas State Historical Society, I had reference to William E. Connelley's very valuable *History of Kansas Newspapers* (Topeka, 1916).

Populist books, articles, pamphlets, or other printed material, of which I used about seven dozen items, ranged from Ignatius Donnelly's novel, *Caesar's Column*, N. A. Dunning's *Farmers' Alliance History*, W. J. Bryan's *The First Battle*, Mrs. S. E. V. Emery's *Seven Financial Conspiracies*, and N. B. Ashby's treatise, *The Riddle of the Sphinx*—none of which were specifically Kansan Populist but which presumably circulated in that state— to Kansas items such as Senator Peffer's articles in the *Forum* and *North American Review*, speeches by Mrs. Lease and others, reform tracts by Lieutenant-Governor Percy Daniels, S. S. King, S. M. Scott, Sam N. Wood, D. C. Zercher, and others, Populist campaign material of various kinds, and some items by such non-Populists as William Allen White, Ed Hoch, and J. K. Hudson. This heterogeneous lot was primarily of value in exhibiting Populist thought and attitudes in a more systematic, extensive, and often more revealing way than the more ephemeral newspapers could afford.

United States public documents consulted in this study included the *Congressional Record* for the Fifty-second and the Fifty-fourth through Fifty-sixth Congresses (1892, 1895–1900); certain *House Reports* and *Senate Reports* of the Fifty-fourth and Fifty-fifth Congresses relating to the immigration restriction bills of Henry Cabot Lodge and others; and the *Eleventh* and *Twelfth Censuses* (1890, 1900). Public documents of the State of Kansas which proved useful included the *Biennial Reports* of the State Board of Agriculture, especially for statistical information; the state *Censuses* of 1885 and 1895; the *House* and *Senate Journals* from 1891 to 1901 and the *Session Laws* of 1891 and 1901, especially on the question of alien ownership of land; and the official abstracts of election returns, from 1880 to 1908 by county and from 1892 to 1908 by precinct or township.

The New York *Tribune Almanac* and Edward McPherson's *Handbook of Politics* provided party platforms and some election data. Semi-official handbooks of the Kansas legislatures of the period, official publications of the state and national Farmers' Alliance, city directories, and the official proceedings of several church organizations, especially the Swedish and German Lutheran synods, were obvious and helpful sources.

With the help of Homer E. Socolofsky's *Kansas History in Graduate Study: A Bibliography of Theses and Dissertations*

(Manhattan, 1959)—a scholarly aid that ought to exist in every state—I was able to find over two dozen unpublished works that were often of considerable pertinence, some of which I would undoubtedly have missed otherwise. The most helpful of these included, among Ph.D. dissertations, Wayne D. Angell, "A Century of Commercial Banking in Kansas, 1856–1956" (University of Kansas, 1957); Donald H. Ecroyd, "An Analysis and Evaluation of Populist Political Campaign Speech Making in Kansas 1890–1894" (State University of Iowa, 1949); Donald L. Kinzer, "The American Protective Association: A Study of Anti-Catholicism" (University of Washington, 1954); Raymond C. Miller, "The Populist Party in Kansas" (University of Chicago, 1928); and Nell B. Waldron, "Colonization in Kansas from 1861 to 1890" (Northwestern University, 1932). Among Master's theses were Lee A. Dew, "Populist Fusion Movements as an Instrument of Political Reform, 1890–1900" (Kansas State College of Pittsburg, 1957); W. P. Harrington, "The Populist Party in Kansas" (University of Kansas, 1924); Rebecca Jean King, "The Identification of Foreign Immigrant Groups in Kansas" (Kansas State University, 1948); Glenn H. Miller, "Financing the Boom in Kansas, 1879 to 1888" (University of Kansas, 1954); and Kermit E. Opperman, "The Political Career of Senator William Alexander Harris" (University of Kansas, 1938).

The views of Populism's recent critics may be found in the footnote citations in chap. i. To clarify such terms as "anti-Semitism," "nativism," "ethnocentrism," "prejudice," and the like, the works of T. W. Adorno, Gordon W. Allport, Bettelheim and Janowitz, and Zawadski, noted in chap. ii, and of Shlomo Bergman, "Some Methodological Errors in the Study of Anti-Semitism" (*Jewish Social Studies*, V [January, 1943], 43–60), helped particularly. The work of John Higham, especially *Strangers in the Land: Patterns of American Nativism, 1860–1925* (New Brunswick, N.J., 1955), "Anti-Semitism in the Gilded Age: A Reinterpretation" (*Mississippi Valley Historical Review*, XLIII [March, 1957], 559–78), "Social Discrimination Against Jews in America, 1830–1930" (*Publication of the American Jewish Historical Society*, XLVII [September, 1957], 1–33), and "Another Look at Nativism" (*American Catholic Historical Review*, XLIV [July, 1958], 147–58), is indispensable to any student of American nativism. For published articles on Kansas history, immigration, and economic conditions, the publications of the Kansas State Historical Society (first called *Transactions*, then *Collections*, and in recent decades the *Kansas Historical Quarterly*) comprise the most useful single source. Of these and other books and articles of a secondary nature, the following stand out for their usefulness from a long list: Allan G. Bogue, *Money at Interest: The Farm Mortgage on the Middle Border* (Ithaca, 1955); John D. Bright (ed.), *Kansas: The First Century* (4 vols.; New York, 1956); Carroll D. Clark and Roy L. Roberts, *People of Kansas* (Topeka, 1936), a demographic study; W. G. Clugston, *Rascals in Democracy* (New York, 1940); Paul W. Gates, *Fifty Million Acres: Conflicts over Kansas Land Policy, 1854–1890* (Ithaca, 1954); Emory K. Lindquist, *Smoky Valley People* (Lindsborg, 1953); James C. Malin, *Winter Wheat in the Golden Belt of Kansas* (Lawrence, 1944); Kirke Mechem (ed.), *The Annals of Kansas* (Topeka, 1954, 1956); William F. Zornow, *Kansas: A History of the Jayhawk State* (Norman, 1957); Barbara Miller Solomon, *Ancestors and Immigrants* (Cambridge, Mass., 1956), for the story of immigration restriction by literacy test in the nineties; Edward N. Saveth, *American Historians and European Immigrants, 1875–1925* (New York, 1948); O. Fritiof Ander, "The Swedish-American Press and the Election of 1892," *Mississippi Valley Historical Review*, XXIII (March, 1937), 533–54; J. Neale Carman, "Critique of Carruth's Articles on Foreign Settlements in Kansas," *Kansas Historical Quarterly*, XXI (Winter, 1960), 386–90; W. H. Carruth, "Foreign Settlements in Kansas," *Kansas University Quarterly*, I (1892–93), 71–84, and *ibid.*, III (October, 1894), 159–63; Fred H. Harrington, "The Anti-Imperialist Movement in the United States, 1898–1900," *Mississippi Valley Historical Review*, XXII (September, 1935), 211–30; John D. Hicks, "The Political Career of Ignatius Donnelly," *ibid.*, VIII (June, 1921), 80–132; James C. Malin, "The Kinsley Boom of the Late Eighties," *Kansas Historical Quarterly*, IV (May, 1935), 164–87, and "The Turnover of Farm Population in Kansas," *ibid.*, IV (November, 1935), 339–72; Edward N. Saveth, "Henry Adams' Norman Ancestors," *Contemporary Jewish Record* (June, 1945), 250–61; Homer E. Socolofsky, "The Scully Land System in Marion County," *Kansas Historical Quarterly*, XVIII (November, 1950), 338–75.

Neither the Populists nor their opponents were careful preservers of manuscripts. Of the relatively few collections available, the most helpful were the papers of Kansas governors and attorneys-general, of the Populist and Republican State Central Committees, one pseudonymous letter by Mary E. Lease (all at the Kansas State Historical Society), and the papers of Bishop Louis M. Fink of Leavenworth (for the Catholic reaction to the Farmers' Alliance; these papers are in the archives of St. Benedict's College, Atchison). Except for the Fink papers, however, these collections were thin, at least for my present purpose. Aside from the above, there are apparently no extant papers of such Kansas Populist leaders as Governor L. D. Lewelling, Senator W. A. Harris, Jerry Simpson, Mary E. Lease, or State Chairman John W. Breidenthal, although some official correspondence of Lewelling's exists and the lack of Breidenthal papers was remedied in part by two very helpful conversations with Breidenthal's elder son, Willard J. Breidenthal, since deceased. For other helpful interviews I must thank Judge Jacob Christian Ruppenthal, of Russell, who was a two-term Populist county attorney in the nineties and a delegate to numerous Populist conventions, and Mrs. Ruppenthal; Judge Ruppenthal's son, Lloyd Ruppenthal, of McPherson, himself a former Republican state chairman; members of the Riordan family, of Solomon, for information on the political behavior of the Irish in the nineties; E. C. Mingenback, of McPherson, son of a founder of the Farmers' Alliance Mutual Insurance group; J.·Neale Carman, of the University of Kansas, for an interview and for very generous use of unpublished material on Kansas foreign-language groups. I am indebted also to H. W. Lutz, of Holton, James C. Malin, of the University of Kansas, Shelly Waterman, of Kansas City, W. G. Clugston, of Topeka, and John Noonan, of Kansas State University, for suggestions or source information.

I wish also to thank the following publishers and journals for permission to quote material: the American Jewish Historical Society, for quotations from articles by Oscar Handlin and John Higham in the *Publication of the American Jewish Historical Society*, XL (1951) and XLVII (1957); the Beacon Press, for quotation from Peter Viereck, *The Unadjusted Man*; Criterion Books, Inc., for quotation from *The New American Right*, edited by Daniel Bell; Alfred A. Knopf, Inc., for quotation from Richard Hofstadter, *The Age of Reform: From Bryan to F.D.R.*, and from Eric F. Goldman, *Rendezvous with Destiny*; *The Journal of Politics*, for quotation from Victor Ferkiss, "Ezra Pound and American Fascism," which appeared in Vol. XVII (1955) of that journal; *The Journal of Southern History*, for quotation from Norman Pollack, "Hofstadter on Populism," which appeared in Vol. XXVI (1960) of that journal; the Macmillan Company, Publishers, for quotation from *The Autobiography of William Allen White*, published by the Macmillan Company, 1946, and from Edward A. Shils, *The Torment of Secrecy*, published by the Free Press of Glencoe, 1956; *The Mississippi Valley Historical Review*, for quotation from John Higham, "Anti-Semitism in the

Gilded Age: A Reinterpretation," which appeared in that journal in Vol. XLIII (1957); the State Historical Society of Iowa, for quotation from Fred E. Haynes, *James Baird Weaver*, published in 1919; the McGraw-Hill Book Co., Inc., for quotations from Oscar Handlin, *Adventure in Freedom* (1954).

INDEX

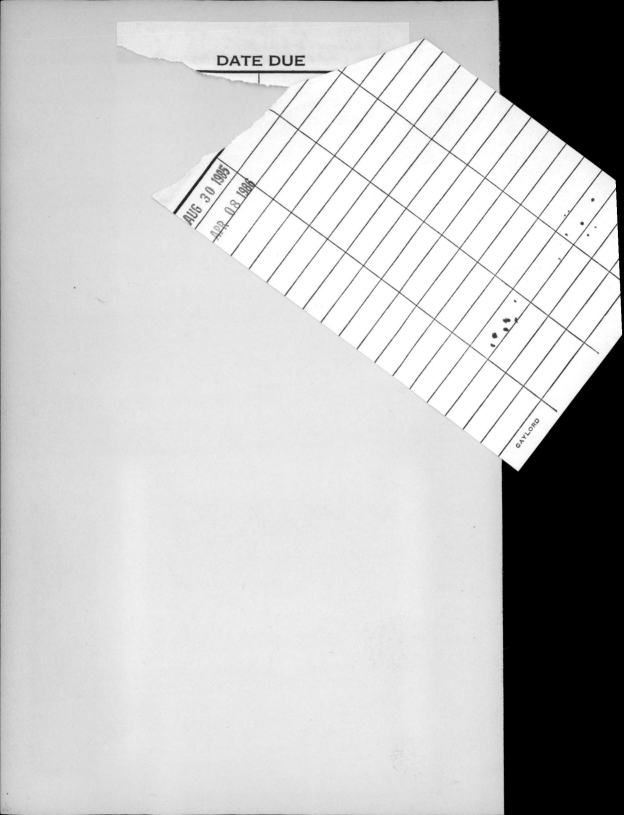

DATE DUE